D0787656

LICENSED ARCHITECT
DAVID MAGLATY
C11375
Exp.
STATE OF CALIFORNIA

BEAUX-ARTS ESTATES

Liisa and Donald Sclare

BEAUX-ARTS ESTATES

A Guide to the Architecture of Long Island

The Viking Press New York

First published in 1980 by The Viking Press
625 Madison Avenue, New York, N.Y. 10022
Published simultaneously in Canada by
Penguin Books Canada Limited

Library of Congress Cataloging in Publication Data

Sclare, Donald.
Beaux-arts estates.

Bibliography: p.
Includes index.
1. Eclecticism in architecture—New York (State)—Long Island. 2. Architecture—New York (State)—Long Island—Guide-books.
I. Sclare, Liisa, joint author. II. Title.
NA730.N42L667 917.47'21 78-26838
ISBN 0-670-34383-8

The main portion of this book appeared originally in 1975 as *Gold Coast Estates, A Guide to Beaux-Arts Architecture on Long Island*, written under a grant awarded in 1974 by the Preservation League of New York State.

Printed in the United States of America

Set in Linotype Bodoni Book

This volume is dedicated to:
Lloyd Morgan, Paris Prize winner, graduate of the Ecole des Beaux-Arts and professor of architecture
Taina Waisman, A.I.A., and the late Sidney L. Katz, F.A.I.A., his students
Vincent Scully and Wayne Andrews, architectural historians
and Ralph Howell, Sr., of E. W. Howell and Company, Babylon, Long Island, master builder

BEAUX-ARTS ESTATES

A Guide to the Architecture of Long Island

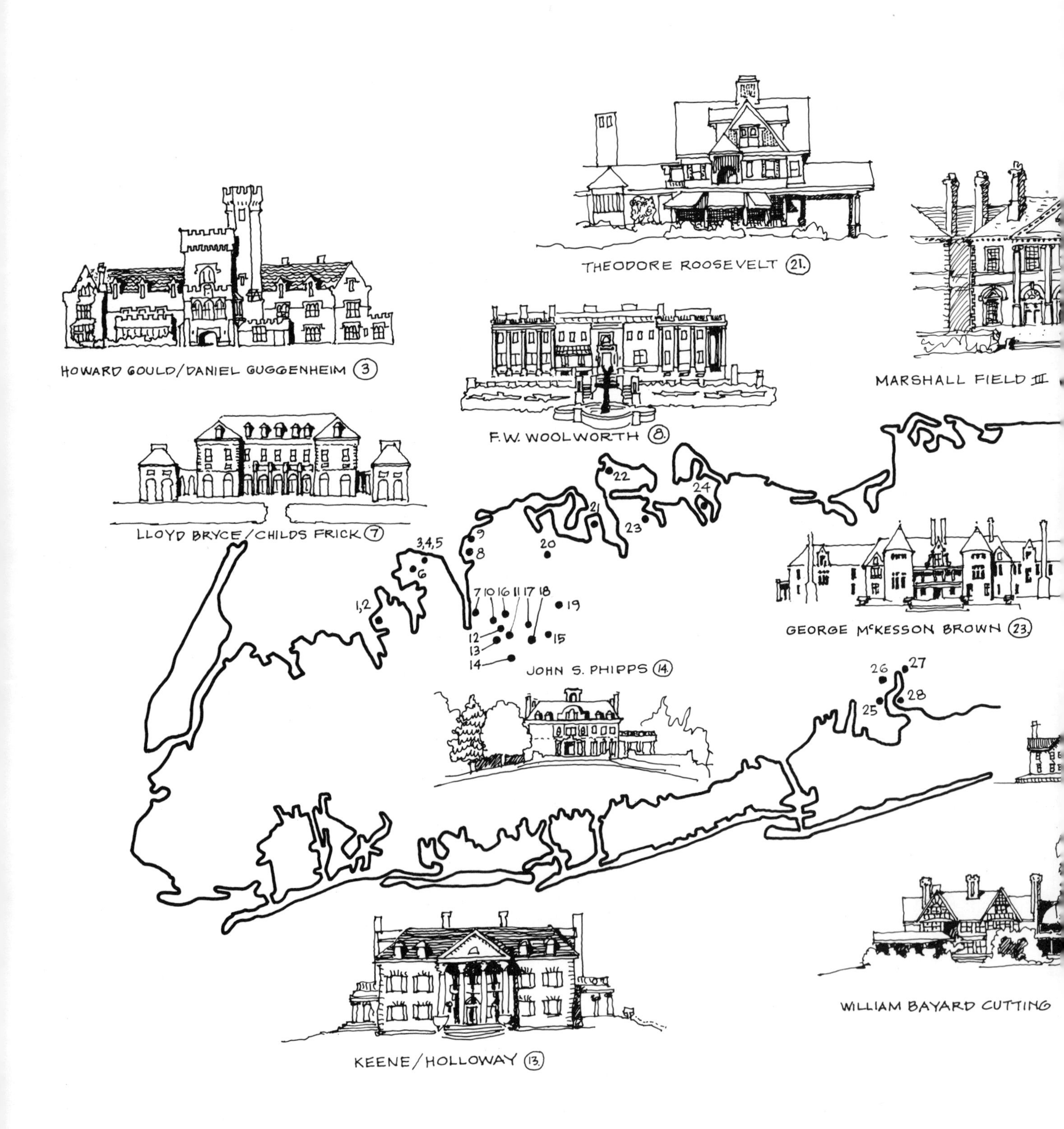

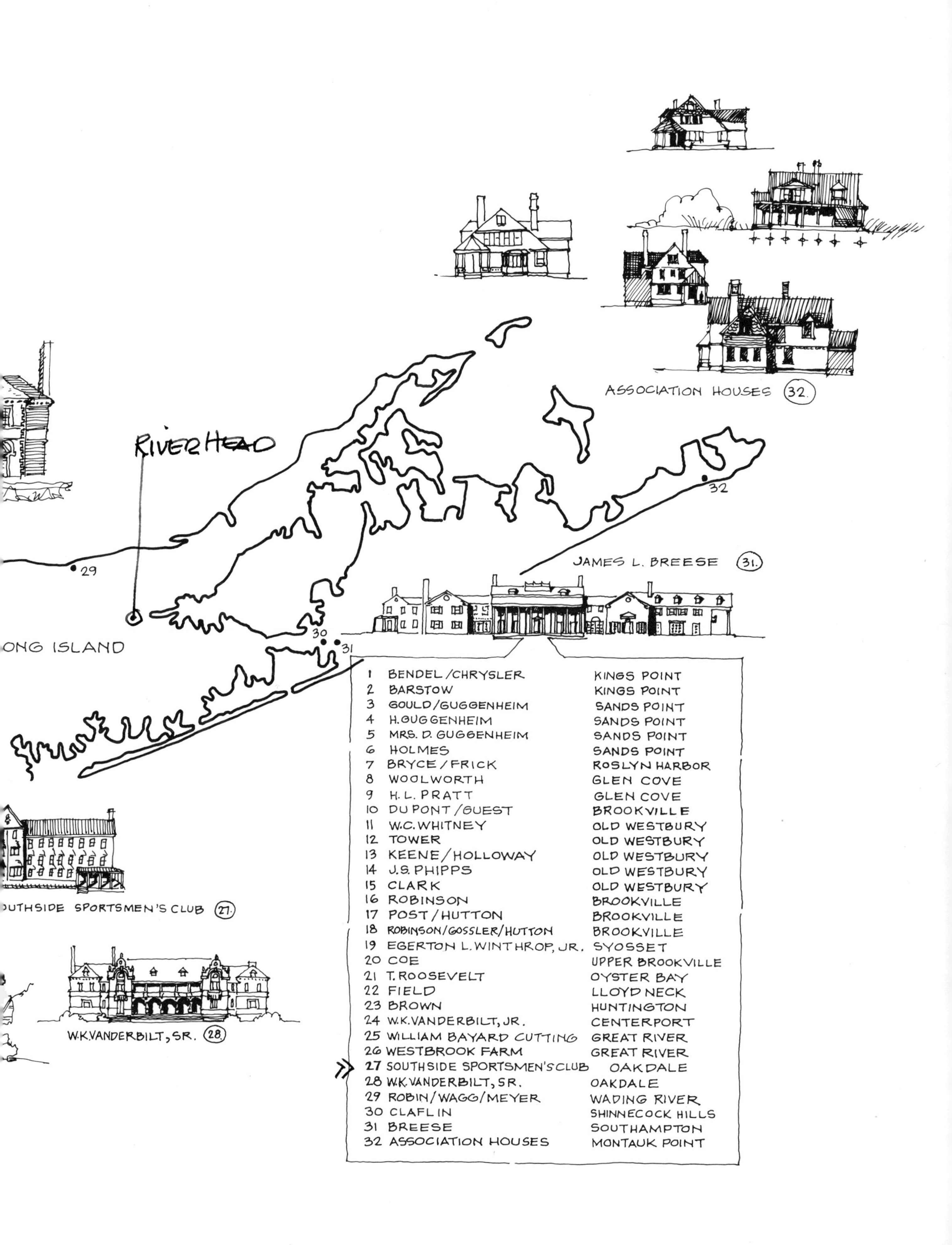
ASSOCIATION HOUSES (32.)
RIVERHEAD
32
JAMES L. BREESE (31.)
29
ONG ISLAND
30
31
OUTHSIDE SPORTSMEN'S CLUB (27.)
W.K.VANDERBILT, SR. (28.)
1 BENDEL/CHRYSLER KINGS POINT
2 BARSTOW KINGS POINT
3 GOULD/GUGGENHEIM SANDS POINT
4 H. GUGGENHEIM SANDS POINT
5 MRS. D. GUGGENHEIM SANDS POINT
6 HOLMES SANDS POINT
7 BRYCE/FRICK ROSLYN HARBOR
8 WOOLWORTH GLEN COVE
9 H. L. PRATT GLEN COVE
10 DU PONT/GUEST BROOKVILLE
11 W.C. WHITNEY OLD WESTBURY
12 TOWER OLD WESTBURY
13 KEENE/HOLLOWAY OLD WESTBURY
14 J.S. PHIPPS OLD WESTBURY
15 CLARK OLD WESTBURY
16 ROBINSON BROOKVILLE
17 POST/HUTTON BROOKVILLE
18 ROBINSON/GOSSLER/HUTTON BROOKVILLE
19 EGERTON L. WINTHROP, JR. SYOSSET
20 COE UPPER BROOKVILLE
21 T. ROOSEVELT OYSTER BAY
22 FIELD LLOYD NECK
23 BROWN HUNTINGTON
24 W.K. VANDERBILT, JR. CENTERPORT
25 WILLIAM BAYARD CUTTING GREAT RIVER
26 WESTBROOK FARM GREAT RIVER
27 SOUTHSIDE SPORTSMEN'S CLUB OAKDALE
28 W.K. VANDERBILT, SR. OAKDALE
29 ROBIN/WAGG/MEYER WADING RIVER
30 CLAFLIN SHINNECOCK HILLS
31 BREESE SOUTHAMPTON
32 ASSOCIATION HOUSES MONTAUK POINT

Preface

With the success of F. Scott Fitzgerald's novel *The Great Gatsby*, published in 1925, Long Island's Gold Coast estates achieved an international reputation. Serving as the country seats of the flappers and Golden Youth of the Jazz Age, these estates had first been developed during an earlier Age of Elegance. Their construction spanned the fifty-year period from the late 1880s to the beginning of the Great Depression, and they represented important social and cultural forces at work in the American democracy. Yet their architectural history, as the physical backdrop of an important era of national industrial expansion and progress, remains virtually undocumented.

The advent of modernism in architecture in the 1930s and 1940s cast a shroud of disdain over the Beaux-Arts principles with which these great estates had been constructed. Although American Colonial architecture of the eighteenth century continued to be acceptable for historical studies, Beaux-Arts architecture was almost banished from architectural history texts and was branded as vulgar, ostentatious, and eclectic. Yet the Beaux-Arts principles of plan and circulation have strongly influenced the development of the modern theories of space and form that have displaced them.

In addition to their architectural significance, the Beaux-Arts estates of Long Island constitute a great historic monument. Together with the estates of the same era in the Hudson River Valley and in Newport, Rhode Island, they make up a distinctive cultural and historic resource comparable in their own way to the plantations of the American South, to the châteaux of the Loire Valley, in France, and to the country manors of Great Britain. Yet there is no comprehensive guidebook that describes these American estates in their original or present form, much less one that attempts to place them in the cultural history of the era in which they were built.

Although many of the great Beaux-Arts mansions on Long Island are now vacant, or sadly deteriorated, and although many have been demolished since the Depression, others remain in good condition. Some of these are publicly owned and are thus accessible to visitors. This guidebook has been written as an introduction to these houses. Its aim is to promote an educated awareness of these historic resources and to encourage the preservation and rehabilitation of such buildings as Driftwood Manor, in Wildwood State Park. This estate is now owned by the public, but it is in a complete state of abandonment and its survival is endangered.

In June 1974 a grant from the Preservation League of New York State and the New York State Council on the Arts enabled us to begin a survey of the thirty-two estates discussed in this guidebook. Most of them are currently owned by schools, museums, or parks, and they are located throughout Long Island. We hope this volume will not only serve as a guide to these overlooked resources of our cultural history but also as an aid in directing national attention to these neglected achievements of the Beaux-Arts period in American architectural history.

Port Washington, New York
September 1978

Acknowledgments

The following people have provided us with original documents and/or valuable information and encouragement: Vincent Anthony, administrator, Old Westbury Gardens Foundation; James E. Arles, assistant commissioner, Long Island State Park Commission; Gil Bergen, supervisor, Connetquot River State Park; Francis Bick, New York; Mark Bilker, State University of New York, College at Old Westbury; Ruth Bolles, reference librarian, Dowling College; Albert G. Coleman, Long Island State Park Commission; Jerry de Marce, assistant superintendent, Sagamore Hill National Historic Site; William Donaldson, superintendent of buildings and grounds, New York Institute of Technology; Dr. Kenneth Ewold, office of campus development, C. W. Post College; James Fairchild, Nassau County Museum; Eleanor Feleppa, director of public relations, Southampton College; Brendan Gill, author and critic, New York; Winston Guest Family; Joseph Halligan, department of buildings and grounds, C. W. Post College; Joseph Hicks, New York Institute of Technology; Caleb Hornbostel, National Institute for Architectural Education; Frank and Helen Hourtal, owners, Sharon's Inn, Montauk Point; Ralph Howell, Sr., senior partner, E. W. Howell and Company, general contractor for the Marjorie Merriweather Post/Edward F. Hutton Estate, Hillwood, and for the Harry F. Guggenheim Estate, Falaise, and for the Mr. and Mrs. Roderick Tower Residence at Old Westbury; Leonard Johnson, supervisor, Sands Point Park and Preserve, Nassau County Museum; Richard Jorgensen, superintendent, Harbor Arts Center; Sidney L. Katz, F.A.I.A., and Taina Waisman, A.I.A., Katz Waisman Weber, Architects, New York; William Love, assistant secretary, Board of Trustees, Long Island University; John Maerhofer, director, Nassau County Office of Cultural Development; M. Carle O'Conner, administrator, Grace Downs School; C. N. Payne, president, Webb Institute of Naval Architecture; Diane F. Perry, Suffolk County Historical Society; Ellen Rosebrock, Roslyn Landmark Society; Martin P. Skrocki, director of external affairs, U.S. Merchant Marine Academy; Edward Smits, director, Nassau County Museum; Daniel G. Tenney Family; Donald Ungarelli, chief librarian, C. W. Post College; Barbara Van Liew, architectural historian, Society for the Preservation of Long Island Antiquities; Santo Vitale, curator, Vanderbilt Museum; Richard Wildt, supervisor, and Harold Aldrich, Wildwood State Park; and Richard A. Winsche, Nassau County Historical Museum.

We would also like to thank the staffs of Avery Library, Columbia University; the New York Public Library, Architectural Division; the Port Washington Public Library; and our editors at The Viking Press, Barbara Burn, Martina D'Alton, Alida Becker, and Ellen Posner.

We are particularly grateful to our editor, John P. O'Neill, for his skill and care in editing this volume.

Contents

INTRODUCTION

The Influence of the Ecole des Beaux-Arts on American Architecture

The French national school of fine arts, the Ecole des Beaux-Arts, located in Paris, has been an international center of art and architectural education for more than three hundred years (see fig. I–1). It traces its origin back to 1671, during the reign of Louis XIV, when its forerunner, the Royal Academy of Architecture, was established, and its educational system owes its widespread influence and longevity to the teaching of a method of work and of a series of design principles rather than to the advocation of any particular artistic style.

This emphasis on method is illustrated by the wide range of styles that was exhibited or influenced by the Royal Academy, which later developed into the Ecole des Beaux-Arts. In the 1670s, Academy students found their main inspiration in the designs made for the Palace of Versailles by the leading French architects Louis Le Vau and Jules Hardouin Mansart and by the landscape architect André Le Nôtre. By the late nineteenth century a new inspiration could be seen in the cast-iron buildings that were then being produced by Ecole des Beaux-Arts graduates, such as Henri Labrouste's Bibliothèque Nationale, Paris, and Dutert & Contamin's Hall of Machines, erected for the Paris Exposition of 1889. The Ecole also exerted its influence on the early works of Prix de Rome-winner Tony Garnier, who designed the now famous *cité industrielle* project (1901–17), and Auguste Perret, whose reinforced concrete apartments at 25 bis Rue Franklin, Paris, were built in 1903. An Ecole student, Perret later trained many important architects in his Paris studio, including Le Corbusier.

The education received by generations of architects at the Ecole des Beaux-Arts was based on an apprenticeship-atelier system of solving design problems in the *atelier*, or studio, of a practicing architect. The teaching method involved the development of the student's own *parti*, or basic general scheme, and an analysis of that scheme based on abstract principles of design, the result being a finished composition. This abstract reference system was used in analyzing projects of varying sizes and functions that employed different types of materials and methods of construction. It was a universal system, independent of artistic styles, and the Beaux-Arts teaching method based on this system is mentioned in the published writings of many French and American Ecole graduates who later taught in the United States, including Ernest Flagg, Thomas Hastings, and Paul Philippe Cret.

The basic design principles stressed the importance of the parti as an expression of functional and spatial relationships in the organization of the overall plan and its component sections. Other crucial concerns were the *progression*, or movement, of the spectator through a series of spaces with interior *axes* and exterior *vistas*, which when seen by the spectator implied an extension of the progression. Thus exterior space was an extension of interior space, and the *grand plan*, involving master planning and landscape design, was an extension of architectural or spatial planning.

French influence on American architecture and planning is not usually recognized until the Second Empire period of the late nineteenth century, when the first American graduates of the Ecole des Beaux-Arts began to develop thriving practices at home. However, earlier influences date back to the French settlements in the Louisiana Territory and to the French colony in Canada. These influences may be seen in some of the older houses and churches of the Vieux Carré, or Old Quarter, of New Orleans, Louisiana, and they are also apparent in the cathedrals and convents erected in Quebec, Canada, in the late seventeenth and the early eighteenth centuries.

More formal French influences can be traced from the Federal period following the American Revolutionary War, when Parisian architect and planner Pierre Charles L'Enfant drew up the master plan for Washington, D.C. His 1791 design was inspired by the master-planning principles used at Versailles, as disseminated by the Ecole des Beaux-Arts. In 1811, Joseph Mangin, a French-born architect who practiced in New York, collaborated with John McComb and won the design competition for New York's City Hall. This building was influenced by the late-eighteenth-century period of French architecture, which had also been popularized by Ecole graduates.

Other French architects worked in the United States during its early years on a variety of projects, both public and private. Joseph Jacques Ramée designed the master plan for Union College (1812–13) in Schenectady, New York, one of the first examples of a completely designed campus and one of the first grand plans executed in the United States. Another student of the Ecole, Jacques Nicolas Bussière de Pouilly, practiced in New Orleans and designed that city's Old St. Louis Hotel in 1835.

After 1850, the French Second Empire period reflected the influence of the Ecole during the reign of Napoleon III in France. This era was exemplified by the works of Napoleon's master town planner, Baron Georges Eugène Haussmann, and by Charles Garnier's design for the Paris

I–1 (above) Entrance courtyard of the Ecole des Beaux-Arts, Paris, with the Arc de Gaillon

I–2 (far left) Richard Morris Hunt, a prominent American Beaux-Arts architect

I–3 (left) Henry Hobson Richardson, one of the first Americans to study at the Ecole des Beaux-Arts

Opéra (1861–75). In the United States, Second Empire influence could be seen in the design for the Old Boston City Hall (c. 1865) by Gridley J. F. Bryant and Arthur D. Gilman. In another collaboration, the sculptor Alexander Milne Calder, who had been educated in Paris and London, joined with John McArthur, Jr., to produce the French Empire designs and ornamentation for Philadelphia's City Hall (1871–1901). In Washington, D.C., the Old State, War, and Navy Building (1871–88), now the Executive Office Building, was designed by architect Alfred B. Mullett in a style derived from the Second Empire.

Earlier, in 1848, Danish-born architect Detlef Lienau, who had trained in the Paris office of Ecole graduate Henri Labrouste, the designer of the Bibliothèque Ste.-Geneviève, established his own studio and office in New York City. There he trained several important American architects, including Henry J. Hardenbergh, who later designed the Dakota Apartments (1882–84) and the Plaza Hotel (1906–1907), both in New York City. Another of Lienau's students was Paul J. Pelz, whose collaboration with J. L. Smithmeyer won the design competition for the new Library of Congress (1886–97) in Washington, D.C.

In the United States, the latter half of the nineteenth century was a period characterized by growing industrial prosperity. During this period American students first succeeded in passing the rigorous French entrance examinations and thereby gaining admission to the Ecole des Beaux-Arts in Paris. There they were to learn a method of work that was far different from any employed at that time in most of the small architectural offices in the United States. They would return home to establish major offices and to handle large-scale projects in the prosperous and expanding business centers of America. At the same time, they would maintain and introduce the highly developed abstract design principles and standards that were taught at the Ecole.

Richard Morris Hunt was the first American-born architect to study at the Ecole des Beaux-Arts (see fig. I–2). After graduation, he remained in Paris at the atelier of Hector Lefuel and worked with him on the Pavillon de la Bibliothèque of the Louvre (1852–55). In 1855 Hunt returned to New York, and in 1857 he established his own office and atelier in that city. Not surprisingly, it was organized in the manner of the Beaux-Arts ateliers in Paris.

Another early student at the Ecole, Henry Hobson Richardson, worked at first in Paris under the French architect Théodore Labrouste (see fig. I–3). After returning to the

United States, Richardson formed an architectural partnership in 1867 with Charles Gambrill, who had apprenticed under Richard Morris Hunt. Richardson, like Hunt, had been trained at the Ecole to function as a teacher, or critic. The older students, or *anciens*, were required to instruct the younger, or *nouveaux*, in the atelier. Richardson's own office was modeled on this atelier system.

The ateliers of Hunt and Richardson form the major roots of America's architectural family tree. Among those who served their apprenticeships with Hunt in New York were William Robert Ware, Henry Van Brunt, George B. Post, and Frank Furness. Others who worked and studied with Richardson in New York and later in his office in Brookline, Massachusetts, included Charles Follen McKim, Stanford White, John Galen Howard, George Shepley, and Charles Coolidge. All of these architects later had large practices of their own, and their offices, in turn, trained succeeding generations of young architects in the design principles of the Ecole des Beaux-Arts.

As more Americans traveled abroad and were educated in Paris, they too returned home to open offices and ateliers. Of these, the most important was that established by the partnership of Charles F. McKim, an Ecole graduate and Richardson protégé, William R. Mead, and Stanford White, who had been trained by Richardson (see fig. I–4). Their office became a dominant force in American architecture for several decades, and the impressive list of architects who worked with McKim, Mead & White or trained in their office includes George F. Babb, Cass Gilbert, John Carrère, Thomas Hastings, and Henry Bacon.

Another of the United States' most influential architects, Louis Sullivan, was exposed to several Beaux-Arts influ-

I–4 McKim, Mead & White, architects, ranked as one of the most important American Beaux-Arts firms in the first quarter of the twentieth century. Left to right: William R. Mead, Charles F. McKim, and Stanford White

ences. After studying at Massachusetts Institute of Technology under William Robert Ware and Ecole graduate Eugene Létang, Sullivan worked for Hunt's former pupil Frank Furness in Philadelphia. In 1874 he attended the atelier Vaudremer at the Ecole and later worked in Chicago for William Le Baron Jenney, who had been educated at Paris' Ecole Centrale in engineering and architecture.

In his *Autobiography of an Idea*, Sullivan recognized the Beaux-Arts method as a reference system rather than a set directive for the appearance or style of any building. For this, he said, each architect would have to develop his own individual solutions and interpretations of style. Sullivan's unique design for the Transportation Building at the World's Columbian Exposition in Chicago in 1893 reflected this philosophy, and this edifice was admired by contemporary French architects as an expression of individuality that simultaneously recognized the abstract principles of spatial organization.

Some of these same design principles may be seen in Sullivan's critical analysis of the work of his protégé Frank Lloyd Wright and in Wright's design for the Imperial Hotel (c. 1916–22) in Tokyo (see fig. I–5), which

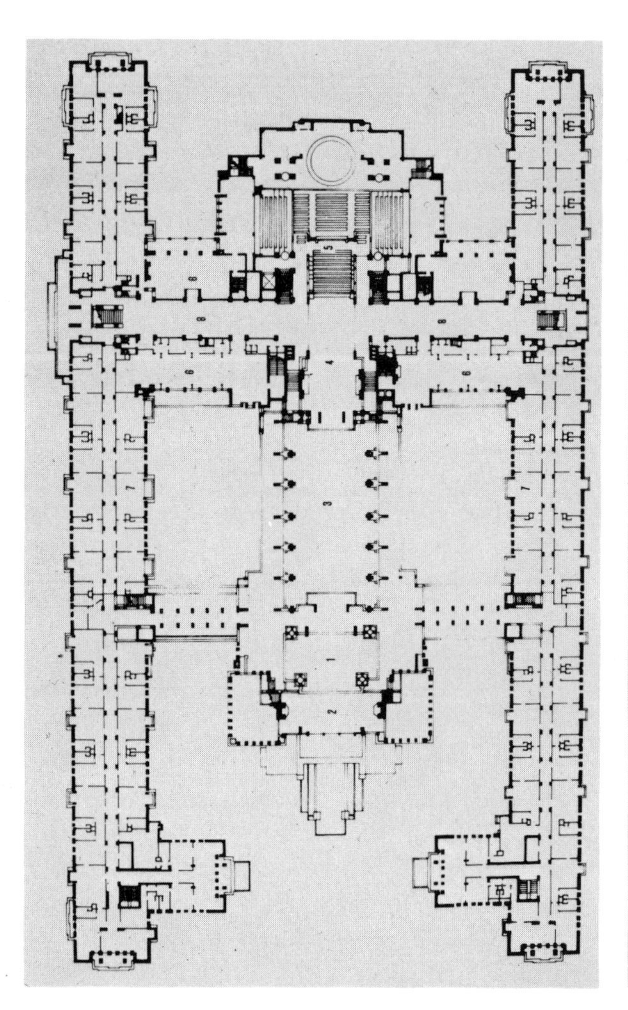

I–5 (left) Imperial Hotel, Tokyo, main-floor plan. Frank Lloyd Wright, architect, 1916–22

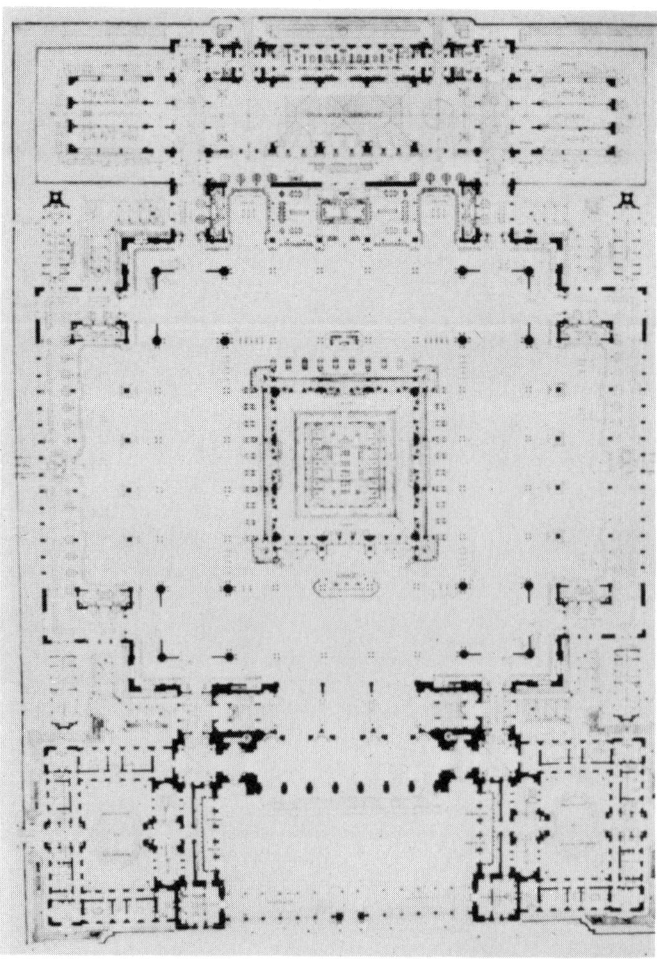

I–6 (right) Project for a national bank, the Prix de Rome-winning design of 1899 by Tony Garnier

was published in *Architectural Record*, April 1923. Sullivan described the importance of the parti to the design and to its development, based on social and functional relationships. He described the concept of a circulatory system to facilitate the accessibility of functional units and the use of a grand promenade to connect the outer, or guest, wings with a central service core. Sullivan also identified in the Imperial Hotel plans the academic concepts of intersecting axes, symmetrical forms, and a progression through a grand plan involving changing terrace levels and vistas.

These spatial and organizational characteristics described by Sullivan can be similarly identified in the design projects of many famous students of the Ecole des Beaux-Arts and its offsprings—from Tony Garnier's Prix de Rome-winning design (1899) for a national bank (see fig. I–6) to the work of students at American schools that were organized according to the Beaux-Arts system. In addition, the grand plan of Wright's Imperial Hotel as described above can be linked to the plan of another —superficially quite dissimilar—Beaux-Arts–influenced hotel, the Waldorf-Astoria (1929–31) in New York, which was designed by Ecole graduate Lloyd Morgan for the New York firm of Schultze & Weaver. Although the exterior physical detailing of this building has an Art Moderne character, the spatial organization of its main plan and section follows the same design principles that were taught at the Ecole and that appear in the work of Sullivan's protégé, Frank Lloyd Wright.

The first American school of architecture was organized at Massachusetts Institute of Technology, Cambridge, in 1866 by William Robert Ware, who modeled it on the program of the Ecole. However, its ateliers were made a part of the school rather than remaining separate, as was usual in the French system. French graduates of the Ecole were recruited to help organize the new programs at M.I.T. and to instruct the students. This procedure was so successful that in 1881 Ware was called upon to organize the School of Architecture at Columbia University, New York. As more schools were established, the Beaux-Arts method provided the basis for architectural education throughout the United States. The system was to remain intact for more than fifty years.

Architectural projects in the American schools, as at the Ecole, stressed principles of design and functional planning rather than a single style. History was not a formal part of the design project, but was studied separately in the form of archaeology projects and in *analytiques* of the various historical orders. The *esquisse*, a nine-hour preliminary-sketch proposal for a subsequent design project (see fig. I–7), and the *esquisse-esquisse*, a twelve- to twenty-four-hour complete sketch problem, were emphasized as a method of initiating a design parti and then of developing it into a *projet rendu*, or a resolved and completed presentation.

In 1894 the Society of Beaux-Arts Architects in America was organized. One of its aims was to develop more ateliers in the offices of practicing architects, thus encouraging them to have a more formal role in architectural education as prescribed by the French system. In 1915 the Society founded the Beaux-Arts Institute of Design in order to formulate educational design competitions that would be open both to students in office-ateliers and to students in architectural schools. The contest results were exhibited and judged at the Institute headquarters in New York. In this way each architectural school and participating office became, in effect, a member atelier of the Beaux-Arts Institute of Design. The winning projects were published in the Institute's monthly journal along with the critiques of the jury of architects. Students could compare their designs not only with the work of others within their own school but also with designs for the same project by students from throughout the country (see fig. I–8).

By the 1920s the Beaux-Arts Institute of Design was coordinating the educational programs of more than thirty-five major architectural schools in the United States and Canada. Complementary programs were also developed for educational training in mural painting and in architectural sculpture. The Beaux-Arts Institute of Design, now known as the National Institute for Architectural Education, still holds its annual Paris Prize competition, which now awards a major traveling scholarship and is open both to architectural students and to graduates.

The peak period of Beaux-Arts influence in American architecture lasted roughly from the 1880s, when the early American schools of architecture were organized in the Beaux-Arts tradition, to the 1930s, when the French method of education began to be displaced by the German, or Bauhaus, system associated with the International Style.

However, many elements of the Beaux-Arts educational system are still employed in American architectural schools, including the idea of a design atelier with professional critics, a jury system of evaluating design projects, a parti of the design, a sketch problem, a final presentation and rendering of the parti, as well as many of the abstract principles used in developing and evaluating a design.

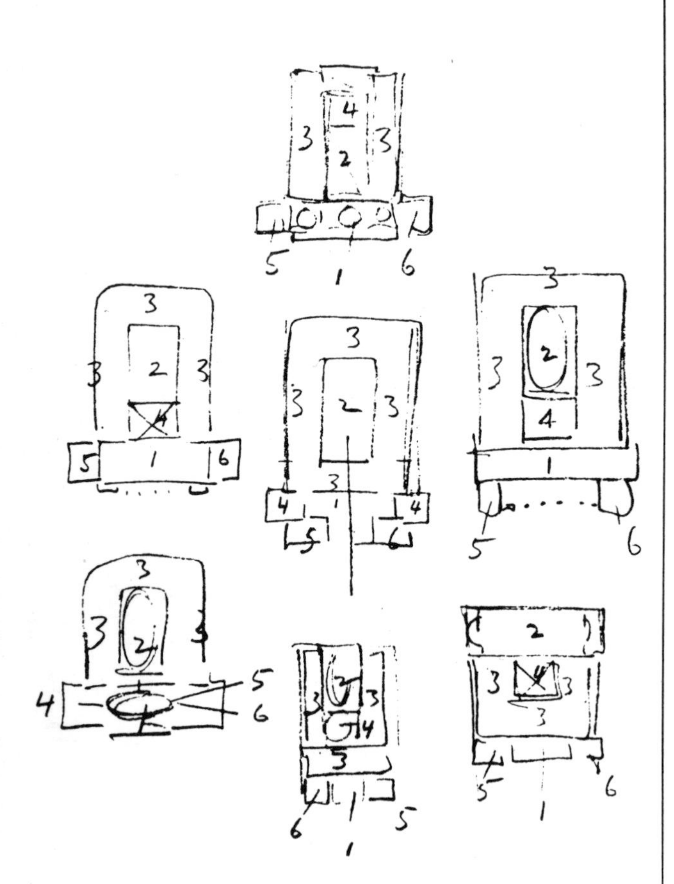

I–7 Sketches showing the development of a parti in an esquisse, *or sketch proposal*

(For a further discussion of these principles, see page 35.)

These principles and Beaux-Arts methods were taught in American architectural schools by such noted critics as Paul P. Cret (University of Pennsylvania), Henry Hornbostel (Columbia University and Carnegie Institute of Technology), Lloyd Morgan (New York University), Jacques Carlu (Massachusetts Institute of Technology), and Jean Labatut (Princeton University).

The influence of Beaux-Arts principles is seen in the designs of all the major graduates of the Beaux-Arts educational system. These architects worked throughout the range of styles that developed in the late nineteenth and in the early twentieth centuries in the United States. They built edifices in the Queen Anne style and in the Shingle Style and later in the Neoclassic and Art Moderne styles. Hunt, Richardson, McKim, Robert Swain Peabody, and other architects who returned home from the Ecole to the United States reacted to the contemporary domestic and

I–8 Design for "A Memorial Tunnel Entrance" by Eero Saarinen. This student drawing won the Spiering Prize at Yale University in 1932

vernacular styles. With their increased awareness of and use of the Beaux-Arts principles of spatial organization, they in turn influenced the development of the emerging Shingle Style and its subsequent variations. Later, William Van Alen and Raymond Hood reacted to the Art Deco and Art Moderne styles and influenced the development of a modern or contemporary American architecture while employing these same Beaux-Arts organizing principles.

A brief survey of the work of notable American architects who were trained under the Beaux-Arts system will provide ample evidence of the depth and breadth of its influence. This consistent influence is identifiable within a great variety of physical styles. In the Northeast, Richard Morris Hunt's work included the new interiors and central open space of the William S. Wetmore Residence, Château-sur-Mer (1872), and Cornelius Vanderbilt's residence, The Breakers (1892–95), which shows the Italian Renaissance influence (see fig. I–9). Both are located in Newport, Rhode Island. A Long Island residence designed by Hunt was the original William K. Vanderbilt, Sr., Estate, Idle Hour (1876), at Oakdale, destroyed by fire in 1899 (see page 209). H. H. Richardson designed Boston's Romanesque-styled Trinity Church (1872), the French-medieval Town Hall (1879–81) in North Easton, Massachusetts (see fig. I–10), and the now-demolished Marshall Field Warehouse (1885–87) in Chicago. McKim, Mead & White produced the Shingle Style Newport Casino (1879–81); the French Renaissance Herman Oelrichs Residence, Rosecliff (1900–1902), in Newport (see fig.

I–9 (far left) Drawing of The Breakers, Newport, Rhode Island. Designed by Richard Morris Hunt, 1892–95

I–10 (left) Drawing of Town Hall, North Easton, Massachusetts. Designed by H. H. Richardson, 1879–81

I–11 (below) Drawing of the entrance hall, Rosecliff, Newport, Rhode Island. Designed by McKim, Mead & White, 1900–1902

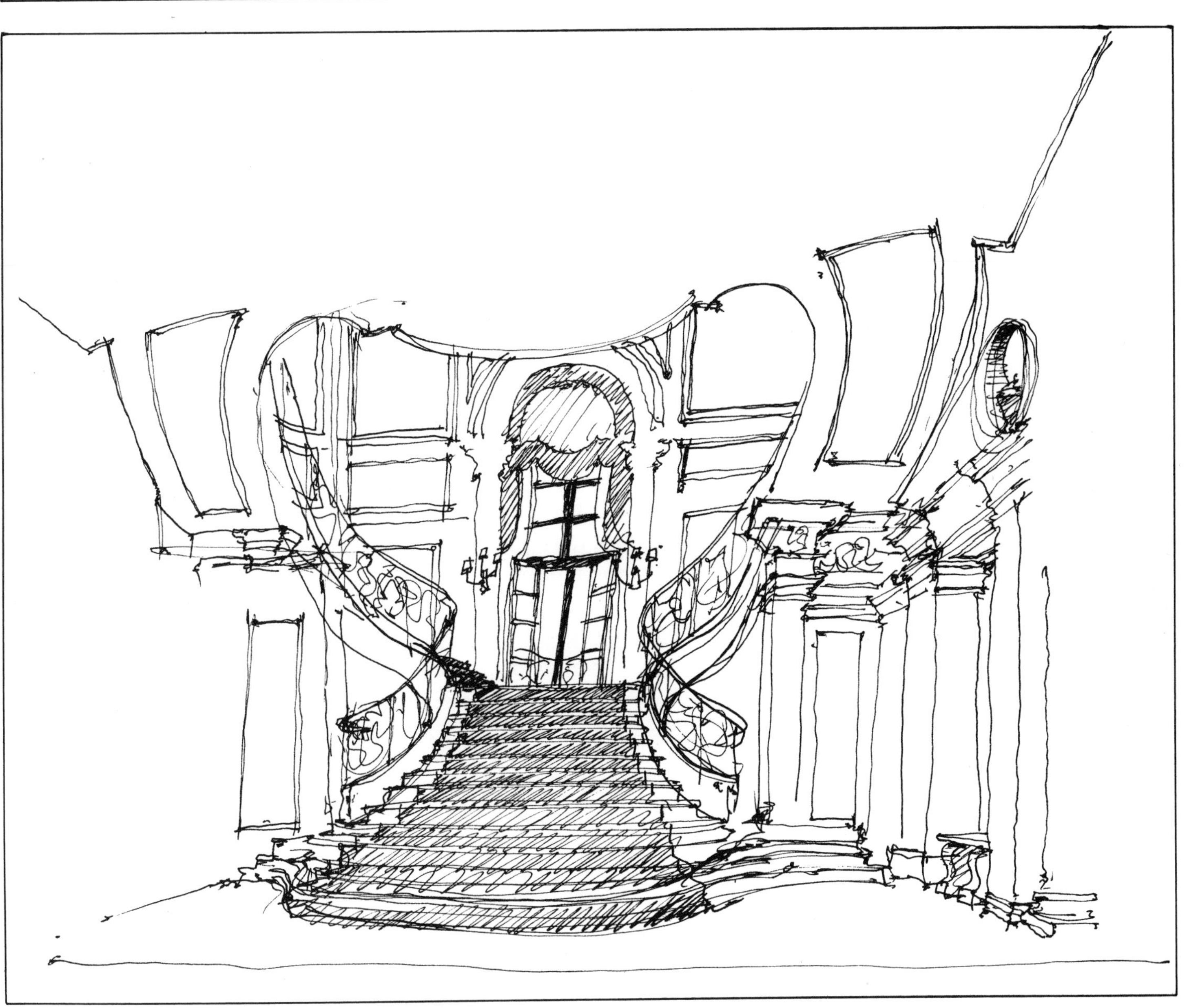

I–12 Drawing of the interior of Grand Central Station, New York. Designed by Warren & Wetmore, in association with Reed & Stem, 1903–13

I–11); and the Italian Renaissance Henry Villard Houses (1882–85) in New York. The James L. Breese Estate, The Orchard (1898–1906), at Southampton was also designed by McKim, Mead & White (see page 229).

Working in Boston, Ecole graduate Robert Swain Peabody of Peabody & Stearns designed the Shingle Style G. N. Black Residence, Kragsyde (1882), in Manchester, Massachusetts, and the Elberon Casino (1885) in Elberon, New Jersey. Important office-ateliers in Boston were also developed by Hunt's students William Robert Ware and Henry Van Brunt and by Richardson's students George Shepley, Charles H. Rutan, and Charles Coolidge.

In New York, several famous graduates of the Ecole

established practices and designed outstanding buildings. The firm of Carrère & Hastings created the plans for the Main Building of the New York Public Library (1902–1909), as well as for the Alfred I. Du Pont/Mrs. Frederick Guest Estate, Templeton (1916–17), at Brookville (see page 101). Whitney Warren of Warren & Wetmore designed New York's famed Grand Central Station (1903–13) in association with the firm of Reed & Stem (see fig. I–12). Warren & Wetmore also planned the William K. Vanderbilt, Jr., Estate, Eagle's Nest (1928), at Centerport (see page 185). Ernest Flagg designed Scribner's Bookstore (1913) on Fifth Avenue; the Singer Office Building and Tower (1897–1906), New York, which has since been demolished; and the Frederick G. Bourne Estate (1902) at Oakdale (see fig. A–7).

Other architects and firms with Beaux-Arts backgrounds who designed major buildings in New York and on Long Island include Delano & Aldrich, who planned the Mr. and Mrs. Roderick Tower Residence (1924) in Old Westbury (see page 114) and the Egerton L. Winthrop, Jr., Estate (1903–1904) in Syosset (see page 149), and John Russell Pope, the designer of the Robinson/Gossler/Hutton Residence (c. 1917–26) in Brookville (see page 144) and the Marshall Field III Estate, Caumsett (c. 1925), in Lloyd Neck (see page 170). Cass Gilbert, the architect of the Woolworth Building (1911–14), William Van Alen, the architect of the Chrysler Building (1929–31) (see fig. I–13), William Lamb of Shreve, Lamb & Harmon, designer of the Empire State Building (1931), and Raymond Hood, one of the principal architects of Rockefeller Center (1931–40), were all graduates of the Ecole. Eero Saarinen, who designed the T.W.A. Terminal at John F. Kennedy International Airport (1960–62), also received a Beaux-Arts education as a student at Yale University (see fig. I–8).

Philadelphia architects who were educated or influenced by the Beaux-Arts system included Hunt's pupil Frank Furness, who designed the Pennsylvania Academy of the Fine Arts (1872–76), and Horace Trumbauer, the architect of the Berwind Residence, The Elms (1901), in Newport. The noted critic Paul P. Cret collaborated with Albert Kelsey on the Pan-American Union Building (1910) in Washington, D.C., and George Howe, who was an Ecole graduate, joined with William E. Lescaze in planning the Philadelphia Savings Fund Society Building (1930). Louis Kahn, who received a Beaux-Arts education at the University of Pennsylvania, Philadelphia, and worked under Paul P. Cret, later designed the Salk Center for

I–13 Drawing of the Chrysler Building, New York. Designed by William Van Alen, 1929–31

Biological Research (1963) in La Jolla, California.

In Washington, D.C., Beaux-Arts–influenced projects include Henry Bacon's Lincoln Memorial (1922), John Russell Pope's Jefferson Memorial (1934–43), and numerous residences and embassies—particularly along Massachusetts Avenue—designed by Jules de Sibour and George Oakly Totton, two Ecole graduates.

The designer of Chicago's Auditorium Building (1887–89), and the Schlesinger & Mayer Department Store (1899–1904), now Carson Pirie & Scott, in Chicago (see fig. I–14), Louis Sullivan trained many important architects in his Chicago office, including William Gray Purcell, George Grant Elmslie, Irving Gill, and Frank Lloyd Wright. Wright was exposed to several other Beaux-Arts influences as well, from his initial development under M.I.T. graduate Joseph Lyman Silsbee to his Oak Park association with another M.I.T. alumnus, Marion Mahony, who in turn was trained under Ecole critic Constant Désiré Despradelle. Wright also collaborated with sculptor and Ecole graduate Richard Bock. Beaux-Arts planning principles can be seen in some of Wright's large-scale projects, including his grand-plan designs for the Wolfe Lake Resort project (1895) and the Midway Gardens (1914), both in Chicago, as well as for the previously discussed Imperial Hotel in Tokyo (see fig. I–5).

Other Beaux-Arts–trained and –influenced architects in the Midwest include Henry Ives Cobb, who apprenticed in the office of Peabody & Stearns, as well as Howard Van Doren Shaw and David Adler, both graduates of the Ecole. The office of Daniel Burnham & Company employed many important designers who were educated at the Ecole or had trained under Beaux-Arts graduates. These included Charles Atwood, who worked on the design of the Reliance Building (1893–94) in Chicago; Edward Bennett and Jules Guerin, who collaborated with Daniel Burnham on the Chicago and San Francisco master plans (1905–1907); and Pierce Anderson, the chief designer on the Union Station project (1902) in Washington, D.C.

Beaux-Arts influence extended farther west with the work of such architects as Ecole graduate James W. Reid, who designed the Hotel del Coronado (c. 1888) in San Diego, California, in association with his brother Merritt Reid. Charles and Henry Greene, who received Beaux-Arts educations at M.I.T., produced the Swan House (1894) and the Culbertson House (1902), both in Pasadena, and the William R. Thorsen Residence (1908) in Berkeley.

Bernard Maybeck was one of the most influential archi-

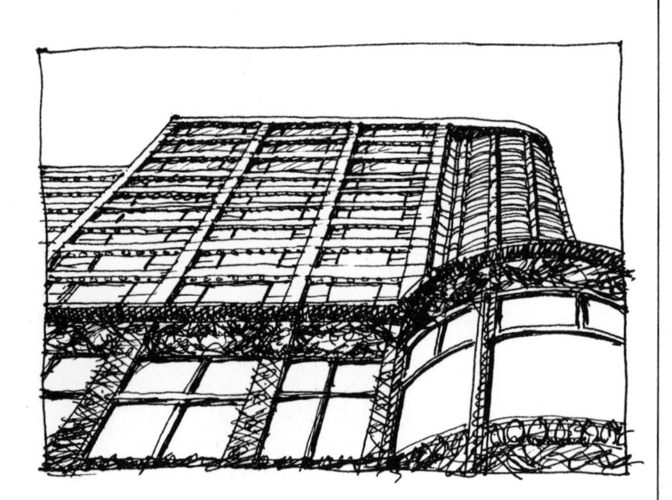

I–14 Drawing of Carson Pirie & Scott Department Store, Chicago, Illinois. Designed by Louis Sullivan, 1899–1904

tects in the West and a founder of San Francisco's Bay Area Style. He had studied in the atelier André at the Ecole during the 1880s and then worked with Carrère & Hastings on the Ponce de Leon Hotel in St. Augustine, Florida, before moving to California. His many projects included the Christian Science Church (1910) in Berkeley, the Palace of Fine Arts (1915) in San Francisco (see fig. I–15), and the half-timbered Roos House (1909) and the shingled Goslinsky House (1909), both in San Francisco.

Another West Coast architect, John Galen Howard, attended the Ecole's atelier Laloux, then trained under H. H. Richardson, and later worked with McKim, Mead & White. He was in charge of the master plan for the University of California at Berkeley (c. 1901) and designed several buildings on the campus, including the Shingle Style Old School of Architecture (1906) and the Renaissance-inspired Mining Building (1907). Willis Polk, who had studied in Paris and headed the San Francisco office of D. H. Burnham & Company, later designed the glass curtain-walled Hallidie Building (1915) in San Francisco and the Crocker Mansion (1913) at Hillsborough.

I–15 Palace of Fine Arts, San Francisco, California. Designed by Bernard Maybeck, 1915

Several other architects carried Beaux-Arts influences to the West Coast. Julia Morgan, designer of William Randolph Hearst's San Simeon Estate (1919–47), graduated from the Ecole following its admission of women in 1897. Ecole graduate Carleton M. Winslow, Sr., was the chief designer in the California office of Cram, Goodhue & Fergusson for the Panama-Californian Exposition in San Diego in 1915. Other Beaux-Arts architects and firms in the region included Bakewell & Brown, designers of the San Francisco City Hall (1913–15), and Myron Hunt, who planned the Henry E. Huntington Estate (1910–20) in San Marino, California.

In the southern United States, major Beaux-Arts projects included the George W. Vanderbilt Estate, Biltmore (1888–95), in Asheville, North Carolina, designed by Richard Morris Hunt (see fig. I–16); the Henry Flagler Estate, Whitehall (1901), in Palm Beach, Florida; and the Ponce de Leon Hotel in St. Augustine. Both of the latter projects were designed by Carrère & Hastings. In Hot Springs, Virginia, The Homestead Hotel was planned by Warren & Wetmore.

Addison Mizner, who was educated at the Ecole, worked primarily in Palm Beach and planned many private houses and estates, clubs and commercial developments there. Lloyd Morgan, another Ecole graduate, designed Palm Beach's The Breakers Hotel (1926) and Miami's Coral Gables Hilton Hotel (c. 1926) for the New York firm of Schultze & Weaver. Just south of Miami lies the Italian Renaissance-styled James Deering Estate, Vizcaya (c. 1912), designed by Ecole-educated architect F. Burrall

I–16 West view of Biltmore, Asheville, North Carolina. Designed by Richard Morris Hunt, 1888–95

I–17 (above) Drawing of the James Deering Estate, Vizcaya, Dade County, Florida. Designed by F. Burrall Hoffman, Jr., c. 1912

I–18 (left) The typical Beaux-Arts studio, view of a drafting room in the office of Carrère & Hastings, New York, c. 1900

Hoffman, Jr., in collaboration with landscape architect Diego Suarez and design consultant Paul Chalfin (see fig. I–17).

From this brief survey, it is obvious that important examples of Beaux-Arts architecture may be found in a multitude of styles throughout the country. American architects who had graduated from the Ecole or from American universities and ateliers modeled on the Beaux-Arts system fused together existing vernacular traditions with contemporary foreign influences by applying to them the basic abstract principles of spatial organization. While the designs of the Beaux-Arts period often reflect various historical influences in styles, the use of these consistent spatial principles combined with a systematic method of work gives this period its ultimate strength and continuity and still affects the way architects teach and work today, both in architectural schools and offices (see fig. I–18). Following the trail of direct and implied links between the buildings produced today and those of the Beaux-Arts period always leads back to these common principles—and simultaneously documents a valuable and often neglected part of our architectural heritage.

The Development of Estates on Long Island

The earliest estates in New York were part of a system of agricultural land grants, or patroonships, that dated from the period of Dutch settlement in the Hudson River Valley and its environs. The extensive Dutch holdings on western Long Island were gradually overshadowed after 1664 by those of English settlers after they seized the region in the name of the duke of York. As part of the royal colony of New York, lands were then purchased and developed as manors, by permission or grant of the English Crown.

Several areas of Long Island still reflect their ties to this early system of land grants. The most famous and long-lived of the English manors is Gardiners Island, granted by the Crown in 1639 to Lion Gardiner and owned today by the seventeenth lord of the manor of the Gardiner family. About 1686, another estate, the Manor of St. George, in Mastic, was granted by King Charles II to William Tangier Smith, whose descendants later founded Smithtown. A third, Sylvester Manor, had been established in 1652 by Nathaniel Sylvester on Shelter Island as a refuge for Quaker settlers. The manor house itself, completed about 1735, is an imposing Georgian mansion with hipped roof and double chimneys.

Other early Long Island estates have been preserved and are open to the public. Sagtikos Manor in Bay Shore, which was developed from 1692 to 1697 by Stephanus Van Cortlandt, a mayor of New York, is now administered by the Sagtikos Historical Society. Another, Lloyd Manor, was established in 1685 by Joseph Lloyd at Lloyd Neck, near Cold Spring Harbor. The manor house, dating from 1722 to 1763, is a white-shingled, Georgian Colonial design with a central hall and gabled roof. It is maintained today by the Society for the Preservation of Long Island Antiquities, which also looks after Rock Hall, located in Lawrence. This building was erected in 1767 by Gerhardus Clowes for Josiah Martin and is an excellent example of a fully developed and delicately detailed Georgian mansion. It too is open to the public.

The English Georgian influence on estate design, along with some Dutch characteristics, continued through the Colonial period and through the Federal period of the new republic and extended well into the early nineteenth century. During the Greek Revival and the Romantic Revival periods in American architecture, lasting from the 1820s through the Civil War, prominent professionals, artists, and writers—as well as wealthy businessmen—began to commission the building of large country residences on Long Island. Although these estates were often self-

KEEP
RIGHT

sufficient, they did not rely on agriculture for their economic existence. The towns and local communities that adjoined them purchased food and provisions from smaller, individually owned farms.

Several of these large country residences are still in existence. The Onderdonck House in Manhasset, a Greek Revival design, was built in the early 1830s for Horatio Gates Onderdonck, a prominent lawyer and judge (see fig. I–19). It is now owned by the Strathmore Village Association. The Benjamin Huntting House in Sag Harbor, dating from 1845–46, is a Greek Revival mansion built by a wealthy whaler, and its design, attributed to Minard Lafever, includes a domed skylight over a prominent central stair. Most fittingly, this building now houses the Suffolk County Whaling Museum. Lafever is also credited with the design of the First Presbyterian, or Old Whalers', Church in Sag Harbor, constructed between 1843 and 1844, and designed with a combination of Greek Revival and Egyptian Revival elements.

The architectural and social developments of the Hudson River Valley often paralleled and influenced similar developments on Long Island. From the initial influences of Dutch manors and farmhouses through the growth of the Hudson River School of Romantic artists, writers, and naturalists, examples of this cross-influence are frequent. The Romantic Revival works of Alexander Jackson Davis along the Hudson, such as the Gothic Revival structure, Lyndhurst (1838–65) in Tarrytown, and the Delamater House (1844) at Rhinebeck, are paralleled by the projects of Calvert Vaux, Frederick Withers, and Jacob Wrey Mould on Long Island. Cedarmere, now owned by the Nassau County Museum, was the Roslyn estate of the Romantic poet and naturalist William Cullen Bryant (see fig. I–20). Developed in 1843, the estate incorporates an earlier eighteenth-century farmhouse with design alterations and additions, including a boathouse and studio. Its design is attributed to Calvert Vaux, an early associate of Andrew Jackson Downing, and parallels Alexander Jackson Davis's work at Rhinebeck. The landscaping and master plan of Cedarmere are attributed to Frederick Law Olmsted, who collaborated with Vaux on the designs for Central Park in New York City and who was responsible for the planning of the most famous naturalistic park systems in the United States.

Other Romantic Revival estate designs on Long Island include Brecknock Hall, a large Italianate stone villa in Greenport, built in 1857 for the whaler David Gelston Floyd. The E. C. Litchfield Mansion, now located in Brook-

I–19 (opposite above) The Onderdonck House in Manhasset, Long Island, a Greek Revival design, c. 1830

I–20 (opposite below) Cedarmere, Roslyn, Long Island, whose design has been attributed to Calvert Vaux, c. 1843

I–21 Drawing of Wenlo, Glenwood Landing, near Roslyn, Long Island. Designed by Jacob Wrey Mould, 1868

lyn's Prospect Park, was designed by Alexander Jackson Davis in 1857 and combines both Italianate and Gothic Revival elements. A later house, Wenlo, at Glenwood Landing, near Roslyn, designed in 1868 for the naval architect Thomas Clapham, also combines Italianate and Victorian Gothic elements in rough stonework similar to that of Brecknock Hall and to that of Château-sur-Mer in Newport, Rhode Island (see fig. I–21). Its architect, Jacob Wrey Mould, collaborated with Calvert Vaux on the design of the classical terrace and esplanade of Central Park and on the original design for the Metropolitan Museum of Art in New York.

Sycamore Lodge in Roslyn Harbor, designed by architect Frederick S. Copley in the 1860s, shows the Dutch influence of Flemish gables combined with Gothic Revival elements. The Cliffs, planned by Henry G. Harrison and constructed in 1836 at Mill Neck as a summer home for James William Beekman, is another important example of Gothic Revival estate architecture on Long Island (see fig. I–22).

The years following the Civil War were characterized by a tremendous growth in industrial development throughout the country, due in part to the impetus the war had provided in production and manufacturing methods. Technological advances included the Bessemer hot-air process, invented in 1855, which made possible the commercial production of steel in large quantity and facilitated the construction of railroads, buildings, and bridges. The discovery of oil deposits in Pennsylvania and of gold and other minerals in the West was accompanied by the rise of industrial and financial empires headed by speculators and entrepreneurs who exploited and developed the country's resources without government limitation or taxation.

This atmosphere of rapid development was glorified by the Philadelphia Centennial Exposition of 1876, at which new American technological achievements were displayed before all the represented foreign countries. The newly designated Captains of Industry—the businessman and the entrepreneur—were satirized by Mark Twain and Charles Dudley Warner in their novel *The Gilded Age*, published in 1873. This volume depicts a ruthless entrepreneur's "get-rich-quick" schemes, which employed industrialized production methods to make goods of questionable value. Twain admonished a society in which he saw gold becoming a substitute for spiritual values and for traditional morals.

As industrial fortunes grew and mobility increased due to the expanding network of railroads, more and more estates were developed on Long Island. New resorts, clubs, and summer residences sprang up in great numbers. The development of resorts elsewhere, such as at Saratoga Springs, Oak Bluffs, Mount Desert Island, Newport, and Elberon, was paralleled on Long Island by developments at Sea Cliff, Lawrence, Islip, Southampton, and Montauk Point. Sea Cliff, near Glen Cove, began in 1871 as a Methodist summer camp and grew into a popular resort in the 1880s. On the South Shore, the Rockaway Hunt Club was established in the 1870s in Cedarhurst. By 1875 the Long Island Rail Road's three main lines, serving the north, south, and interior sections of Long Island, were essentially complete. In the following years large summer residences and clubs were erected in central Long Island and on its East End. The Southside Sportsmen's Club, established in 1864 at Oakdale, near Islip, had its own railroad station (see page 203) and was adjacent to the grandiose summer estates of Pierre Lorillard and of William K. Vanderbilt, Sr. (see page 209). The Wyandanch Club, a major hunting preserve, was founded in 1880 near Smithtown. During the 1880s and 1890s, summer homes proliferated farther out on the island at Southampton, East Hampton, and Montauk Point.

Early designs of this period reflected the influences of the French Second Empire, or Mansardic, Style and later ones the Queen Anne Style with Tudor elements. The Second Empire Style in resort design was epitomized by the Grand Union Hotel (1872) in Saratoga Springs, and on Long Island this style could be seen in the Wyandanch Club. The French Mansardic influence was also evident in the 1868 design for H. H. Richardson's own house on Staten Island. In 1872 the William S. Wetmore residence, Château-sur-Mer, in Newport was altered and renovated by Richard Morris Hunt, who developed a central Beaux-Arts–inspired grand interior space that was set within a French Mansardic exterior.

The work of both Hunt and Richardson reflected these architects' formal training in French design and was combined with their personal adaptation of the vernacular Second Empire Style in the United States. Domestic Queen Anne and Tudor influences were also interpreted by Richardson, in the Watts Sherman House (1874) at Newport, and by Hunt, in St. Mark's Church (1878–80) in Islip (see fig. A–1), as well as in the original William K. Vanderbilt, Sr., Estate, Idle Hour (1876), at Oakdale (see page 209).

The transition from the Queen Anne Style to the Shingle Style may be seen on Long Island in three estates that have

I–22 Drawings of The Cliffs, Oyster Bay, Long Island, an example of Gothic Revival estate architecture, c. 1863

I–23 Drawings of the Adams/Derby House, Oyster Bay, Long Island. Designed by Potter & Robertson, 1878

remained in private hands—the Adams/Derby House (1878) in Oyster Bay, designed by Potter & Robertson (see fig. I–23); the Mrs. Anna C. Alden House (1879–80) at Lloyd Neck, by McKim, Mead & Bigelow; and the Alice Roosevelt House (1882) in Oyster Bay, designed by Bruce Price. This development can also be seen in the Association Houses (1882–84) at Montauk Point, by McKim, Mead & White (see page 237). These houses are somewhat related in design to Edna Villa (1881–82), Isaac Bell's Newport home, which was also designed about the same time by McKim, Mead & White.

During this transitional era, French design influence continued to be seen in large residential and resort designs, most notably in the French Château Style of the William K. Vanderbilt, Sr., Mansion (1881) in New York, by Richard Morris Hunt, and in the Ogden Goelet summer residence, Ochre Court (1889–91) in Newport, also designed by Hunt. The Narragansett Casino (1881–84) and the Charles J. Osborn Estate (1884–85), in Mamaroneck, New York, both planned by McKim, Mead & White, also exhibited French influences. However, by the 1890s, this design influence had largely been replaced on Long Island by the Shingle Style, which dominated residential architectural designs at that time. Important examples of estates in the Queen Anne and Shingle styles on Long Island include the now-demolished Sunset Hall (1883) in Lawrence, by Lamb & Rich; Theodore Roosevelt's Residence, Sagamore Hill (1884–86), in Oyster Bay, also designed by Lamb & Rich (see page 163); and Westbrook (1886), at Great River, designed by Charles C. Haight for William Bayard Cutting (see page 191).

As the era of American industrial expansion and development progressed, great empires were built and unprecedentedly large industrial fortunes were amassed—by Commodore Cornelius Vanderbilt in railroads; by Henry Clay Frick, J. P. Morgan, and Henry Phipps in steel; by John D. Rockefeller and Charles Pratt in petroleum; by Daniel Guggenheim and Clarence H. Mackay in metals; by Jay Gould and Otto Kahn in finance; and, later, by Walter P. Chrysler and Henry Ford in the new automobile industry. Mark Twain's satirical epithet "the Gilded Age" gradually became the name of an entire period, and equally satirical phrases that described the manners, mores, and habitats of "high society" at the turn of the century became current.

The term "Gold Coast" satirized the development of large estates along the shore of ocean or lake by industrial moguls whose wealth had been amassed during the Gilded Age. While a Gold Coast community of large estates developed on the North Shore of Long Island, similar Gold Coasts of opulent residences emerged along other shores—on Lake Michigan north of Chicago and in such communities north of Boston as Beverly, Swampscott, and Manchester-by-the-Sea. That the name "Gold Coast" also evoked the imperialistic nature of the Gold Coast of Africa, a symbol of mining and speculative interests, was ironically appropriate.

As the Gilded Age came to represent both a social structure and an era, the term "Gold Coast" came to symbolize the environment of large country homes and estates on or near the waterfront, country extensions of the city mansions and town houses of the well-to-do. Gold Coast estates also were erected on the South Shore and the East End of Long Island, and examples of these, as well as of some transitional, early Queen Anne and Shingle Style houses, have been included in this guide in order to give a more complete picture of the development of the Gold Coast era of estate architecture on Long Island.

Social life at country residences, resorts, and city mansions during this period was documented by novelist Edith Wharton in her books *The Age of Innocence* (1920) and *The House of Mirth* (1905) and by Maxfield Parrish and Charles Dana Gibson in their illustrations. Society figures sat for their portraits to such artists as Thomas Eakins and

John Singer Sargent, and in their residences they hung landscapes by William Merritt Chase, among other artists, for whom McKim, Mead & White had designed (attributed) the Shinnecock Art School, near Southampton, about 1892 (see page 223).

Sport and recreation formed an important part of Gold Coast social life. In 1895 McKim, Mead & White planned the Shinnecock Hills Golf Club in the Shingle Style, combined with later Colonial Revival elements. Other major clubs built on Long Island during this era included the Seawanhaka-Corinthian Yacht Club, founded in 1871 at Oyster Bay, and the Meadowbrook Polo Club, whose Colonial Revival structure was designed by John Russell Pope in 1906 at Jericho. In 1903 Belmont Racing Park was established near Floral Park, and in 1908 the Long Island Motor Parkway, constructed by William K. Vanderbilt, Jr., was completed (see page 185).

The Shingle Style phase in Long Island estate design gradually developed into the Colonial Revival style, largely due to the influence of McKim, Mead & White. This development can be seen in this firm's plans for the Edwin D. Morgan Estate (1891–1900) at Wheatley Hills, which has been demolished except for three small fragments that have been converted into separate buildings (see fig. I–24). The original design combined a large shingled residence with Colonial Revival detailing—classic column orders, denticulated eaves with painted exterior trim—and a major courtyard development of formally aligned gardens and vistas. McKim, Mead & White had used similar themes in their 1889 design for Edwin D. Morgan's Newport Mansion, Beacon Rock, a large Palladian villa built on a rocky outcropping surrounded by water.

The Mrs. K. A. Wetherill House (1894–96) at St. James, designed by McKim, Mead & White, is a smaller example of the transition to the Colonial Revival Style, as is Stanford White's own residence, Box Hill (1892–1902), also in St. James, which incorporates an earlier farmhouse (see fig. I–25). White was also responsible for another major Beaux-Arts interpretation of the Colonial Revival Style on Long Island, the James L. Breese Estate, The Orchard (1898–1906), in Southampton, a structure that also incorporates an earlier farmhouse (see page 229). The grand ballroom, or music room, addition to this mansion combines a large-scale, Tudor Eclectic interior with the smaller scale of a Colonial country house on the exterior.

The French Château (or Francis I) influence in estate design gradually changed to the more formal French and

I–24 (opposite above) Edwin D. Morgan Estate, Wheatley Hills, Long Island. Designed by McKim, Mead & White, 1891–1900

I–25 (opposite below) View from the garden of Stanford White's own residence, Box Hill, St. James, Long Island. Designed by the architect, 1892–1902, and still owned by members of his family

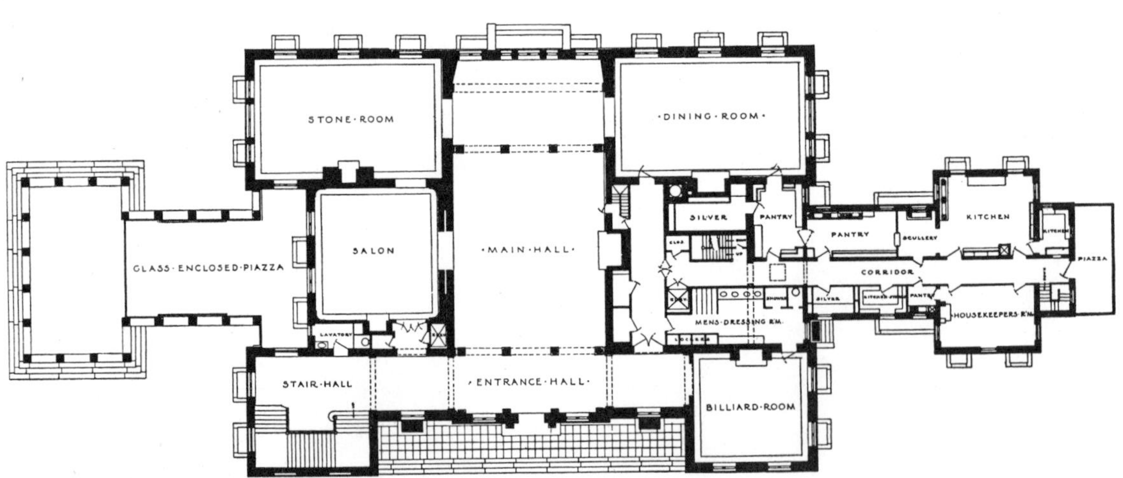

I–26 Clarence H. Mackay Estate, Harbor Hill, Roslyn, Long Island. Entrance elevation and main-floor plan. The house was designed by McKim, Mead & White, 1902–1905

Italian Renaissance Eclectic styles. The Clarence H. Mackay Estate (1902–1905) in Roslyn, designed by McKim, Mead & White, now no longer standing, employed both medieval French Château and French Renaissance design elements in a symmetrical monumental composition (see fig. I–26). This contrasted with the earlier Colonial Revival residential scale of the Edwin D. Morgan Residence at Wheatley Hills, although the Morgan Estate, with its enclosed courtyards and gardens, was actually a larger development. McKim, Mead & White also designed the large French Renaissance Herman Oelrichs Residence, Rosecliff (1900–1902), in Newport, well known today as the setting for the 1974 Hollywood film version of F. Scott Fitzgerald's *The Great Gatsby* (see fig. I–11). Two of the best-known examples of Renaissance Eclectic Style were designed by Richard Morris Hunt at Newport—Marble House (1892) for William K. Vanderbilt, Sr., and The Breakers (1892–95) for Cornelius Vanderbilt (see fig. I–9).

Examples of French Renaissance influences on Long Island included the now-demolished Château des Beaux-Arts Casino (1905) at Huntington, designed by Delano & Aldrich; the F. W. Woolworth Estate, Winfield Hall (1916), at Glen Cove, planned by C. P. H. Gilbert (see page 91); and the Otto Kahn Estate (c. 1923) in Woodbury, also designed by Delano & Aldrich and now owned by Eastern Military Academy. The George McKesson Brown Estate (1910–11) at Huntington, designed by Clarence Luce, is a late example of the French Château Style on Long Island (see page 177).

With the desire for more formal period or eclectic styles at the turn of the century, the Colonial Revival influence soon led to more elaborate and larger-scaled English Georgian and Palladian styles. This transition is seen in the design of the Lloyd Bryce/Childs Frick Estate, Clayton (1895), at Roslyn Harbor, by Ogden Codman, Jr., an architect who was associated with novelist Edith Wharton in formulating the theories of interior design propounded in *The Decoration of Houses* (see page 86). In 1902 the New York architect Ernest Flagg designed Frederick G. Bourne's Georgian-Palladian estate at Oakdale, now La-Salle Military Academy (see fig. A–7), and in 1906 the English designer George Crawley created Westbury House, a mansion in the style of a Charles II country manor, for John S. Phipps at Old Westbury, with a grandiose system of terraces and axes extending into formal gardens and grand vistas (see page 123).

The Eclectic Tudor and English medieval styles that de-

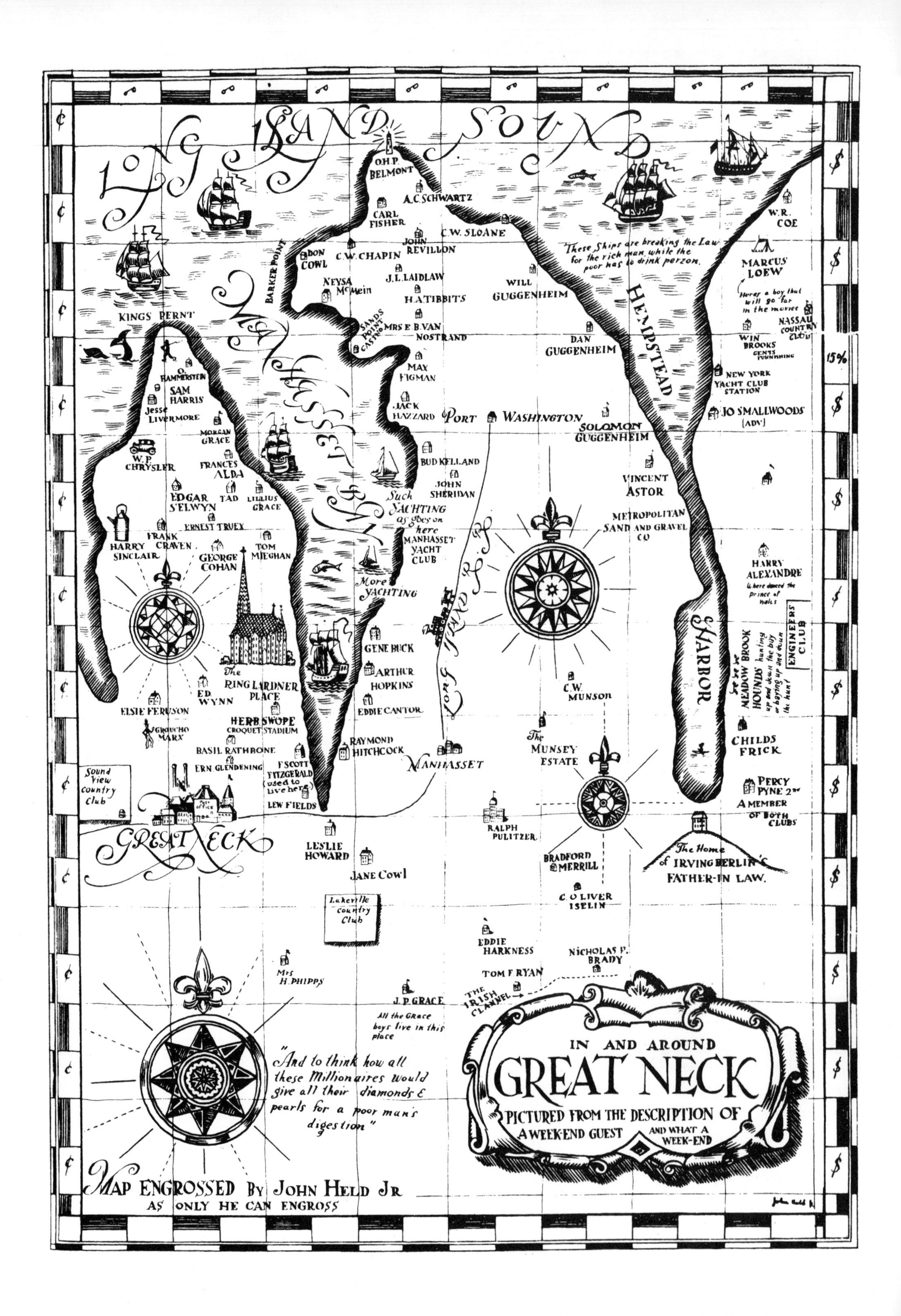

LONG ISLAND SOUND
O.H.P. BELMONT
A.C. SCHWARTZ
CARL FISHER
JOHN REVILLON
C.W. SLOANE
W.R. COE
These Ships are breaking the Law for the rich man while the poor has to drink perzon.
DON COWL
C.W. CHAPIN
BARKER POINT
NEYSA McMein
J.L. LAIDLAW
H.A. TIBBITS
WILL GUGGENHEIM
MARCUS LOEW
Here's a boy that will go far in the movies
NASSAU COUNTRY CLUB
KINGS PERNT
SANDS POINT CASINO
MRS E.B. VAN NOSTRAND
MANHASSET BAY
DAN GUGGENHEIM
HEMPSTEAD HARBOR
WIN BROOKS GENTS FURNISHING
15%
O. HAMMERSTEIN
MAX FIGMAN
NEW YORK YACHT CLUB STATION
SAM HARRIS
JESSE LIVERMORE
JACK HAZZARD
PORT WASHINGTON
SOLOMON GUGGENHEIM
JO SMALLWOODS (ADV)
MORGAN GRACE
W.P. CHRYSLER
FRANCES ALDA
BUD KELLAND
JOHN SHERIDAN
VINCENT ASTOR
EDGAR S'ELWYN
TAD
LILLIUS GRACE
Such YACHTING as goes on here
METROPOLITAN SAND AND GRAVEL CO
ERNEST TRUEX
FRANK CRAVEN
HARRY SINCLAIR
GEORGE COHAN
TOM MIEGHAN
MANHASSET YACHT CLUB
HARRY ALEXANDRE
Where danced the Prince of Wales
More YACHTING
LONG ISLAND R.R.
ENGINEERS' CLUB
GENE BUCK
MEADOW BROOK HOUNDS hunting up and down the buy or buying up and down the hunt
The RING LARDNER PLACE
ARTHUR HOPKINS
C.W. MUNSON
ED WYNN
ELSIE FERUSON
EDDIE CANTOR
HERB SWOPE CROQUET STADIUM
GROUCHO MARX
RAYMOND HITCHCOCK
The MUNSEY ESTATE
CHILDS FRICK
BASIL RATHBONE
ERN GLENDENING
F SCOTT FITZGERALD (used to live here)
MANHASSET
Sound View Country Club
LEW FIELDS
PERCY PYNE 2nd A MEMBER OF BOTH CLUBS
RALPH PULITZER
GREAT NECK
LESLIE HOWARD
JANE COWL
BRADFORD MERRILL
The Home of IRVING BERLIN'S FATHER-IN LAW.
C. OLIVER ISELIN
Lakeville Country Club
EDDIE HARKNESS
NICHOLAS F. BRADY
Mrs H. PHIPPS
TOM F RYAN
THE IRISH CHANNEL
J.P. GRACE
All the Grace boys live in this place
IN AND AROUND
GREAT NECK
PICTURED FROM THE DESCRIPTION OF A WEEK-END GUEST AND WHAT A WEEK-END
"And to think how all these Millionaires would give all their diamonds & pearls for a poor man's digestion"
MAP ENGROSSED BY JOHN HELD JR AS ONLY HE CAN ENGROSS

veloped during this period were elaborate departures from the earlier Tudor influences of the Queen Anne Style in country residences, the scale again becoming greater and the compositions more formal. The William C. Whitney Estate at Old Westbury, designed about 1902 by McKim, Mead & White, was an example of this developing trend. In 1898–99 George A. Freeman had planned the William C. Whitney Racing Stables and Gymnasium, both of which have a Queen Anne and Tudor character (see page 109), but the main house, now demolished, was designed in a large-scale Eclectic Tudor Style. The Eclectic Tudor Style was accompanied by the rise of equally imposing designs for English medieval manor houses and Jacobean palaces. Good examples include the Howard Gould/Daniel Guggenheim Estate, Castlegould (1909) in Sands Point, planned by Hunt & Hunt (see page 58), and the Herbert L. Pratt Estate, The Braes (1912), in Glen Cove, designed by James Brite (see page 95).

Later, during the 1920s, the French Provincial Eclectic Style began to reflect a different trend toward smaller-scale and less formal compositions, as in the irregular massing and intimate dimensions of the Harry F. Guggenheim Estate, Falaise (1923), at Sands Point, designed by Frederick J. Sterner, in association with Polhemus & Coffin (see page 67). The Spanish Colonial Style also became popular during these years and provided an appropriate historical context for the growing use of reinforced concrete in residential design. The William K. Vanderbilt, Jr., Estate, Eagle's Nest (1928; 1934–36), at Centerport, planned by Warren & Wetmore, is one of the most important examples of the Spanish Colonial influence on Long Island estate design (see page 185).

Between 1910 and 1930, literary and theatrical residential communities became a much-publicized part of Long Island life. Long Beach, on the South Shore, boasted the summer homes of Florenz Ziegfeld, Eddie Foy, and George Murphy, and Great Neck, on the North Shore, had the country residences of Lillian Russell, George M. Cohan, Leslie Howard, Eddie Cantor, Oscar Hammerstein, Ring Lardner, Sinclair Lewis, and F. Scott Fitzgerald.

These celebrities continued the social depiction of the Gold Coast era, which had first been described in the works of Edith Wharton and later were documented in Theodore Dreiser's *Twelve Men* (see page 216). The estates formed the settings of the plays of Philip Barry, and the image of the Gold Coast was employed in George S. Kaufman's *Merrily We Roll Along*, in such musicals as George and Ira Gershwin's *Oh, Kay!*, and in the illustrations of John

I–27 (opposite) Map of Great Neck, Long Island, by John Held, Jr., first published in The New Yorker *in 1927. Great Neck, Sands Point, and Port Washington inspired the principal setting of F. Scott Fitzgerald's* The Great Gatsby, *published in 1925*

Held, Jr. (see fig. I–27). The era's image culminated in F. Scott Fitzgerald's novel *The Great Gatsby*, whose story unfolded on opulent estates in Great Neck and Sands Point.

Soon after this Golden Age, the Great Depression of the 1930s and the traumatic onset of World War II brought an end to the Gold Coast as it had flourished during the Beaux-Arts period of estate design. Changing social and economic conditions required federal and local governments and society in general to deal with the urgent problems of poverty, unemployment, need for low-cost housing, and the necessary development of industrialized, rather than handcrafted, building techniques. The Gold Coast and its privileged way of life succumbed to the pressures and realities of a modern postwar society, but many of its great estates have had a more enduring existence than the socioeconomic conditions that permitted their creation.

This guide is a handbook to thirty-two Long Island estates, all of which have survived in some form and most of which are open to or visible to the public.

Elements of Beaux-Arts Estate Design

The appearance and the growth of estates on Long Island have been briefly traced, and related social and historical events leading up to the development of the Gold Coast have been summarized. It is now important to review some of the major design elements that relate these great houses of the Gold Coast era to one another. Many of the academic principles that may be identified in the Beaux-Arts designs of these estates are equally important to contemporary architectural projects.

The concept of *interpenetrating spaces* can be identified in the plan of the Howard Gould/Daniel Guggenheim Estate, Castlegould, at Sands Point (see fig. I–28). This concept is employed in the overlapping spatial relationships between the living hall, the skylighted palm court, and the vaulted stair hall. Other estates illustrate this principle as well—for example, the Henri Bendel/Walter P. Chrysler Estate at Kings Point (see page 51) in the open mezzanine off the two-story-high central hall space and the Foxhall Keene/William Grace Holloway Estate at Old Westbury (see page 118) in the interconnected main-floor living spaces. A sense of *transparency*, when exterior spaces become the implied extension or development of interior spaces, may be seen in the Marshall Field III Estate, Caumsett, at Lloyd Neck (see page 170), where an exterior covered loggia projects into the form of the house, creating an extension of the interior central hall. In the William K. Vanderbilt, Sr., Estate, Idle Hour, at Oakdale, an open courtyard and a waterfront porch serve as spatial extensions to either side of the main living hall (see fig. I–29).

The use of openings and changes in levels to define spaces, as opposed to the use of solid walls, can be identified in the Howard Gould/Daniel Guggenheim Estate, Castlegould, at Sands Point (see page 58), where the interior skylighted court is defined by changes in level and in lighting, and where the glass-enclosed terrace is separated from the living hall by an open screen of columns. This device is also used in the William K. Vanderbilt, Sr., Estate, Idle Hour, at Oakdale, where the men's drawing or smoking room is separated from the circulation of the adjacent corridor by a colonnaded wood screen (see fig. I–30).

The influence of interior functions and spaces on exterior forms is seen in the generous covered porches of the Theodore Roosevelt Residence, Sagamore Hill, at Oyster Bay (see page 163), and in the William Bayard Cutting Estate, at Great River (see page 191), as well as in the Lloyd Bryce/Childs Frick Estate, Clayton, at Roslyn Harbor (see page 83). The porches both serve and extend the major

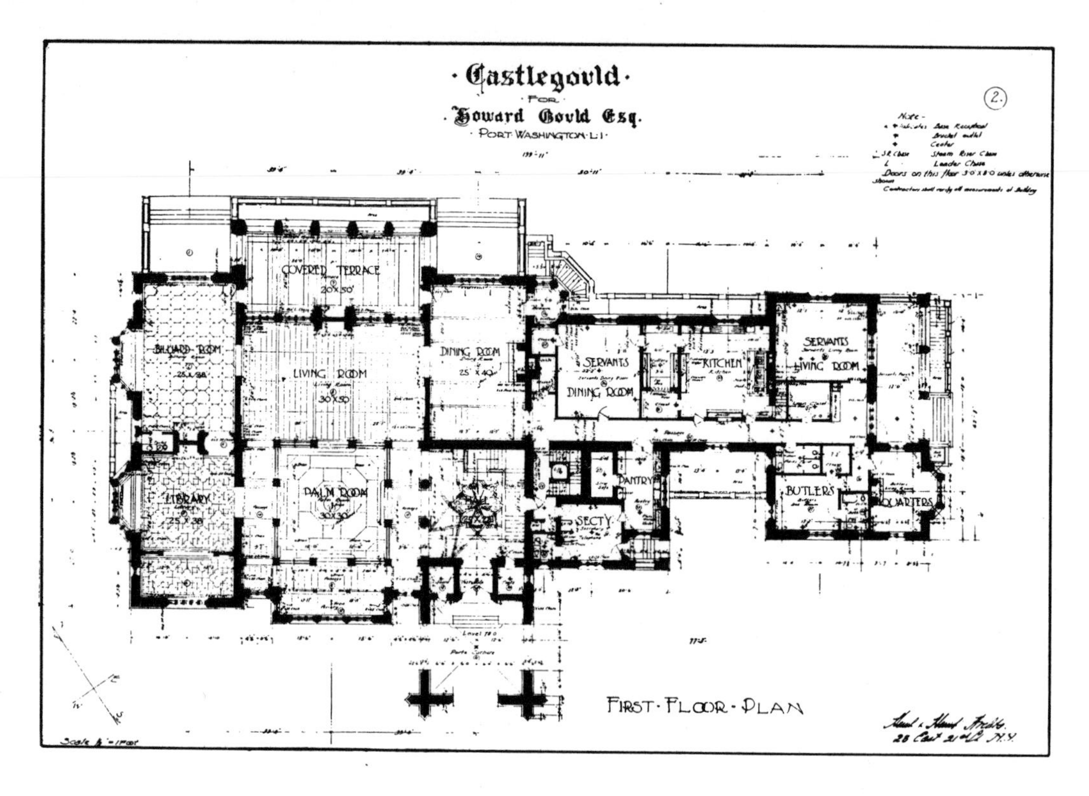

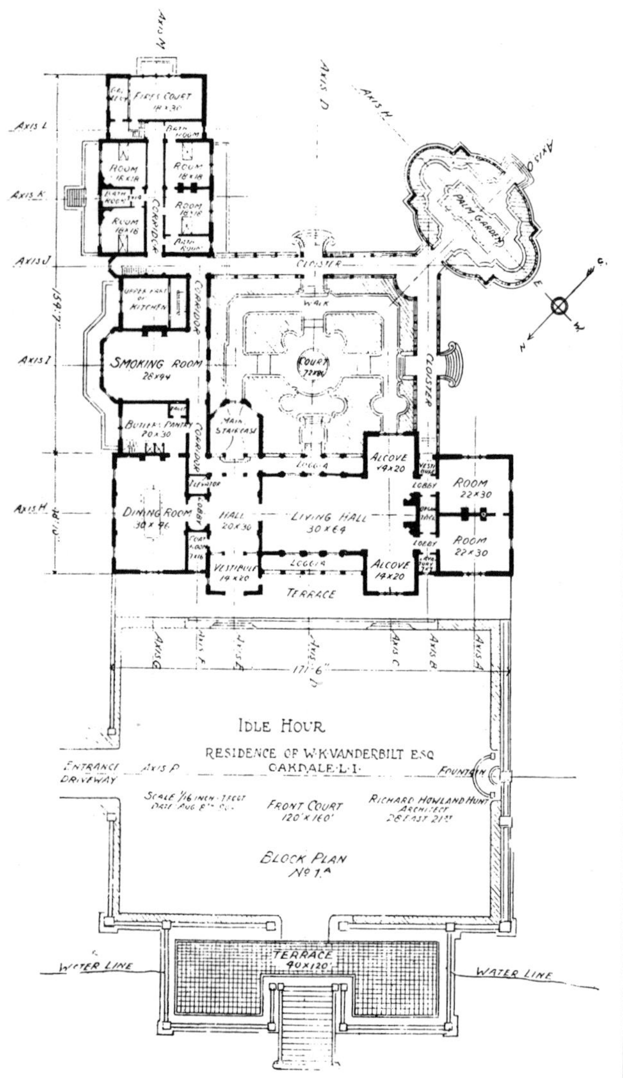

living areas of each of these houses. Both the Howard Gould/Daniel Guggenheim Estate, Castlegould, at Sands Point (see page 58), and the F. W. Woolworth Estate, Winfield Hall, at Glen Cove (see page 91), have prominent entrance porte cocheres that also serve to define and to extend interior spaces in the entry and reception areas. The articulation of differing interior functions is well illustrated in the large service wing of the William R. Coe Estate, Planting Fields, in Upper Brookville (see page 155), which is set at an angle to the main portion of the house and is designed with a completely different physical character. The importance of functional relationships in the *parti* or layout of the house, particularly the separation of service elements from social areas, may be seen in many other designs. In the Alfred I. Du Pont/Mrs. Frederick Guest Estate, Templeton, at Brookville (see page 101), and in the Harry F. Guggenheim Estate, Falaise, at Sands Point (see page 67), service circulations within the houses were entirely separate, with independent service-access courtyards. In the Lloyd Bryce/Childs Frick Estate, Clayton, at Roslyn Harbor (see page 83), and in the J. Randolph Robinson Residence, Brookville (see page 135), these service wings were designed as physically independent forms.

The sense of *hierarchy* of form, or the design of major elements or functions in the exterior expression of the house, can be seen in the elevation of the James L. Breese Estate, The Orchard, at Southampton (see page 229),

where the central or main living unit was designed to be physically dominant over the large service and social wings to each side. Even though the music room is actually a larger space, in the elevation its form is subsidiary to the central block. In the William C. Whitney Gymnasium at Old Westbury (see page 109), a major two-story-high space within the building is identified on the exterior by prominent triangular roof gables over the central hall that are perpendicular to the long gable roof over the rest of the structure.

The design *consistency* of window openings and of wall configurations, and the grouping of openings in order further to articulate and extend interior spaces, may be seen in the elevations of the Mrs. Christian R. Holmes Estate, The Chimneys, at Sands Point (see page 79); the Herbert L. Pratt Estate, The Braes, at Glen Cove (see page 95); and the Theodore Roosevelt Residence, Sagamore Hill, at Oyster Bay (see page 163). The definition of exterior spaces by the juxtaposition of solids and voids can be identified in the defined open spaces created by the projecting wings and terraces of the Herbert L. Pratt Estate; in the interior courtyard space of the Mrs. Daniel Guggenheim Residence, Mille Fleurs, at Sands Point (see page 73); and in the garden terrace formed by the service dependencies of the Lloyd Bryce/Childs Frick Estate, Clayton, at Roslyn Harbor (see page 83).

A variety of spatial relationships is employed in the various layouts or *partis* of the residences. In the *central-*

I–28 (opposite above) Howard Gould/Daniel Guggenheim Estate, Castlegould, Sands Point. The main-floor plan, provides a good illustration of interpenetrating spaces and the use of axes

I–29 (opposite below) William K. Vanderbilt, Sr., Estate, Idle Hour, Oakdale. The main-floor plan illustrates both the transparency and the interpenetration of interior and exterior spaces

I–30 (above) William K. Vanderbilt, Sr., Estate, Idle Hour, Oakdale. The men's smoking room is separated from the adjacent corridor by a colonnaded wood screen

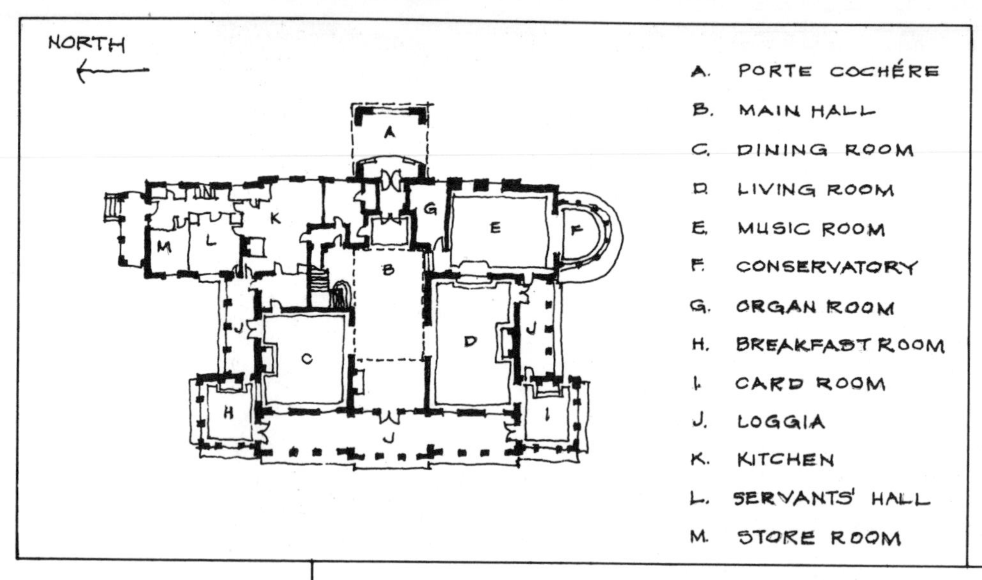
NORTH
A. PORTE COCHÈRE
B. MAIN HALL
C. DINING ROOM
D. LIVING ROOM
E. MUSIC ROOM
F. CONSERVATORY
G. ORGAN ROOM
H. BREAKFAST ROOM
I. CARD ROOM
J. LOGGIA
K. KITCHEN
L. SERVANTS' HALL
M. STORE ROOM

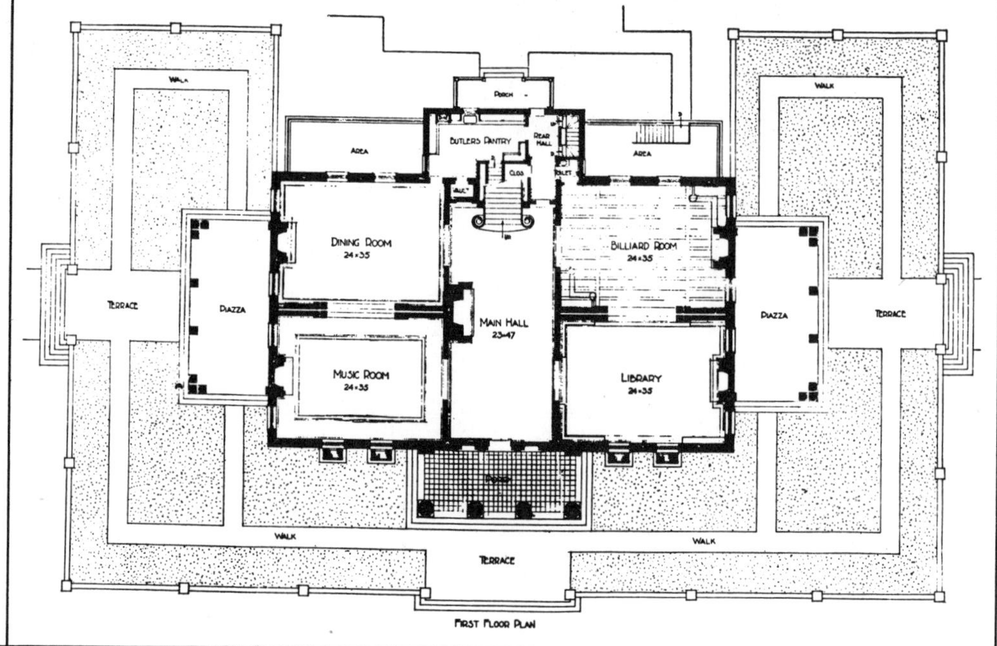
WALK
PORCH
BUTLERS PANTRY
REAR HALL
AREA
AREA
DINING ROOM
24×35
BILLIARD ROOM
24×35
TERRACE
PIAZZA
MAIN HALL
23×47
PIAZZA
TERRACE
MUSIC ROOM
24×35
LIBRARY
24×35
WALK
WALK
TERRACE
FIRST FLOOR PLAN

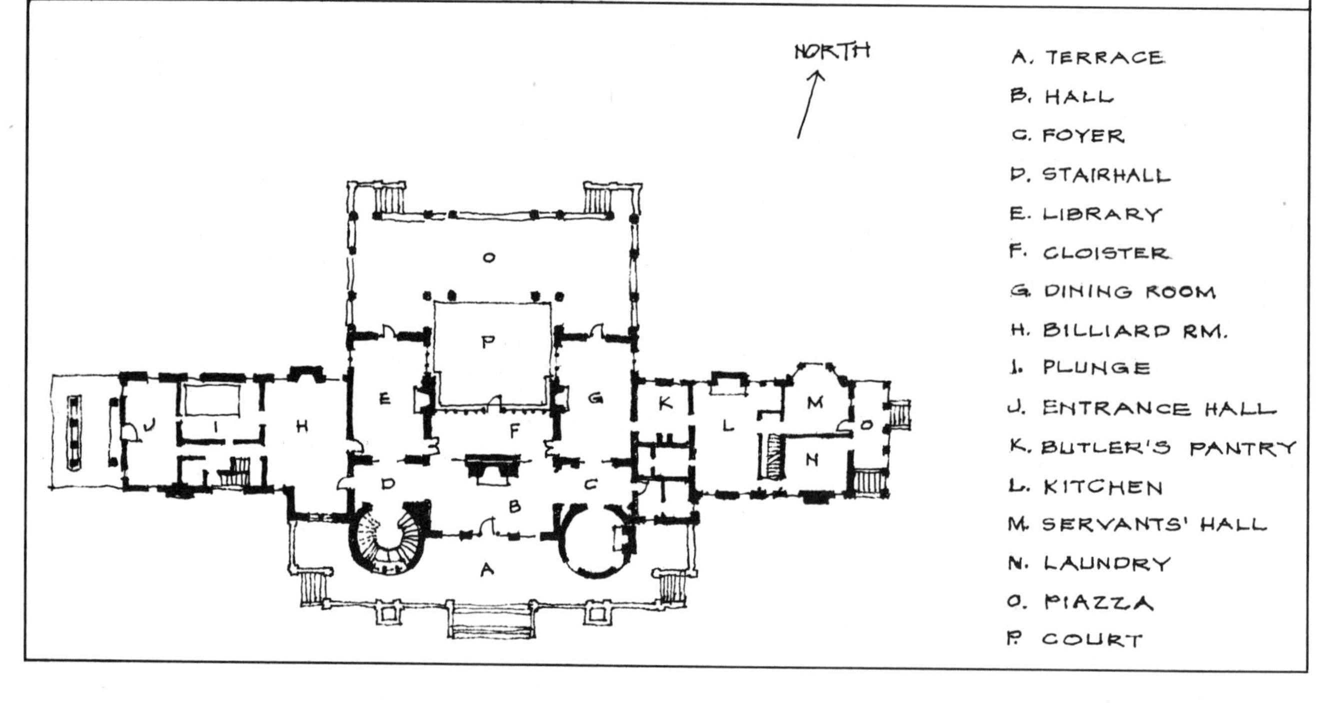
NORTH
A. TERRACE
B. HALL
C. FOYER
D. STAIRHALL
E. LIBRARY
F. CLOISTER
G. DINING ROOM
H. BILLIARD RM.
I. PLUNGE
J. ENTRANCE HALL
K. BUTLER'S PANTRY
L. KITCHEN
M. SERVANTS' HALL
N. LAUNDRY
O. PIAZZA
P. COURT

hall parti a major interior hallway, occasionally combined with the main living spaces, is used to organize the plan. The Henri Bendel/Walter P. Chrysler Estate at Kings Point (see fig. I–31), with its two-story-high living hall, the Foxhall Keene/William Grace Holloway Estate at Old Westbury (see fig. I–32), and the Egerton L. Winthrop, Jr., Estate at Syosset (see page 149) illustrate the use of this type of parti. The *courtyard parti* employs a central exterior space about which its design is organized. It can be identified in the William K. Vanderbilt, Jr., Estate, Eagle's Nest, at Centerport (see page 185), in the William K. Vanderbilt, Sr., Estate, Idle Hour, at Oakdale (see page 209), and in the George McKesson Brown Estate in Huntington (see fig. I–33). Other basic partis include a *linear* organization, as in the Harry F. Guggenheim Estate, Falaise, at Sands Point (see page 67), and in the Southside Sportsmen's Club, at Oakdale (see page 203), and an *elemental* type of parti, in which the plan is expressed with physically separate units, as in the Lloyd Bryce/Childs Frick Estate, Clayton, at Roslyn Harbor (see fig. I–34) and in the J. Randolph Robinson Residence at Brookville (see page 135).

The systems of movement or *circulation* in the designs were studied through the use of interior *axes* and exterior *vistas*. Individuals moving into and through a building were intended to progress through a definite sequence or series of spaces. At the intersections of spaces, minor *cross-axes*, or secondary patterns of movement, were used to articulate the circulation further. In the Howard Gould/Daniel Guggenheim Estate, Castlegould, at Sands Point (see page 58), and in the William K. Vanderbilt, Sr.,

I–31 (opposite above) Henri Bendel/Walter P. Chrysler Estate, Kings Point. The main-floor plan is a good illustration of the central-hall type of parti

I–32 (opposite center) Foxhall Keene/William Grace Holloway Estate, Old Westbury. The main-floor plan provides another good example of the central-hall type of parti

I–33 (opposite below) George McKesson Brown Estate, Huntington. The main-floor plan illustrates the courtyard type of parti, in which the design has been organized about a central exterior space

I–34 (below) Lloyd Bryce/Childs Frick Estate, Clayton, Roslyn Harbor. The main-floor plan illustrates the elemental type of parti, in which the plan is expressed with physically separate units

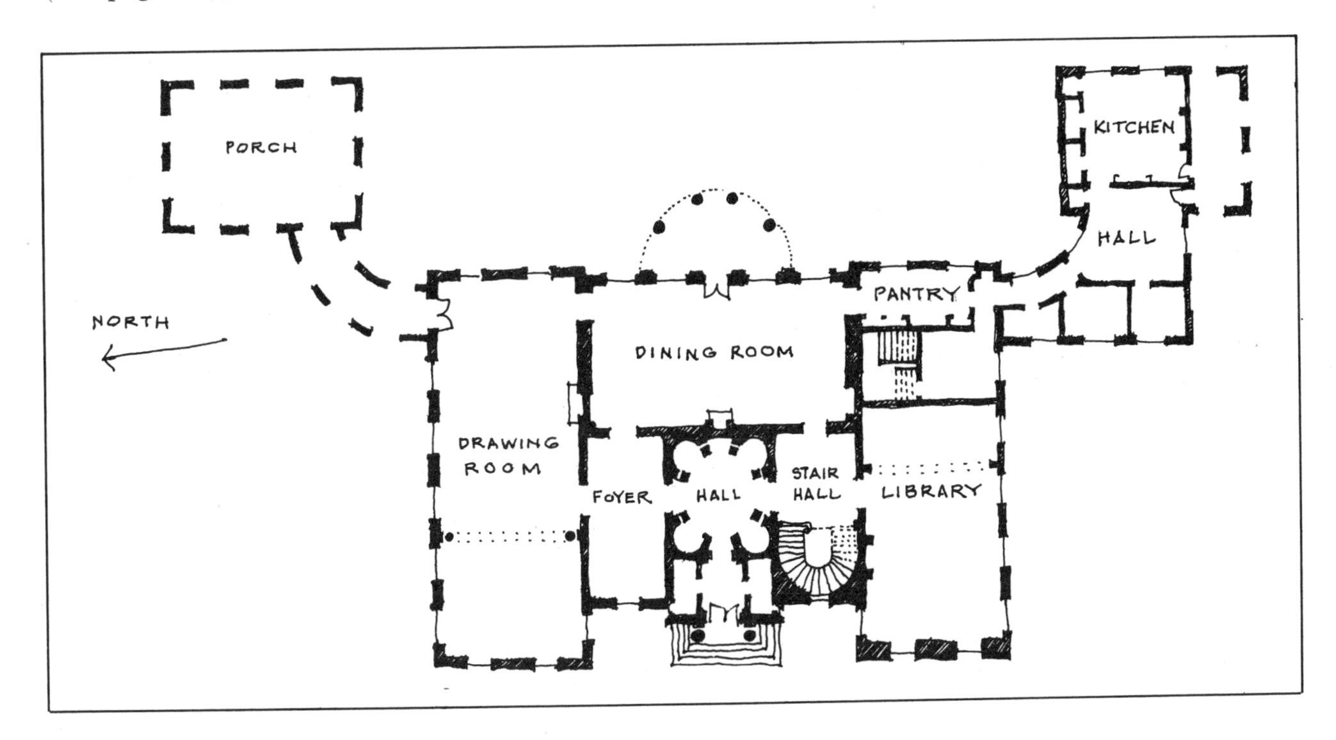

I–35 (opposite above) William Bayard Cutting Estate, Westbrook, Great River. The main-floor plan illustrates an asymmetrical, or irregular, design

I–36 (opposite below) Marjorie Merriweather Post/Edward F. Hutton Estate, Hillwood, Brookville. The main-floor plan provides another illustration of an asymmetrical design

Estate, Idle Hour, at Oakdale (see page 209), the use of axes in the interior spatial organization was an important device. Exterior axial vistas were equally important in the layout of the Herbert L. Pratt Estate, The Braes, at Glen Cove (see page 95) and in the John S. Phipps Estate, Westbury House, at Old Westbury (see page 123), as well as in the master plans of the Egerton L. Winthrop, Jr., Estate at Syosset (see page 149) and the William R. Coe Estate, Planting Fields, at Upper Brookville (see page 155).

Theories of *proportion* and balance, such as the Golden Mean, were used as reference tools to refine physical measurements, just as Le Corbusier's Modular System is employed today. *Symmetry* was another reference tool used to investigate or emphasize the visual balance or proportion of masses. Although designs might be *asymmetrical*, or irregular, the relative proportion of masses was still studied in order to achieve a visual balance. Examples of *symmetrical* schemes include the George McKesson Brown Estate at Huntington (see page 177); the Foxhall Keene/William Grace Holloway Estate at Old Westbury (see page 118); and the Herbert L. Pratt Estate, The Braes, at Glen Cove (see page 95). *Asymmetrical*, or irregular, schemes include the William R. Coe Estate, Planting Fields, at Upper Brookville (see page 155); the William Bayard Cutting Estate, Westbrook, at Great River (see fig. I–35); and the Marjorie Merriweather Post/Edward F. Hutton Estate, Hillwood, at Brookville (see fig. I–36).

The development of an overall *master plan* or site layout was an integral part of the estate design. It began with the relationship of the buildings to the particular characteristics of the site. This concept is illustrated in the positioning of the George McKesson Brown Residence at Huntington (see page 177) on the crest of a hill that slopes down to a large boat harbor. Another good example is the relationship of the Marshall Field III Residence, Caumsett, at Lloyd Neck (see page 170), to a lagoon that opens onto Long Island Sound. The Harry F. Guggenheim Residence, Falaise, at Sands Point (see page 67), is perched dramatically on a steep cliff overlooking the water, and the Robinson/Gossler/Hutton Residence, at Brookville (see page 144), sits atop a hill overlooking a vast meadow and farmland.

The *approach* to the main building was an important element of the master plan. A long, axial entry drive leads to the F. W. Woolworth Residence, Winfield Hall, at Glen Cove (see page 91), and a grand, tree-lined *allée* is the main approach to the John S. Phipps Residence, Westbury

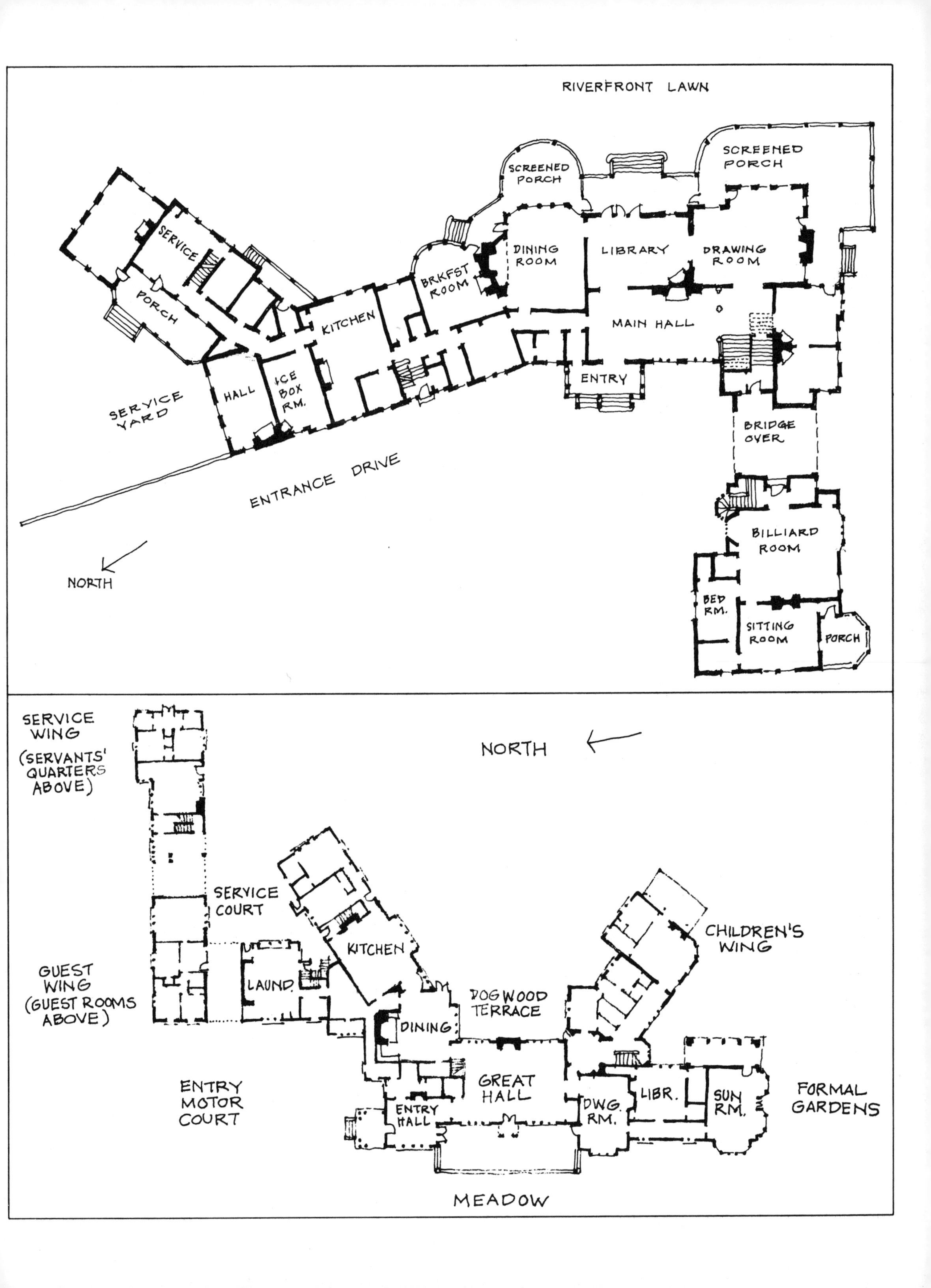

RIVERFRONT LAWN
SCREENED PORCH
SCREENED PORCH
SERVICE
PORCH
DINING ROOM
LIBRARY
DRAWING ROOM
BRKFST ROOM
KITCHEN
MAIN HALL
ENTRY
HALL
ICE BOX RM.
SERVICE YARD
BRIDGE OVER
ENTRANCE DRIVE
NORTH
BILLIARD ROOM
BED RM.
SITTING ROOM
PORCH
SERVICE WING (SERVANTS' QUARTERS ABOVE)
NORTH
SERVICE COURT
KITCHEN
CHILDREN'S WING
GUEST WING (GUEST ROOMS ABOVE)
LAUND.
DOGWOOD TERRACE
DINING
GREAT HALL
ENTRY MOTOR COURT
ENTRY HALL
DWG. RM.
LIBR.
SUN RM.
FORMAL GARDENS
MEADOW

House, at Old Westbury (see page 123). Formal entrance courtyards often form part of the site plan, as in the fore-court of the Herbert L. Pratt Estate, The Braes, at Glen Cove (see page 95), and in the walled entry courts of the Mr. and Mrs. Roderick Tower Residence at Old Westbury (see page 114); the Harry F. Guggenheim Estate, Falaise, at Sands Point (see page 67); and the William K. Vanderbilt, Sr., Estate, Idle Hour, at Oakdale (see page 209). Approaches or driveways were sometimes visually framed by service buildings on the site. The stables of the Egerton L. Winthrop, Jr., Estate at Syosset (see fig. I–37) serve this purpose. Wings of the main residence itself can also create a framed impression, as in the entry drive to the William Bayard Cutting Estate, Westbrook, at Great River (see fig. I–38), and the William K. Vanderbilt, Jr., Estate, Eagle's Nest, at Centerport (see page 185).

The estates of Long Island were often agriculturally self-sufficient, and their master plans included stables for horses, dairy barns, greenhouses, and garages, as well as boathouses, athletic facilities, and gatehouses. These buildings were sometimes placed formally or geometrically in relation to one another, but more often they were positioned

I–37 (opposite above) Egerton L. Winthrop, Jr., Estate, Syosset. The stables serve as a visual frame to the approach to the main house

I–38 (opposite below) William Bayard Cutting Estate, Westbrook, Great River. The entrance drive is visually framed by the wings of the main house

I–39 (above) William Bayard Cutting Estate, Westbrook, Great River. The view of the house and lawn gives an idea of the importance of landscape design in the master plan. The naturalistic landscaping of Westbrook was designed by Frederick Law Olmsted

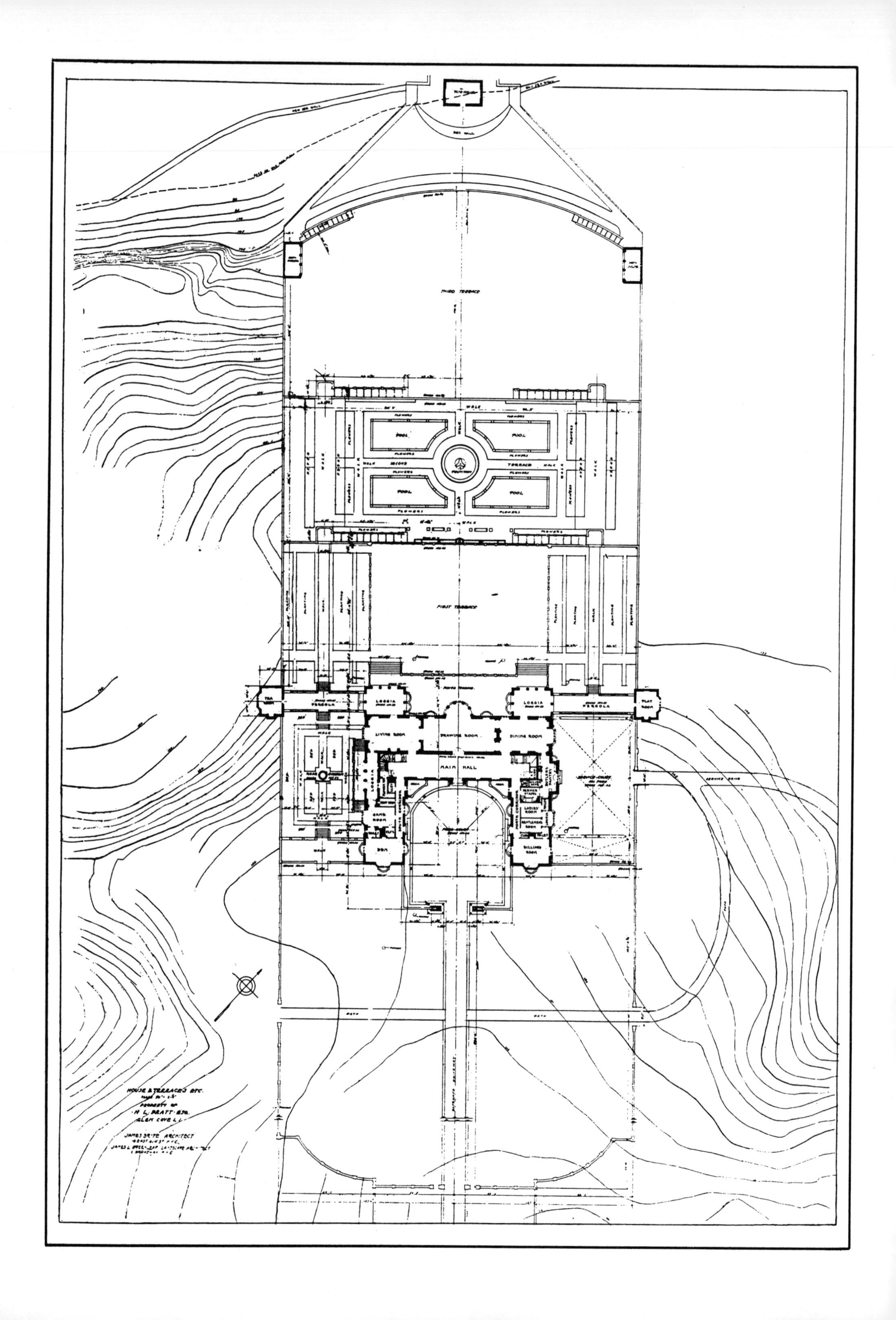
THIRD TERRACE
POOL
POOL
POOL
POOL
FOUNTAIN
SECOND
TERRACE
WALK
FLOWERS
PLANTING
FIRST TERRACE
TEA
PERGOLA
LOGGIA
LOGGIA
PERGOLA
PLAY ROOM
LIVING ROOM
DRAWING ROOM
DINING ROOM
MAIN HALL
SERVICE STAIRS
LADIES ROOM
GENTLEMENS ROOM
BILLIARD ROOM
DEN
SERVICE DRIVE
PATH
HOUSE & TERRACES ETC.
PROPERTY OF
H L PRATT ESQ.
GLEN COVE L I
JAMES BRITE ARCHITECT

according to the nature and size of the site and the contours of the land. The circulation between the service buildings and the main residence was also an important part of the master plan. The William K. Vanderbilt, Sr., Estate, Idle Hour, at Oakdale (see page 209), and the Marshall Field III Estate, Caumsett, at Lloyd Neck (see page 170), were laid out along the scale of town plans.

Landscape design, as a part of a master plan, contained both geometric, or *classical*, elements as well as naturalistic, or *picturesque*, elements, occasionally in the same site. Examples of naturalistic landscape designs include the William Bayard Cutting Estate, Westbrook, at Great River (see fig. I–39), planned by Frederick Law Olmsted; the William R. Coe Estate, Planting Fields, at Upper Brookville (see page 155), designed by the Olmsted Brothers; and the gardens of the Marshall Field III Estate, Caumsett, at Lloyd Neck (see page 170), by Marian C. Coffin. The employment of more formal landscaping and of grand terraces is illustrated in the design of the gardens of the Herbert L. Pratt Estate, The Braes, at Glen Cove (see page 95), planned by James Leal Greenleaf, as well as in the waterfront landscaping of the Henri Bendel/Walter P. Chrysler Estate at Kings Point (see page 51), by Charles W. Leavitt, and in the gardens of the Robinson/Gossler/Hutton Residence at Brookville (see page 144), by Ellen B. Shipman.

Formal landscapes were based on the development of a *grand plan* with *axial vistas*, as in the Herbert L. Pratt Estate, The Braes, at Glen Cove (see fig. I–40). Terraces and architecturally aligned exterior spaces were used with geometric planting configurations and with classical or period garden forms, as in the gardens of the John S. Phipps Estate, Westbury House, at Old Westbury (see fig. I–41). These gardens are now known as Old Westbury Gardens and are open to the public. Naturalistic landscaping, as at the William Bayard Cutting Estate, Westbrook, at Great River (see fig. I–39), included the development of the native physical characteristics of the site in order to reinforce the style and location of plantings and open spaces. Irregular or picturesque groupings of plants and flowers were maintained and/or emphasized. Many of the estate designs included both formal and informal elements, as seen in the master plans for the Marjorie Merriweather Post/Edward F. Hutton Estate, Hillwood, at Brookville (see page 138); for the Egerton L. Winthrop, Jr., Estate at Syosset (see page 149); and for the James L. Breese Estate, The Orchard, at Southampton (see page 229).

In recent years many estates on Long Island have been

I–40 (opposite) Herbert L. Pratt Estate, The Braes, Glen Cove. The site and main-floor plans show the importance of exterior axial vistas in the layout of the estate

I–41 (above) John S. Phipps Estate, Westbury House, Old Westbury. The view of the gardens and terraces furnishes a good example of formal landscaping

I–42 (right) Landon K. Thorne Estate, Bay Shore, was designed by William F. Dominick, and its landscape architects were Ferruccio Vitale and Alfred Geiffert, Jr. This house was demolished in 1976

Gottscho

destroyed, most lamentably the famous Edwin D. Morgan Estate at Wheatley Hills (see fig. I–24) and the Clarence H. Mackay Estate at Roslyn (see fig. I–26). Others now on the endangered list include the F. W. Woolworth Estate, Winfield Hall, at Glen Cove (see page 91), and the James L. Breese Estate, The Orchard, at Southampton (see page 229). The Landon K. Thorne Estate in Bay Shore (see fig. I–42), designed by William F. Dominick, has recently been demolished. The need grows steadily for publicly available information on the historic value of all the Beaux-Arts estates of Long Island. The houses discussed and illustrated in this book, most of which are now community resources and are open to or visible to the public, must serve to create an awareness of the useful potential of the other landmarks of this period now endangered.

The academic principles and methods that the Beaux-Arts system employed continue to exert their influence on the way architects work today. It is in this sense that the Beaux-Arts era has participated in the development of contemporary architecture. The full influence of the Beaux-Arts system in the United States, in general spanning the period between 1880 and 1930, has yet to be completely analyzed. The omission of this period, as it so often is, from architectural histories serves only to give an inaccurate and incomplete picture of the American heritage and its resources. It is this lack of awareness that has resulted in the casual destruction of so many important examples of American architecture.

THE ESTATES

1
Henri Bendel/ Walter P. Chrysler Estate, Kings Point

Henry Otis Chapman, architect, 1916; Charles W. Leavitt, landscape architect, c. 1929; estate now part of the U.S. Merchant Marine Academy; grounds open to the public; located off Steamboat Road

Henri Bendel (1867–1936) came to New York from his native Louisiana in 1899 and established a small millinery shop. From this modest beginning, Bendel's grew to become one of the city's most luxurious and fashionable stores. Its relocation near the intersection of Fifty-seventh Street and Fifth Avenue in 1911 helped to establish that uptown area as a new center of high-society shopping.

In 1916 Bendel commissioned Henry Otis Chapman to design a residence for him at Kings Point. Walter P. Chrysler (1875–1940), founder of the Chrysler Corporation, purchased the estate in 1923 as a summer home. Chrysler had begun his career as a machinist's apprentice, quickly advancing to plant manager and then to president of the Buick Motor Company. After serving as vice-president of General Motors, he created his own firm from the former Maxwell Motor Corporation and in 1920 absorbed Dodge Brothers, another automobile manufacturer. In order to house his company's expanded offices, he commissioned William Van Alen to design the Chrysler Building (1929–31) in New York. This edifice was the world's tallest building for a short time until the completion of the Empire State Building a few blocks distant.

The Chrysler Estate at Kings Point was purchased by the federal government in 1938 after the death of Mrs. Walter P. Chrysler. In 1943 the United States Merchant Marine Academy established itself there, and the main house is now Wiley Hall Administration Center.

Henry Otis Chapman's design for the Bendel/Chrysler Estate is based on a Beaux-Arts version of French Renaissance elements and is related in style to the F. W. Woolworth Estate, Winfield Hall, in Glen Cove by C. P. H. Gilbert (see page 91). The overall plan offers an excellent example of the concept of progression along a central axis, as represented by the central hall, with the main spaces of the house disposed symmetrically along the axis. Vistas leading out to the water, as well as to the formal entrance and gardens, serve as extensions of the central axis.

The house was originally approached along a drive lined with elaborate flower gardens. Today, surrounded by Academy buildings, the entrance is marked by a ship's gun and by a flagpole. The entrance elevation of the house is carefully modeled to appear symmetrical (although it is not), through the use of a surface break with quoins at both ends of the building. In this way the visual length of the wall is shortened, defining the basic square plan of the design and keeping the distance from the entry equal on

1-1 (opposite) Garden retaining wall and west lawn and elevation

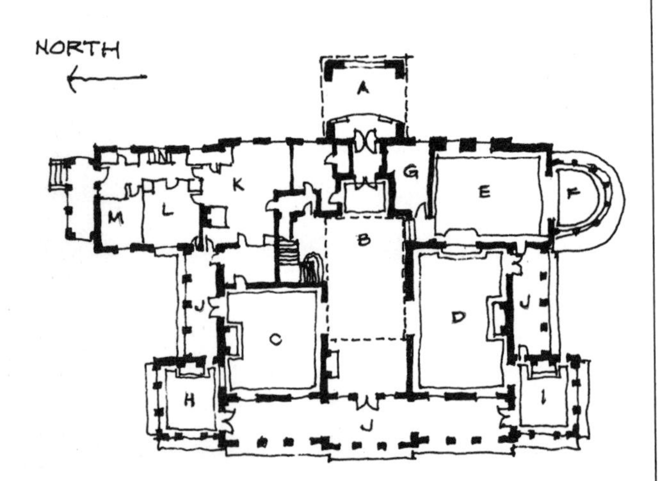

A. PORTE COCHÉRE
B. MAIN HALL
C. DINING ROOM
D. LIVING ROOM
E. MUSIC ROOM
F. CONSERVATORY
G. ORGAN ROOM
H. BREAKFAST ROOM
I. CARD ROOM
J. LOGGIA
K. KITCHEN
L. SERVANTS' HALL
M. STORE ROOM

1–2 (above) Main-floor plan

1–3 (opposite above) Entrance or east elevation

1–4 (opposite below) Waterfront or west elevation

both sides. A lowered roof line, in addition to the surface break in the wall elevation, defines and separates the adjacent service wing.

The wide rectangular porte cochere on the front exterior acts as an extension of the two-story central hall space and mezzanine within. Defined by a series of spaces that penetrate each other both vertically and horizontally, this central hall ascends in height from the level of the soffit, or underside of the mezzanine floor, up to the high ceiling level above the second-floor arcaded gallery. The hall serves as a major circulation space, in plan as well as in section, with a series of alcoves or secondary spaces leading to galleries in each direction. The main stair is also treated as an alcove, and the spaces beneath the mezzanine lead to the vestibule and porte cochere at one end of the hall and to the waterside terrace at the other.

The waterfront elevation is designed with an arcaded gallery or loggia on the first floor. This is dominated by a central, vertical bay with a classic "Palladian" motif—it is characterized by a prominent arched opening with a smaller, square-headed opening on either side. The glass-enclosed loggia, originally open to the air, was designed to create deep shadows in contrast to the unrelieved, white-stuccoed, exterior walls. Broad terrace steps lead down from the loggia toward the waterfront.

Most of the existing landscape design, by Charles W. Leavitt & Sons, dates from during the period of Walter P. Chrysler's ownership (c. 1929) and includes a descending series of paved and grass terraces, defined by garden pergolas and retaining walls, which ends in an elaborate seawall and dockside development.

Henry Otis Chapman (1862–1929) practiced architecture in New York City after concluding his studies at Cornell University and in Europe. He designed several large office and bank buildings in New York, including two branches of the United States Mortgage and Trust Company (1922–26) and the Vantine Office Building (1914) at Fifth Avenue and Thirty-ninth Street. Chapman also designed the F. C. Gilsey Residence in Great Neck and the Broadway Tabernacle Church in New York City. His son, Henry Otis Chapman, Jr., trained as an architect and practiced with his father, later forming the large New York firm of Chapman, Evans & Delahanty.

Charles W. Leavitt was a prominent landscape architect who had also worked on the William C. Whitney Estate at Old Westbury (see page 109) and on the Foxhall Keene/William Grace Holloway Estate at Old Westbury

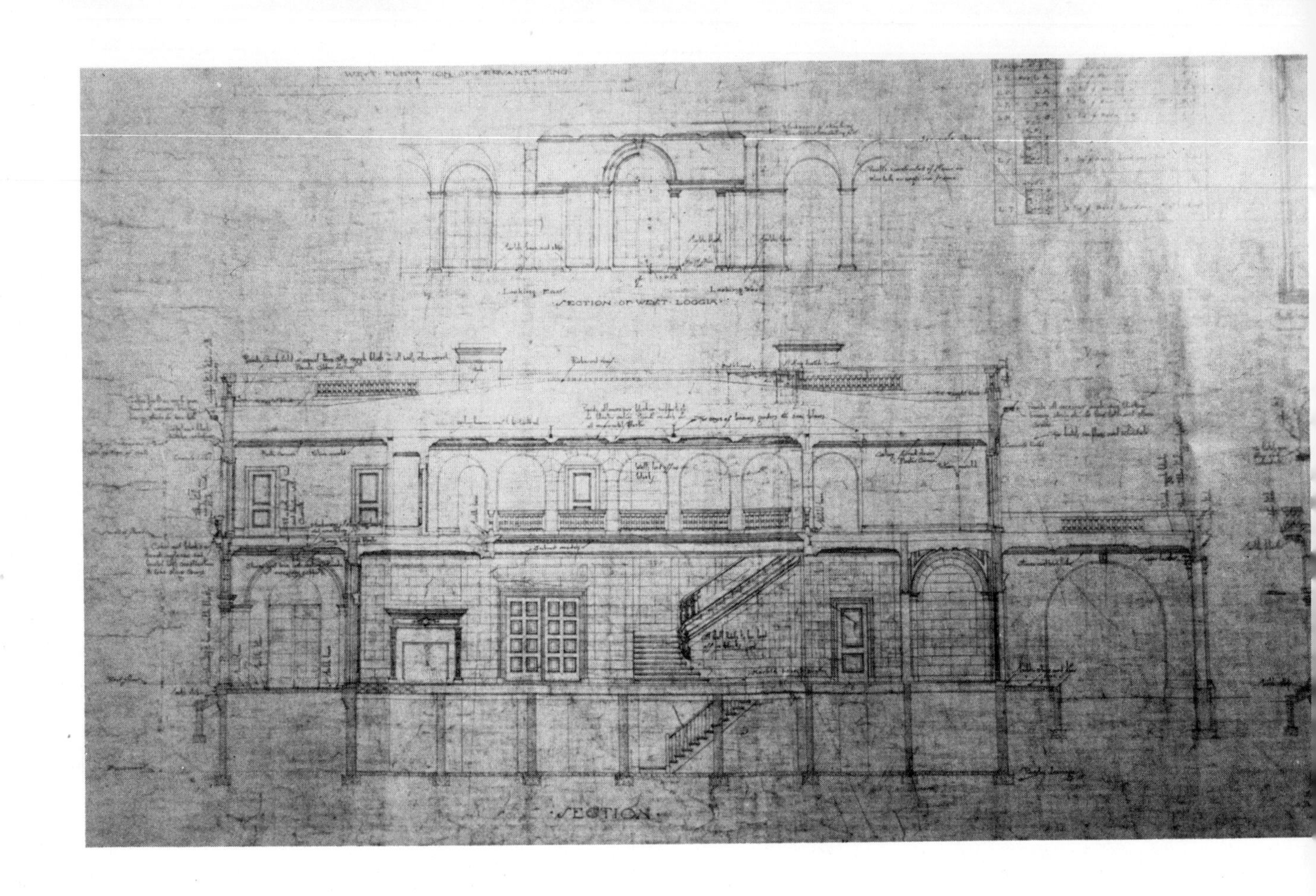

1–5 *Cross-section through main hall*

(see page 118). Leavitt served as the civil engineer and landscape architect for the Palisades Interstate Parkway, one of the prototypes of modern parkway design. He also planned several well-known racetracks, including those at Saratoga Springs, New York, and at Belmont Park, Long Island.

2
William S. Barstow Residence, Kings Point

Original architect unknown, c. 1917; 1929 addition, Greville Rickard, architect; residence now owned by the U.S. Merchant Marine Academy; property under development as a campus facility; located off Steamboat Road

William S. Barstow (1866–1942) was an electrical engineer and inventor. Born in Brooklyn, New York, and educated at Columbia University, Barstow began working at the Edison Machine Works in 1887 and became both a friend and an associate of Thomas A. Edison. He served as general manager of the Edison Electric Illuminating Company through 1901 and later organized the General Gas and Electric Company, serving as that firm's president through 1929. He also operated his own engineering firm, Barstow Campbell & Co., and was the first mayor of Kings Point.

The Barstow Residence was later purchased by Frederick W. I. Lundy, owner of the well-known Lundy's seafood restaurant in Sheepshead Bay, Brooklyn. Lundy sold the property to the U.S. Merchant Marine Academy in 1975.

The design of the Barstow house was influenced by elements of sixteenth-century Lombard and Tuscan architecture. These influences may be seen in the plain, stuccoed, and ochre-colored surfaces of the main three-story central block, the shallow attic windows beneath the tiled roof, and the arched openings with projecting balconies supported by prominent brackets. Characteristic ornamental details include the use of triangular window pediments and articulated masonry corner courses.

One- and two-story projections from the central block of the house contain glass-enclosed porches and sun rooms. A large addition to the house, consisting of a music room, a solarium, and a service wing, complements the Italian Renaissance character of the original design. Built in 1929, the addition was designed by architect Greville Rickard. It is not known whether he had also worked on the original design for the house. The delicate bronze and glass detailing of the solarium contrasts with the original "blocky" design of the exterior while simultaneously extending the arched window pattern of the waterfront elevation. Each elevation is designed to open onto a separate landscape, defined by dense planting and site grading and by the use of separated entry and service courts. The house itself is set on a terraced level carved into a sloping hillside and overlooks the water, and the service buildings and garages, located farther up the hill, are approached from upper entrance levels.

The main living room and music room spaces of the interior are parallel to the waterfront view and are separated from the dining and kitchen areas of the house by a central storage and service core, located behind the main stair. An elaborate three-level stair and entry hall make good use

of the building's height. The interiors of the house were lavishly decorated, and many of the original installations are still there, such as unusual electric fittings for entertainment that include a push-button console for selecting musical pieces to be played on an automatic organ and a fully equipped cinema room in the basement. Although the house remains relatively unchanged since Barstow first occupied it, the U.S. Merchant Marine Academy is now planning its new use as a campus facility, and some interior alterations will probably be made.

Architect Greville Rickard (1890–1956) was born in Denver, Colorado, and educated at Yale University. After working in architectural offices in both Denver and New York, he established his own practice in New York. Rickard designed many estates and country homes in the New York area, including the John Eden Residence (1927) in Great Neck; the Charles Larkin Residence (1925) in Middlebury, Connecticut; the Tudor Style Raymond Brooks Estate (1928) in Greenwich, Connecticut; and the Ruth Gunster Estate (1932), also in Greenwich, for which he received an Award of Merit.

[*Authors' note: The Barstow Residence has recently been opened to the public as the American Merchant Marine Museum.*]

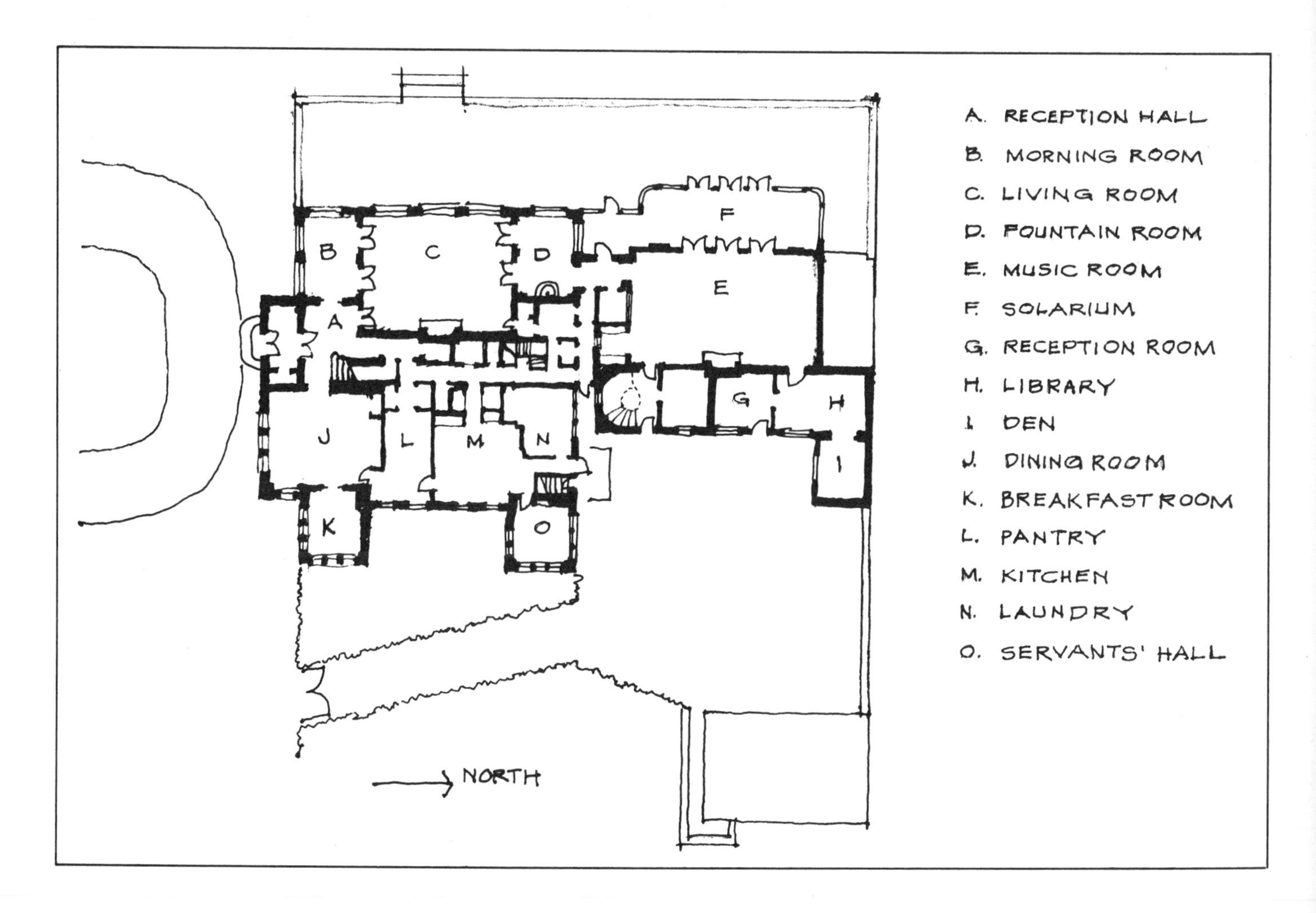

2–1 (opposite) Waterfront or west elevation

2–2 (above) Main-floor plan

2–3 (left) Entrance or east elevation

3
Howard Gould/ Daniel Guggenheim Estate, Castlegould, Sands Point

Hunt & Hunt, architects, 1909; stables, Augustus N. Allen, architect, 1902; estate now part of Sands Point Park and Preserve, administered by the Nassau County Museum; property under development; grounds open to the public for nature walks; located off Middle Neck Road

Howard Gould (1871–1959), the son of stockbroker and financier Jay Gould, inherited extensive holdings in railroads and utilities following the death of his father in 1892. These included controlling stock in the Erie Railroad, the Union Pacific Railroad, the New York Elevated Railroad, and Western Union Telegraph, as well as ownership of the *New York World* newspaper. In 1898, despite strong family objections, Gould married Katherine Clemmons, an actress. While traveling in Ireland, Katherine was impressed with Kilkenny Castle and decided to use its medieval design as the scheme for her and her husband's new home on Long Island. Gould was also sympathetic to the idea of a medieval-period design, having grown up at Lyndhurst (1838–65), the Gothic Revival mansion at Tarrytown, New York, that had been designed by Alexander Jackson Davis (1803–92) and purchased by Jay Gould.

In 1901 Howard Gould sent architect Abner J. Haydel to Ireland for several months in order to study Kilkenny Castle and to prepare designs for his new house. However, the Haydel plans were eventually rejected by Katherine after the architect had refused to make certain changes in them. A lawsuit ensued, and the Haydel proposal was never realized.

In 1902 the Goulds hired architect Augustus N. Allen of New York to lay out the site plan for their estate, which they christened Castlegould, and to design various service buildings for their Sands Point property. While these buildings were under construction, the Goulds lived in an existing frame house on the grounds, named Waterside, which had belonged to the previous owners of the property (the Burdett family) and which was demolished after their new residence was completed.

In 1907 Gould separated from Katherine, but he decided to continue developing Castlegould, this time using his own plans for a new house. In 1909, however, he commissioned New York architects Hunt & Hunt to develop a design for a residence in the style of an English medieval manor house. After Castlegould was finally completed, Gould left for Europe, but his wife refused to grant him a divorce despite their legal separation. Gould seldom used the house, eventually selling the property, in 1917, to Daniel Guggenheim.

Daniel Guggenheim (1856–1930), along with his father, Meyer, and his brothers Isaac, Murray, Solomon, and Simon, operated the Guggenheim Brothers mining empire during the late nineteenth century. Meyer had arrived in the United States in 1847, and he had worked his way up from a door-to-door peddler to become a manufacturer, a merchant, and an importer. He had invested his savings in lead and silver mines in Colorado and then built metal smelteries with the profits.

Daniel, the second oldest of eight sons, became manager of the Guggenheim Brothers enterprises and president of the American Smelting and Refining Company. This firm grew to incorporate smelting, refining, exploration, and mining operations throughout the Americas and abroad, including tin mines in Bolivia, gold mines in the Yukon, diamond fields in the Congo, and copper mines in Alaska, Chile, and Utah that later became the basis of the Anaconda Copper Company.

Two of Daniel's brothers, Isaac and William, owned large estates at Sands Point, and Daniel decided to rent a home there for the summer of 1916. The next year he purchased the Gould Estate as his permanent residence, renaming it Hempstead House because it overlooked Hempstead Harbor in Long Island Sound.

Guggenheim lived there with his family until his death in 1930. His wife, the former Florence Schloss, later built a smaller house elsewhere on the property (see page 73). In 1940 Hempstead House was used as a center for refugee

3–1 Main house, principal entrance

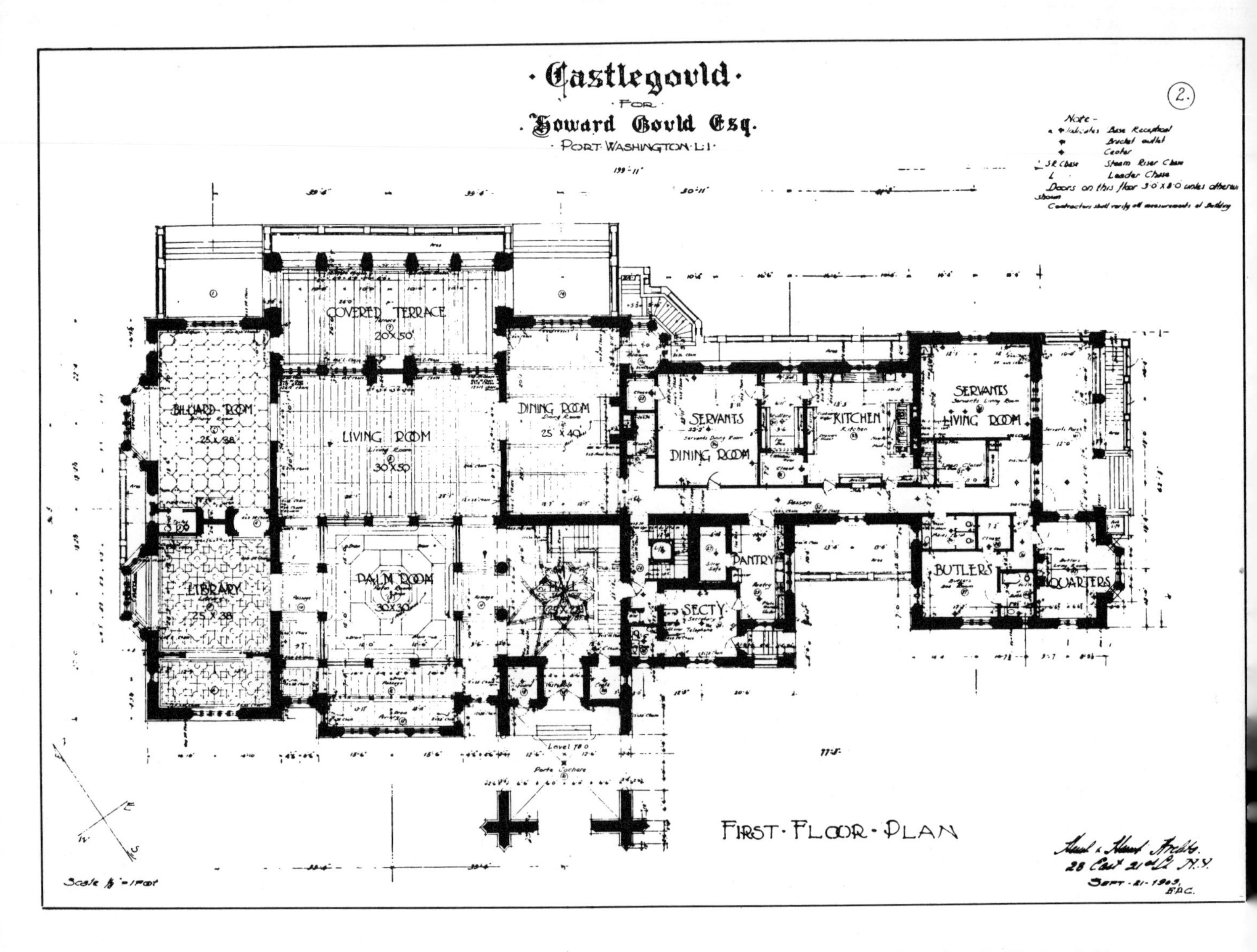

children by the Committee for the Relief of European Children, and in 1942 the estate was donated by Mrs. Guggenheim to the Institute of Aeronautical Sciences, continuing her family's ongoing sponsorship of scientific research and development projects.

The United States Navy acquired the property for its Naval Training Devices Center in 1946, and in 1971, after the federal government had relocated the Navy base, the property was deeded to Nassau County. The Nassau County Museum plans to restore the main house as a museum, and the property is under development as a park and nature preserve and will form part of Sands Point Park and Preserve. The stables presently serve as the museum administration center.

3–2 (preceding pages) Main house, waterfront or northeast elevation

3–3 (above) Main house, first-floor plan

3–4 (opposite) Main house, glass-enclosed loggia off the living room

The design for the main house created much excitement among architects when it was first published in contemporary journals because it illustrated, in a grandiose manner, many of the influential Beaux-Arts principles of

spatial planning. The great hall of the house is a tremendous space that runs from east to west and is composed of three intermediate spaces—a skylighted palm court, a large living room, and a glass-enclosed terrace facing the water. These three areas are defined within the overall space by changes in light, by changes in level, and by open screens of columns rather than by solid walls. The transparent, overlapping character of the interior and exterior spaces is seen in the open relationship of the glass-walled terrace, or loggia, to the living room and of the glass-roofed palm court to the great hall. All the other major living areas on the ground floor open onto and are connected by the great hall—the library and billiard room to the north and the dining room and stair hall to the south. This sense of open space made a great impression on architects of the day, and the house was complimented by *Architecture* magazine in 1912 for its spatial "divisions suggested rather than actually constructed."

The second floor of the house also uses changes in level

instead of walls to subdivide and define spaces. Level changes, as well as an open screen of columns, separate the stair-hall space from a large glass-walled sitting room to one side, above the entrance, and an open gallery that leads to the master bedrooms on the other side, facing the water. Many of the original interiors, designed by William Baumgarten and Company, were altered after the U.S. Navy acquired the property in 1946. Medieval antiques from England, France, and Spain, which had been incorporated into the designs of the rooms, were either destroyed or removed during the Navy's occupation, although the museum hopes to restore some of these spaces to their original condition.

Castlegould was designed by Richard Howland Hunt (1862–1931) of the firm of Hunt & Hunt. The son of Richard Morris Hunt, Richard Howland Hunt was born in Paris and was educated at Massachusetts Institute of Technology and at the Ecole des Beaux-Arts in Paris. He worked with his father, eventually becoming his associate, and practiced jointly with him until his father's death in 1895. In 1901 Hunt formed a partnership with his younger brother Joseph (1870–1924), who had also trained at the Ecole as an architect, and together they practiced under the firm name of Hunt & Hunt.

Among Richard Howland Hunt's credits are the completion of the drawings for New York's Metropolitan Museum of Art (1895–1902), which his father had begun, and the completion of the designs for the George W. Vanderbilt Estate, Biltmore (1888–95), in Asheville, North Carolina. Several design elements of Biltmore, including the character of the great skylighted palm court and its distinctive medieval detailing, can also be seen in Castlegould.

Hunt also designed the Margaret Shepard Residence (1900) in New York City (now the Lotos Club) and the George Blumenthal Residence (1902) there (now the offices of the Museum of Modern Art). The firm became well known for its large country and urban residences, including the William K. Vanderbilt, Sr., Estate, Idle Hour, at Oakdale (see page 209); the J. H. Fisher Estate in Greenwich, Connecticut; and the George W. Vanderbilt Residence (c. 1906) in New York City. Hunt also designed buildings for several major educational institutions, including Vanderbilt University at Nashville, Tennessee, and Vassar College at Poughkeepsie, New York.

Augustus N. Allen (1868–1958) designed the enormous stable complex at Castlegould, which also included garages and servants' quarters, in the crenellated style of an Irish

3–5 (opposite above) Main house, interior view of skylighted palm court. Drawing by Sidney L. Katz, F.A.I.A.

3–6 (opposite below) Stables, drawing of the west elevation

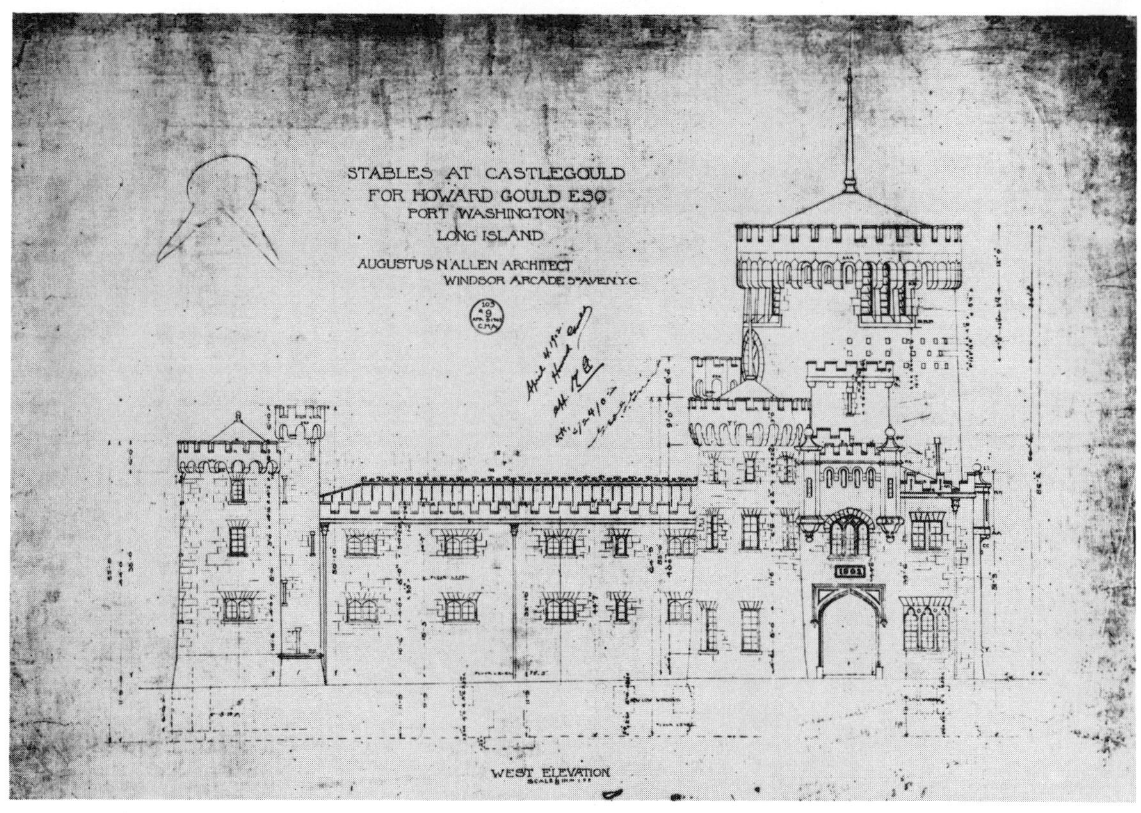
STABLES AT CASTLEGOULD
FOR HOWARD GOULD ESQ
PORT WASHINGTON
LONG ISLAND
AUGUSTUS N ALLEN ARCHITECT
WINDSOR ARCADE 5th AVE N.Y.C.
WEST ELEVATION

castle on the exterior and with high, vaulted ceilings constructed of Guastavino tiles on the interior. He also designed the still-extant dairy farm with its elaborate cow barns, a waterfront casino, guest lodges, and several gatehouses, all in the same heavy, rusticated stonework. Allen graduated from Columbia University School of Architecture in 1891. He also drew the plans for several other country houses and residences on Long Island, including the Max Fleischmann Estate, The Lindens (1910), on Middle Neck Road, near Castlegould, and the Timothy Woodruff Residence in Garden City. Allen designed the Henry Trevor Residence and the Johns Manville Office Building, both in New York City, and the Russell Sage Library in Sag Harbor, which employs Guastavino tile vaults similar to those used in the stable complex at Castlegould.

[*Authors' note: The Castlegould stables are now open to the public and display a portion of the Nassau County Museum antique collection.*]

3–7 Stables, south elevation

4

Harry F. Guggenheim Estate, Falaise, Sands Point

Frederick J. Sterner, architect, Polhemus & Coffin, associate architects, 1923; estate now part of Sands Point Park and Preserve, administered by the Nassau County Museum; open by appointment; located off Middle Neck Road

Another member of the Guggenheim family to settle on Long Island was Harry F. Guggenheim (1890–1971), the son of Daniel and Florence Guggenheim. He was a business executive, diplomat and philanthropist and had received his education at Yale University and at Cambridge University in England. His career began in his family's American Smelting and Refining Company, which controlled smelting, refining, exploring, and mining operations throughout the Americas and abroad (see page 59).

During World War I, Harry F. Guggenheim served as an aviator in the U.S. Navy and developed a lifelong interest in aviation and in aeronautical research. In 1927 he met Charles A. Lindbergh before his historic flight to France, and later he became Lindbergh's close friend and benefactor. He also organized the Guggenheim Foundation for Aeronautical Research, which sponsored many flight research projects, including those of Dr. Robert H. Goddard, a pioneer scientist in rocketry.

In 1923 Guggenheim married Carol Morton, an artist and the daughter of Paul Morton, who had been Secretary of the Navy during Theodore Roosevelt's presidency. As a wedding present, Harry's father, Daniel, gave the couple ninety acres of his Sands Point estate, and Harry commissioned architect Frederick J. Sterner to design a new home there, which he named Falaise. Polhemus & Coffin were associate architects on the project (see page 73), and the house was constructed in 1923–24 by E. W. Howell and Company of Babylon, Long Island.

Falaise was the scene of many meetings between Harry F. Guggenheim and his friends and associates in the field of aviation. After he served as United States Ambassador to Cuba in 1929, he also invited members of the diplomatic corps to his country estate. Frequent guests included Averell Harriman, Adlai Stevenson, Bernard Baruch, and James Doolittle, in addition to Dr. Robert H. Goddard and Charles A. Lindbergh. While a guest at Falaise, Lindbergh wrote much of his autobiographical volume, *We*, which described his flight across the Atlantic Ocean from Roosevelt Field, New York. Later, his wife, Anne Morrow Lindbergh, described life at Falaise in a book of her own, *Bring Me a Unicorn.*

In 1939 Guggenheim married Alicia Patterson, daughter of Joseph Medill Patterson, the publisher of the *New York Daily News.* A pilot, she shared his love of aviation and established a women's aviation record in 1931 on a flight between New York and Philadelphia. The former Miss Patterson was also a journalist who had worked both

4–1 *(above) Entrance or southwest elevation*

4–2 *(opposite above) Main-floor plan*

4–3 *(opposite below) Drawing of waterfront or southeast elevation*

for the *New York Daily News* as a reporter and for *Liberty* magazine. In 1940 she founded *Newsday*, Long Island's daily newspaper. Harry served as publisher and Alicia as editor-in-chief of this publication until her death in 1963. In addition, Harry became president of the Solomon R. Guggenheim Foundation, and in this capacity he completed the Solomon R. Guggenheim Museum of Art in New York, with Frank Lloyd Wright as architect, after the death of his uncle Solomon.

Harry F. Guggenheim also maintained a prize-winning racing stable, and under the Cain Hoy stable name, his horse Dark Star won the Kentucky Derby in 1953. Guggenheim's horses were raised at his plantation in South Carolina and brought north annually for the racing season. They could often be seen exercising on the grounds of Falaise, off Middle Neck Road. The rusticated stone stables that still stand there were designed by Augustus N. Allen as part of the dairy farm of the Howard Gould/Daniel Guggenheim Estate, Castlegould (see page 58).

The main house at Falaise contains Guggenheim's personal collection of furniture, drawings, and trophies and

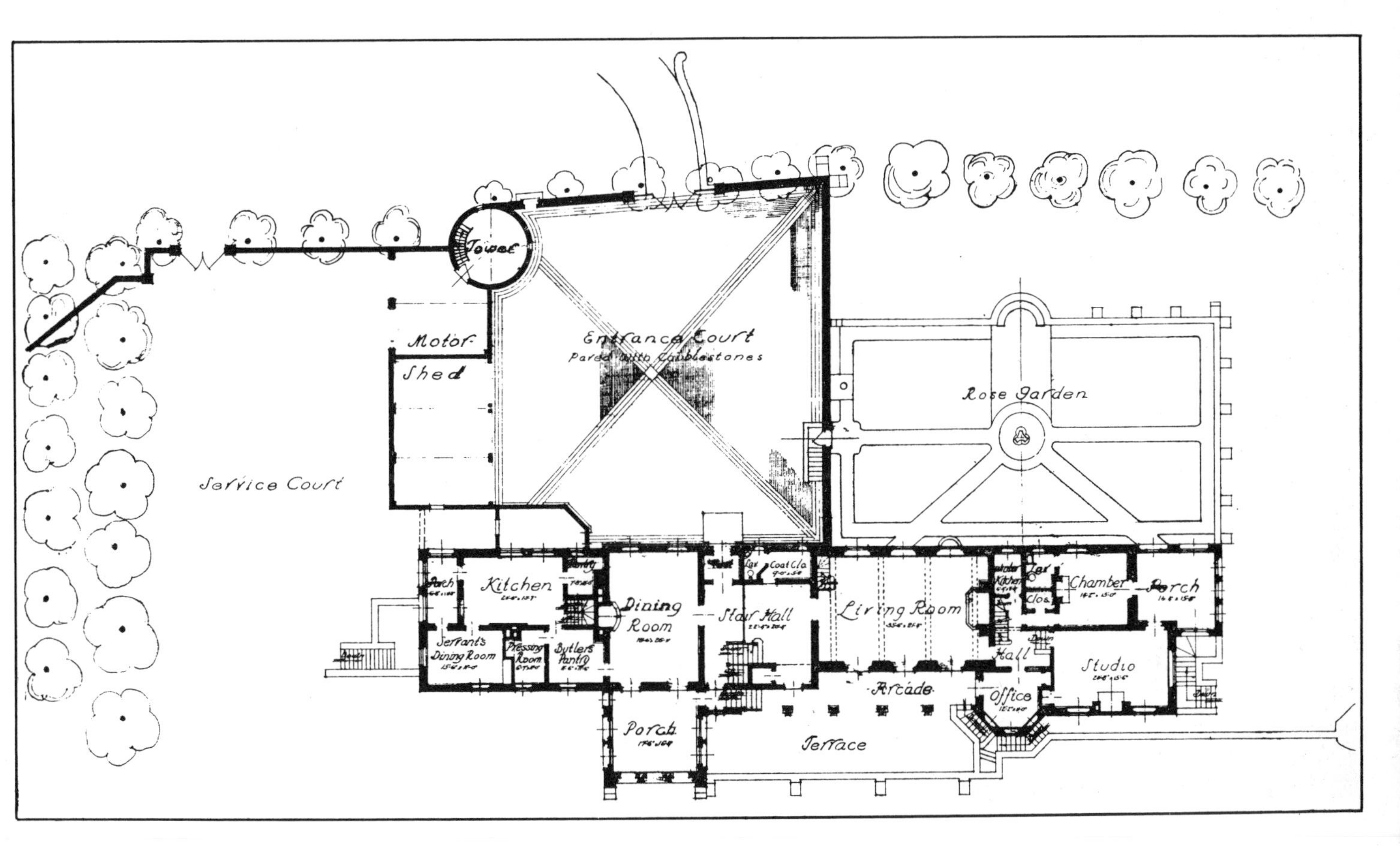
Tower
Motor
Shed
Entrance Court
Paved with Cobblestones
Rose Garden
Service Court
Porch
Kitchen
Servant's Dining Room
Pressing Room
Butlers Pantry
Dining Room
Stair Hall
Coat Clo.
Living Room
Chamber
Porch
Clos.
Hall
Studio
Arcade
Office
Porch
Terrace

4–4 View of the roofs, looking north

4–5 (opposite) View from the northeast, looking up from the water

Charles A. Lindbergh's donated library. It is open to the public, with tours of the estate conducted by appointment with the Nassau County Museum.

Falaise was designed to resemble a French Norman manor house, and it derived its name from the French word for "cliff," as well as from the name of the town of Falaise in Normandy. The "cliff" name is appropriately reflected in the dramatic design of the house, based on a linear progression of spaces, stretching out along a high cliff's edge. The structure of the house is supported by high, battered-brick retaining walls, which are built into the side of the cliff. The French Norman design influence may be seen in the use of prominent, high-pitched, tiled roofs, with projecting round and polygonal towers, and in the employment of low-scaled arcades defined by brick walls and enclosed courtyards.

On the inland side of the house, three walled courtyards separate the building from the adjacent woods and enclose the entrance motor court, the service court, and the swimming-pool court (originally the rose garden). The main entrance is off the motor court and leads into an open central stair hall, midway along the length of the house. The hall is elevated, with stairs leading up to the floor above and down to the main living level. Together with the surrounding open mezzanine, the stairs and hall create a feeling of great spatial depth and vertical height. The service courtyard and service wing of the building, approached from the side of the stair hall opposite the living areas, are designed to function independently of the social and formal areas of the house.

Narrow steps located in the motor court lead down to a small opening in one of the brick walls. This opening serves as a "secret" passage to the swimming-pool courtyard. From here the high rim of the cliff outside, stretching along the waterfront, can be seen through a glass-enclosed arcade at the far end of the pool. This pool landscape is a unified composition of house and protective screen walls ornamented with decorative tiles and brickwork, lush planting, and garden sculpture, all bathed in meditative water reflections. It creates a *Paradise Lost* retreat, especially when compared to the rugged and windy openness of the waterfront view.

The living room with its high French windows is a long, rectangular, airy space sitting on the ridge astride these two vistas—the cloistered pool on one side and on the other the projecting waterfront terrace. The interiors of the living room and of other rooms in the house were designed to

incorporate the antiques and art treasures that were acquired by Harry F. Guggenheim and his first wife on their honeymoon in Europe.

The architect of Falaise, Frederick J. Sterner (1876–1931), was born in England and educated in the United States. He practiced in Denver, Colorado, as a partner in the firm of Sterner & Varian, and he worked on both public buildings and private homes there. Sterner's early work included the William J. Palmer Estate, Glen Eyrie (c. 1910), a large English medieval "castle," near Colorado Springs, in which he capitalized on the dramatic nature of the site as he did later in his design for Falaise. He also designed Colorado Springs' Antlers Hotel (c. 1910), and with architect George Williamson he drew the plans for the Fisher Tower office building (c. 1912) in Denver.

After 1915 Sterner practiced independently in New York City and was the architect of several homes there, including the Stephen C. Clark House (1912), at 46 East Seventieth Street, now owned by the Explorers' Club. He also planned "The Block Beautiful" (1920s), a model rehabilitation and restoration project at Nineteenth Street and Irving Place in New York City, and he designed several summer residences at Belle Terre, Long Island. During the late 1920s Sterner lived in Europe, spending several years in London. His two brothers were also well known in the arts: Albert C. Sterner was a designer and portrait painter, and Lawrence Sterner was a Hollywood scenarist.

4–6 Stair hall and main entrance

5
Mrs. Daniel Guggenheim Residence, Mille Fleurs, Sands Point

Polhemus & Coffin, architects, 1932; house now part of Sands Point Park and Preserve, administered by the Nassau County Museum; property undergoing restoration; located off Middle Neck Road

In 1884 Daniel Guggenheim, the mining and smelting heir, and Florence Schloss were married. The couple had three children, Meyer, Harry, and Gladys, and in 1917 the family purchased Castlegould, the Howard Gould Estate in Sands Point (see page 58), where they lived until Daniel's death in 1930.

Mrs. Daniel Guggenheim was an avid philanthropist and is best remembered for establishing the Guggenheim Memorial Concerts, which are still held every summer in New York City's parks. After her husband's death, their home, which they had renamed Hempstead House, was too large for her to maintain for herself, and she decided to build a smaller house elsewhere on the same property. The site selected had originally been planned as a golf course and was adjacent to Falaise, the estate of her son Harry F. Guggenheim. The architectural firm of Polhemus & Coffin of New York City was commissioned to design Mrs. Guggenheim's new residence, Mille Fleurs, and in 1932 the house was constructed by E. W. Howell and Company of Babylon, Long Island.

Mille Fleurs, with its very private, intimate scale, provides a tremendous contrast to cavernous Hempstead House. Mrs. Guggenheim lived there until her death in 1944. The house was later rented for several summers to Bernard Baruch, a close friend of the Guggenheim family. It is now being restored by the Nassau County Museum as a part of Sands Point Park and Preserve.

Originally designed with a whitewashed finish on its exterior brick walls, Mille Fleurs retains the character of a French country manor house. A central, two-story-high block, facing the water, contains the main living spaces of the house. Two lower wings, at either side, contain bedrooms and service areas, respectively. These wings are symmetrically disposed about a central axis, which passes through the entry court and central interior hall and leads out to a waterfront terrace and vista.

Outside, the side wings and central section of the house create an enclosed, landscaped garden court. This garden forms part of a series of outdoor terraces and courtyards of varying proportions that extend in a progression toward the house. Each one is quite deliberately defined. The outer courtyard, the motor courtyard, is separated from the interior court by a brick garden wall with entrance gates. The waterfront lawn terrace is defined by garden walls and distinctive "guard-booth" towers. Thus the house appears surrounded by intentionally quiet and secluded outdoor spaces.

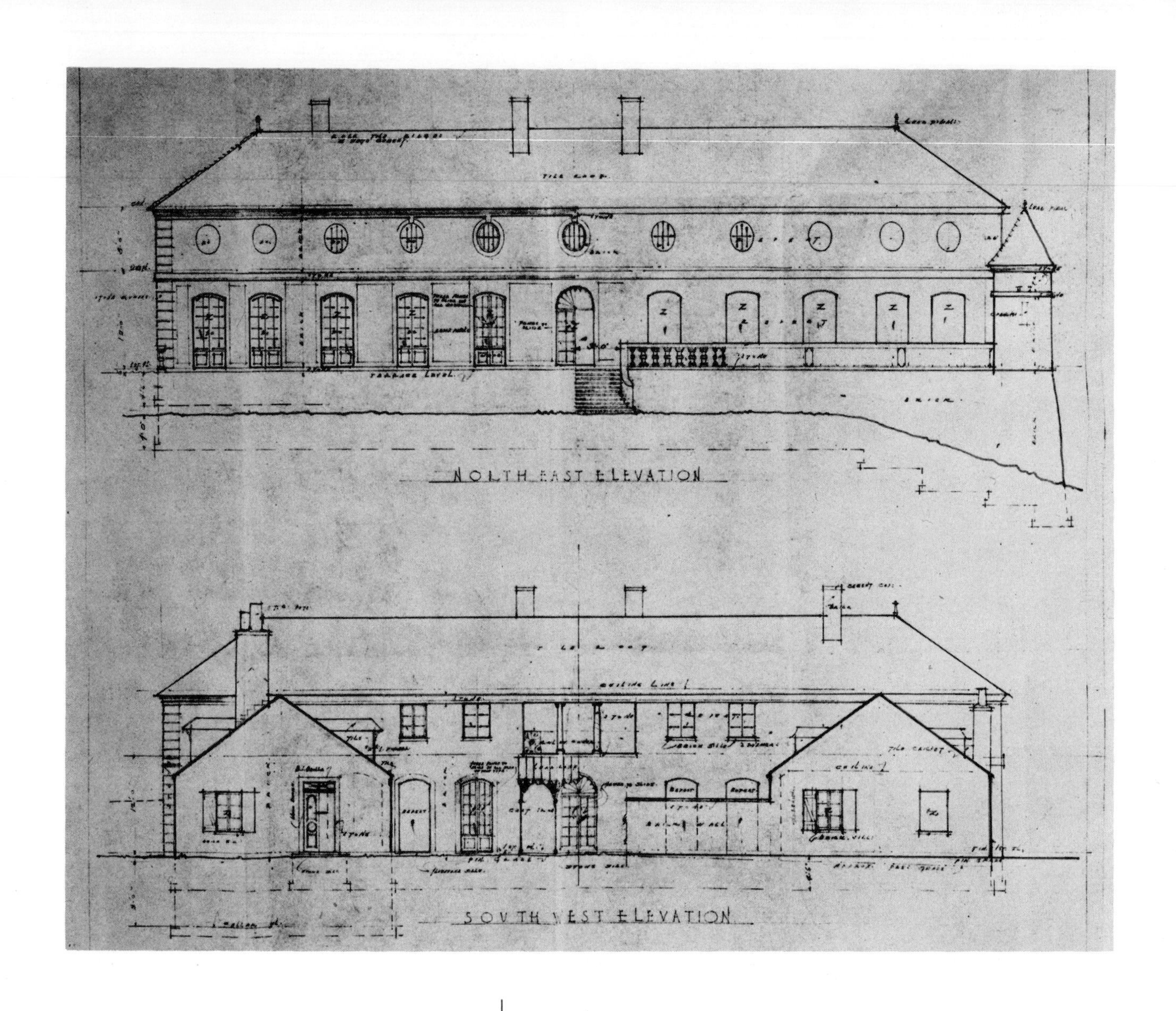

5–1 Architect's drawing of northeast and southwest elevations

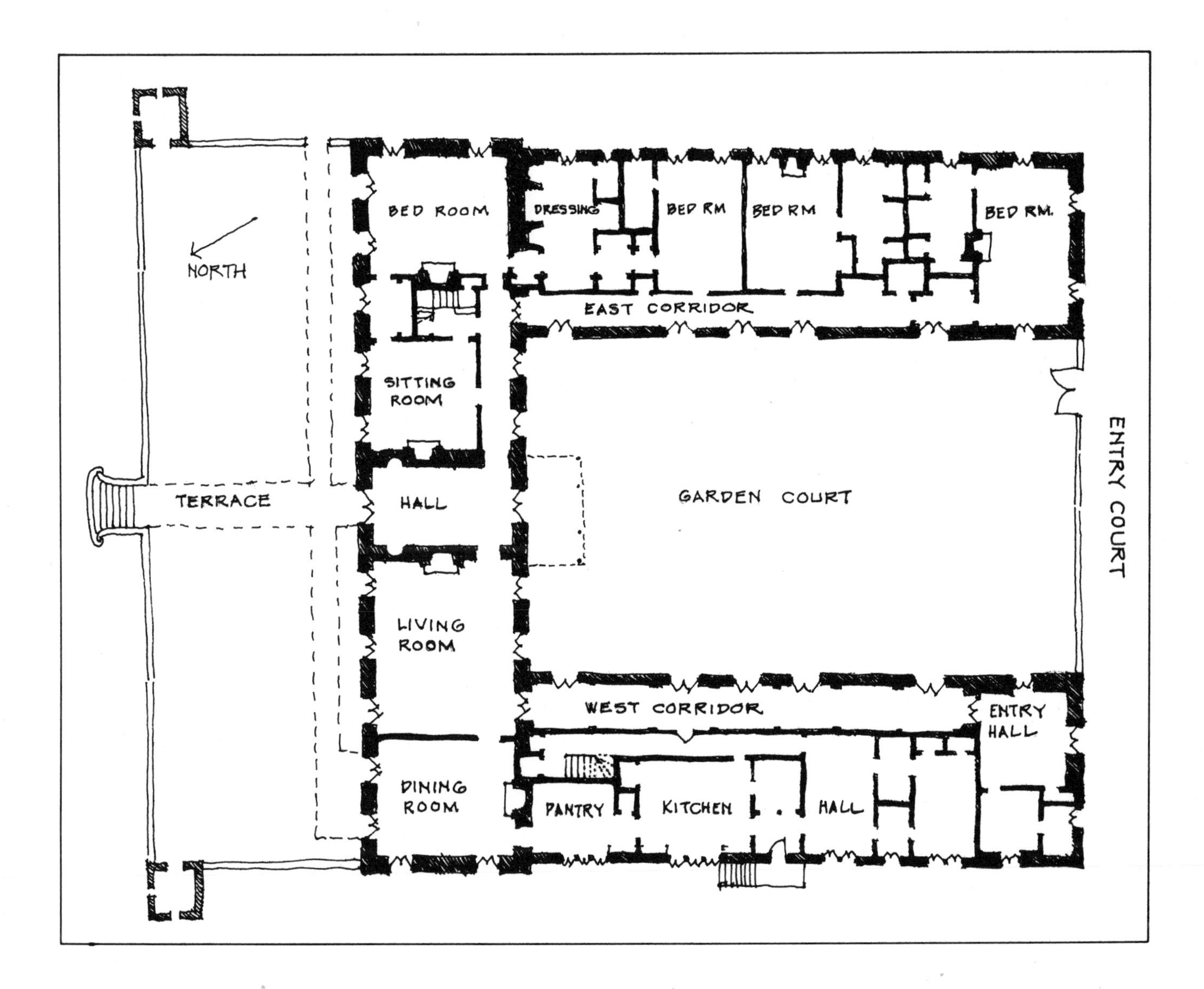

French doors and windows open off the main living spaces of the house onto the waterfront terrace. The bedrooms above, on the second floor, look out to the water through porthole windows, giving each room an individually framed, circular view. Similar windows appear in Georgian period designs and in the work of many Beaux-Arts architects (as in Delano & Aldrich's Willard Straight Residence in New York City). The separation of service functions from social functions, as in the separate service-wing circulation and in the service access court, is also a characteristic element of many Beaux-Arts designs.

Henry M. Polhemus (1891–1970), of the firm of Polhemus & Coffin, was an associate architect on Falaise, which Frederick J. Sterner designed (see page 67). In addition to Mille Fleurs, the firm designed many other country houses on Long Island, including the William S. Jenney Residence (c. 1923) at East Hampton, the Vernon Brown

5–2 Main-floor plan

5–3 *Partial view of northeast elevation and terrace*

5–4 *(opposite) Entrance to the garden court*

and Allen Bakewell residences at Southampton (c. 1935), and the Charles A. Blackwell Estate (c. 1926) in Brookville. Polhemus & Coffin also designed Champs Soleil (1929), a French Provincial mansion in Newport, Rhode Island, which has a courtyard parti similar to that of Mille Fleurs. In New York City the firm planned several projects for Columbia University, including the Baker Field Boathouse (1930) and the Barnard College Memorial Gates (c. 1926), in addition to other designs for urban residences and commercial projects.

6

Mrs. Christian R. Holmes Estate, The Chimneys, Sands Point

Edgar I. Williams, architect, 1929; estate now owned by the Community Synagogue, Sands Point; services and scheduled events open to the public; located off Middle Neck Road

Christian R. Holmes was born in Denmark in 1857 and was educated in both Europe and the United States. Trained as a physician, he became dean of the Medical School of the University of Cincinnati in Cincinnati, Ohio. In 1892 Holmes married Bettie Fleischmann, the daughter of Charles Fleischmann (1834–97), a wealthy American businessman. Fleischmann had emigrated from Hungary to the United States in the 1870s and, with his brother Henry, started a bakery business that later developed into the Fleischmann yeast and margarine industry.

Mrs. Holmes's brother, Max Fleischmann, lived in Sands Point on a country estate designed by Augustus N. Allen called The Lindens (1910). After Christian R. Holmes died in the early 1920s, Mrs. Holmes decided to build a new home, which she named The Chimneys, for herself and for her son and his family in Sands Point not far from her brother's house. A children's wing was later added when her second son and his family also moved to the estate.

The family occupied The Chimneys until Mrs. Holmes's death in 1941. For the next thirteen years the property was used by the U.S. Naval Training Devices Center as a naval officers' club. In 1954 the Sands Point Community Synagogue purchased the estate. A new sanctuary addition to one side of the main house was designed by the firm of Katz Waisman Weber of New York City, and the original building was converted into school classrooms and meeting rooms. Several of the service buildings and cottages located along Tudor Lane to the rear of the estate property are now private residences.

The Chimneys was planned by architect Edgar I. Williams. Its design was based on the style of an English Tudor country house, and many antiques and authentic architectural elements were imported from Great Britain and incorporated into the structure.

The estate derived its name from the large number of ornamented brick and terra-cotta chimneys that rise above the sloping roof of the main house. These chimneys, both single- and multiple-flued, are made of imported bricks laid in a variety of corbeled and spiraled patterns. Each chimney has an individual design, a treatment common in Tudor houses, recalling the individual seals of medieval guild craftsmen.

The entrance to the house is beneath a heavy timber colonnade, which is located off the cobblestoned motor court. The vestibule space opens into a great hall, which extends the full depth of the house and leads to a broad

6–1 (opposite) Main house reflected in a landscaped lake

South Elevation of THE CHIMNEYS. The Residence of
Mrs CHRISTIAN R. HOLMES
at Sands Point, Port Washington, Long Island
Edgar I. Williams, Architect, New York.

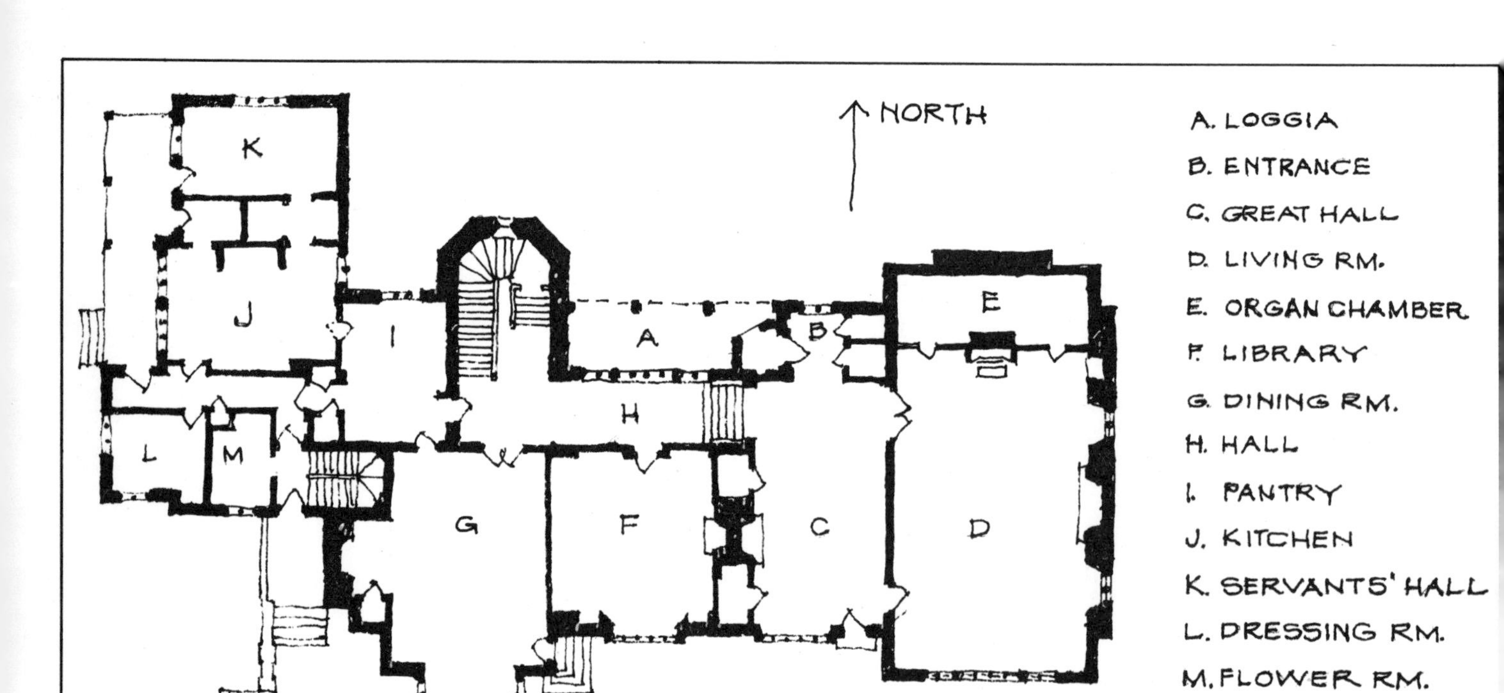
NORTH
A
B
C
D
E
F
G
H
I
J
K
L
M
A. LOGGIA
B. ENTRANCE
C. GREAT HALL
D. LIVING RM.
E. ORGAN CHAMBER
F. LIBRARY
G. DINING RM.
H. HALL
I. PANTRY
J. KITCHEN
K. SERVANTS' HALL
L. DRESSING RM.
M. FLOWER RM.

outdoor terrace and an impressive vista. All the main living areas of the house open onto this garden terrace, which is slightly raised above the sloping grade level. The terrace overlooks a vast rolling lawn designed in the English "picturesque" manner, with specimen plantings and trees that include English hollies and cedars of Lebanon. The lawn slopes gently away from the house toward a reflecting pond, or artificial lake.

Grouped window and door openings on the garden elevation of the house create a sense of openness and movement between the living spaces and the outdoor terrace. The interior circulation of the house is along the courtyard side of the plan, with a glazed gallery containing hand-painted, stained-glass windows. Changes in level along this gallery create a hierarchy of interior spaces, from the low-ceilinged area outside the dining room down several steps to the high-ceilinged great-hall and living-room spaces.

The cobblestoned entrance courtyard is designed in keeping with the Tudor character of the exterior elevations, but beneath this court is a cellar extension to the house that contains a swimming pool, nightclub, bowling alley, and squash court, all designed in the Art Deco Style popular during the 1920s. The swimming pool is designed as an "Alaskan Room" and is embellished with elaborate, original Eskimo totem poles.

6–2 (opposite above) Garden or south elevation. Drawing by Edgar I. Williams, architect

6–3 (opposite below) Main-floor plan

6–4 (above) Entrance or north elevation and entrance court

The master plan for the estate, encompassing approximately twenty-five acres, included the main house with forty-two rooms, a garage and servants' quarters complex, an outdoor pool and teahouse, supervisors' and gardeners' cottages, service buildings, greenhouses, and formal gardens. Forty to sixty staff members at one time lived or worked in the buildings on the estate grounds.

The architect of The Chimneys, Edgar I. Williams (1884–1974), was the brother of the noted American poet William Carlos Williams. Born in Rutherford, New Jersey, and educated both in Switzerland and in the United States, Williams graduated from Massachusetts Institute of Technology School of Architecture in 1908. A year later, he won the coveted Rome Prize competition, which was the highest design award that a young American architect could receive at that time. The award included a scholarship that financed his further studies at the American Academy in Rome (1909–12).

After working in New York under Beaux-Arts graduate Welles Bosworth and in the office of architect Guy Lowell, Williams began his own practice in New York City in 1920 as a partner in the firm of Williams & Barrett. However, beginning in 1928, he practiced independently. He was also a professor of architecture at Columbia University for twenty-five years. In addition to The Chimneys, he designed the Starrett Estate (1927) in Greenwich, Connecticut, and was associate architect of the Donnell Library Center (1946) at 20 West Fifty-third Street in New York City. Williams served as consulting architect to the New York Public Library and was president of the New York chapter of the American Institute of Architects (1942–43). In 1955 he was elected to the National Academy of Design.

7
Lloyd Bryce/Childs Frick Estate, Clayton, Roslyn Harbor

Ogden Codman, Jr., architect, 1895; 1919 additions, Sir Charles Carrick Allom, architect; Marian C. Coffin, landscape architect, 1930; estate now maintained by the Nassau County Office of Cultural Development; under development as the Nassau County Fine Arts Center; open to the public for scheduled events and exhibits; located off Northern Boulevard

Lloyd Bryce (1851–1917), statesman, diplomat, editor, and author, was born in New York City and raised in Georgetown, a suburb of Washington, D.C. Bryce was educated at Oxford University in England and studied law at Columbia University. After serving a term in the U.S. Congress (1887–89), he became owner and editor of the *North American Review*, an influential literary journal. Bryce published many articles and critical essays in the *Review* and was also the author of several books.

Bryce's wife, the former Edith Cooper, was a descendant of Peter Cooper, a well-known inventor and the founder of Cooper Union in New York City. The Bryces built their estate between 1893 and 1895 during the period that Bryce was editor of the *Review*. As he was surrounded by a circle of literary friends, it seemed only natural that Bryce should purchase land from the estate of poet and editor William Cullen Bryant, who had died in 1878. Bryant had once lived at Cedarmere, a residence on an adjacent property, which has recently been acquired as an historic landmark site by the Nassau County Museum (see fig. I–20). After restoration it will be open to the public. It also seemed appropriate that Bryce should select novelist Edith Wharton's associate, architect Ogden Codman, Jr., to design his new residence.

Bryce lived in this house until his death in 1917. The property was then purchased by Childs Frick, who christened the estate Clayton and in 1919 hired Sir Charles Carrick Allom, an English architect, to alter the house for him. Childs Frick's father, Henry Clay Frick, was a partner of Andrew Carnegie and the chairman of the board of the Carnegie Steel Company (which later became the United States Steel Corporation). The elder Frick also assembled a valuable art collection, which is installed in his former mansion, now the Frick Museum, in New York City. The younger Frick was a paleontologist who studied the classification of geological periods through the examination of fossils. He was also a philanthropist and a sponsor of the American Museum of Natural History in New York City.

Clayton is now maintained by the Nassau County Office of Cultural Development and will be the home of the Nassau County Fine Arts Center. Indoor and outdoor exhibits, concerts, and lectures are scheduled regularly.

The design of the Bryce Residence is based on English Renaissance and Palladian prototypes. The two-story main block of the building is a tripartite design, with the central

section of this block containing the entry hall, foyer, and grand stair, as well as the original dining room, which opens onto an expansive sloping lawn recalling an English naturalistic landscape. The dining-room space was later redesigned into a library.

To one side of the central hall at the northern end of the house is a large drawing room on the scale of a ballroom. This space leads out through a curving arcade to a freestanding, covered outdoor "porch" or pavilion. To the other side of the central hall, the original library space, which later was remodeled into a study, leads to a large

service addition and to a formal dining-room pavilion, located in the former kitchen wing.

Full-length French windows topped by enclosed arches simulate the appearance of an arcade extending across the garden elevation of the house and continuing out into open arcades on either side of the main block. These arcades lead to the flanking porch and kitchen (later dining) dependencies or pavilions. The pavilions are located forward of the main house in a Palladian fashion and form a defined space for the outdoor terrace, which is raised slightly above the sloping lawn. This arrangement of a central

7–1 Garden or east elevation

building with flanking dependencies was quite common in the design of Georgian Colonial and Federal country houses, including Mount Vernon in Virginia and Mount Pleasant in Philadelphia, Pennsylvania.

The elemental parti of the two-story block with subsidiary, symmetrical, one-story wings has been preserved from the original Codman design for the house. In 1919 Sir Charles Carrick Allom made several changes in the plan of the house for the Fricks. These included altering the main entrance hall from a circular space with rounded niches into a more conventional rectangular space. He also added a large breakfast and service wing to the south of the house and a covered, open loggia, or colonnaded porch, running across the entrance elevation. Virtually no changes were made in the garden elevation.

Several buildings on the estate date from the period of Frick's ownership, including a gatehouse added in 1925 and a garage and a large laboratory building, where he worked and stored his collections, put up in 1936. Much of the extensive landscaping was designed in 1930, according to the plan of landscape architect Marian C. Coffin. It was revised and expanded by landscape architect Dorothy Nicholas in 1947. North Cottage is also on the grounds of the estate; it was built in 1862 after a design by architect Frederick S. Copley as a gardener's house. This Stick Style cottage was originally part of the nearby estate of William Cullen Bryant.

Ogden Codman, Jr. (1863–1951) received his early education in France and later studied under the Beaux-Arts system at the School of Architecture at Massachusetts Institute of Technology (1882). After working in both Boston and New York, Codman, in 1893, redesigned the interiors of Edith Wharton's Land's End, at Newport, Rhode Island. Together Codman and Edith Wharton formulated a theory of interior design that was based on classic simplicity and that eliminated Victorian clutter. They both favored formal Renaissance and English Georgian precedents in the design of country houses. These theories were published in *The Decoration of Houses*, which they co-authored. Codman was also the architect of Mrs. Charles Coolidge Pomeroy's Residence, designed in 1883 and similar to the Bryce Residence, and Maxim Karolik's Berkeley Villa (1910), a later example of Georgian influence on his work. Both of these houses were at Newport. Other country estates designed by Codman include Nathaniel Thayer's Estate (c. 1903) in Lancaster, Massachusetts, and Walter Maynard's Residence (1916), in Jericho, Long Island. The Maynard Residence shows

7–2 (opposite above) Main-floor plan, showing the original design of Ogden Codman, Jr., architect, 1895

7–3 (opposite below) Entrance or west elevation

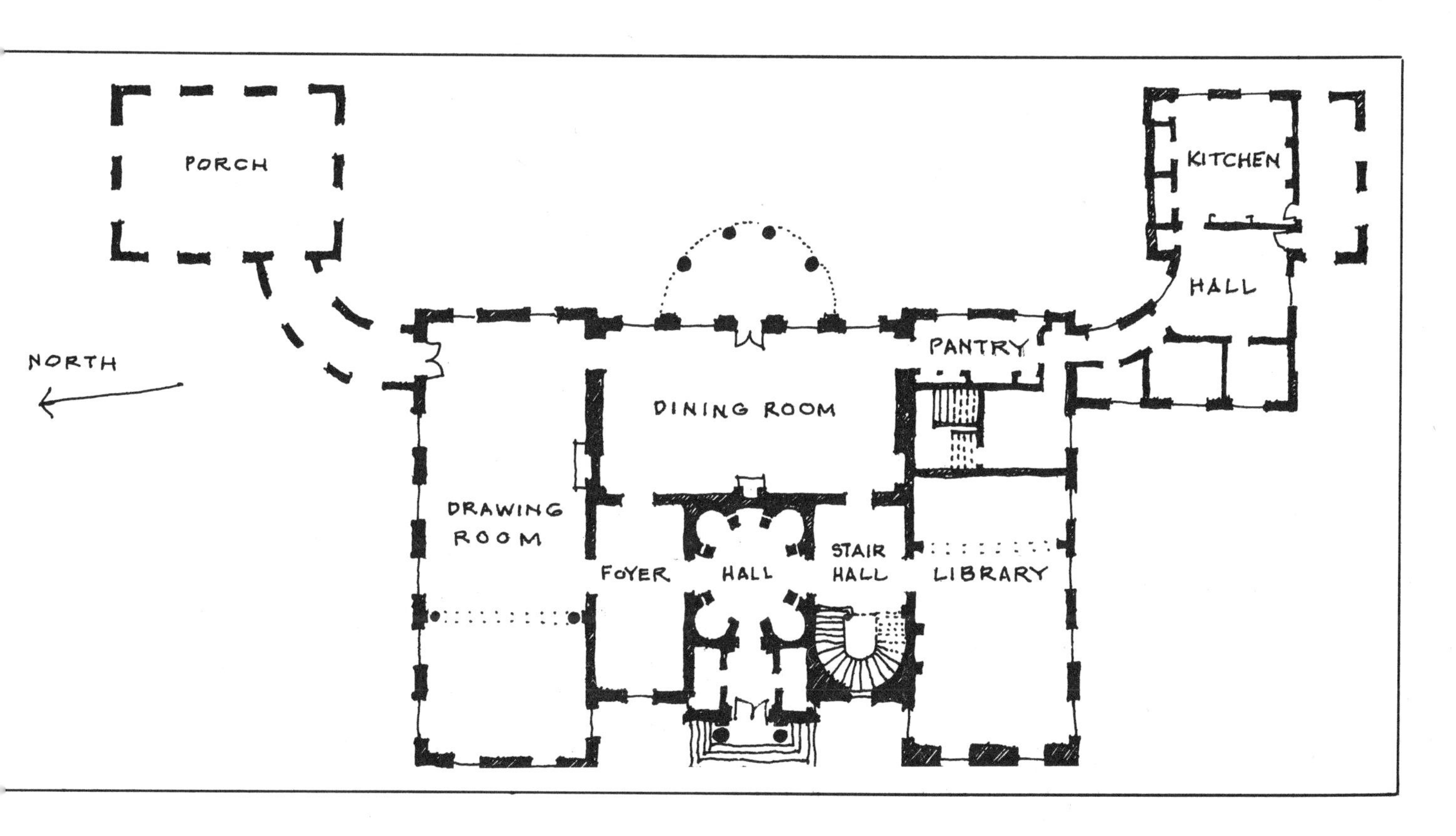
PORCH
KITCHEN
HALL
PANTRY
NORTH
DINING ROOM
DRAWING ROOM
FOYER
HALL
STAIR HALL
LIBRARY

the additional design influence of French country houses and contains Codman's frequently used arched window openings with rounded shutters. In New York City Codman designed several town houses, including Woodward Haven's Residence (1908) at 18 East Seventy-ninth Street, his own city residence (1913) at 7 East Ninety-sixth Street (now Manhattan Country School), and the nearby house (1913) at 12 East Ninety-sixth Street (now Emerson School).

Sir Charles Carrick Allom (1865–1947), who designed the additions and alterations to the Bryce Residence, was educated at the Royal College of Arts in London and also studied in France and Italy. Allom was associated with the New York architectural firm of Murphy & Dana, an office that became well known for its Colonial and Georgian designs. The work of landscape architect Marian C. Coffin is described further in the article on the Marjorie Merriweather Post/Edward F. Hutton Estate, Hillwood, at Brookville (see page 138). Mrs. Coffin also worked at Caumsett, the estate of Marshall Field III at Lloyd Neck (see page 170).

7–4 (opposite above) Sketch of west elevation showing entrance porch

7–5 (opposite below) View of loggia and covered sun porch

8

F. W. Woolworth Estate, Winfield Hall, Glen Cove

C. P. H. Gilbert, architect, 1916; estate recently occupied by the Grace Downs School, not open to the public; located off Crescent Beach Road (property for sale; endangered)

Frank W. Woolworth (1852–1919) was born in Rodman, New York, and attended a local business college in Watertown. After working as a clerk in a grocery store, he opened his first five-and-dime store in Utica in 1879. His merchandising empire, the F. W. Woolworth Company, grew to include more than a thousand stores in the United States, Canada, and Great Britain. In 1911 Woolworth commissioned architect Cass Gilbert (1859–1934) to design the Woolworth Building in New York City, which remains one of the best-known skyscrapers in the history of American architecture.

Another architect, Charles Pierrepont H. Gilbert (1863–1952), was commissioned to design Woolworth's country residence, Winfield Hall, in Glen Cove. The house was built in 1916–17 on the site of an older house of a previous owner that had been destroyed by fire. At the time of its construction Winfield Hall was considered to be one of the last "palaces" to be designed in the manner of the large Newport estates. Woolworth died two years after his house was completed, and the estate has since had a number of owners. It has most recently been occupied by the Grace Downs School, a commercial business school for girls. The house was put on the market by the school in 1976. A private group purchased the property, and it is again for sale.

The design of the Woolworth Residence was based on French and Italian Renaissance prototypes. The Renaissance influence can be seen in the plain wall surfaces (stuccoed on the exterior and sheathed in marble on the interior), the attached columns or wall pilasters with Corinthian capitals, the flat, unbroken roof line with a balustraded parapet, and the high open portico with freestanding classical columns. The attached wall pilasters break up the surface of the exterior wall planes and create the rhythm of a colonnade, with the open portico, located off the living room, as the last bay. Another Renaissance characteristic is seen in the formal garden landscaping, which includes both rectilinear and elliptical terraces. The house is situated on a hilltop. Its main portico looks out over an extended axial progression of descending, terraced hillside gardens, with pools and garden stairs framing the vista out to Long Island Sound. Years of overgrowth and untrimmed plantings have, however, obscured this view.

Another axis extends from the house along the entry drive across an elongated great lawn ending in a distant belvedere—a semicircular, colonnaded garden area, designed with ornamental sculptures. A curving preliminary

8–1 (opposite) Southwest loggia and garden terrace steps

roadway, which creates a transition or separation from the "outside world," precedes the final imposing axial drive up to the porte cochere, or covered entrance, to the house. The building is symmetrically designed about this axis, which continues through the central hall of the interior and out again to a formal garden containing an elaborate fountain and a vine-covered pavilion or shelter.

The main block of the house is similar to those of the Grand Trianon and the Petit Trianon at Versailles, but the window arrangement and detailing are far from a scholastic borrowing, with distinctively American picture windows in the living room, and a greenhouse-style breakfast room, both designed to take advantage of the dramatic view. The interiors of the house are lavish and continue the theme of Renaissance detailing, with marble finishes and a hand-carved, octagonally coffered ceiling in the central hall and grand stair. The huge living room, or music room, to one side of the central hall also has an ornate gilded and coffered ceiling and an intricately carved wood pipe-organ screen. This space opens onto an outdoor loggia or portico. To the other side of the central hall is the large dining room facing the formal gardens, with a kitchen and service wing beyond.

Winfield Hall can be compared to the Henri Bendel/ Walter P. Chrysler Estate at Kings Point, designed by Henry Otis Chapman (see page 51). Though somewhat smaller, the Bendel Residence was designed in the same year and has some similar characteristics, including its

8–2 (below) Main-floor plan

8–3 (opposite above) Entrance or southeast elevation

8–4 (opposite below) Partial view of garden or northwest elevation

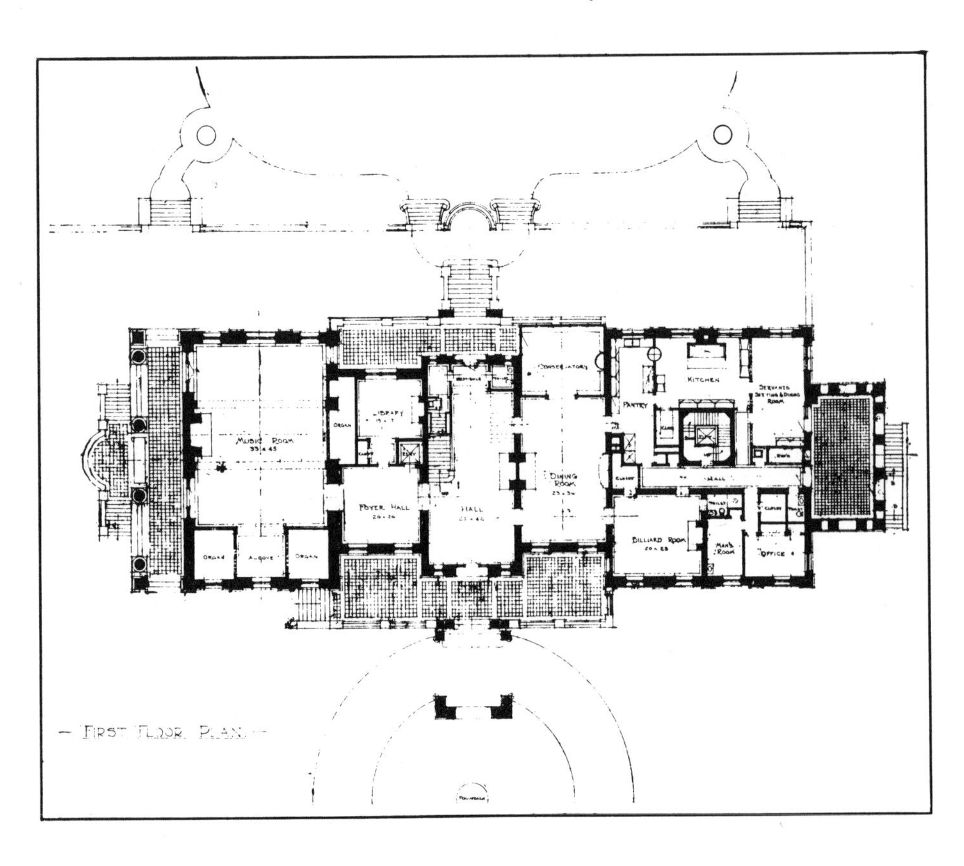

8–5 *Drawing of garden or northwest elevation*

severe rectangularity and its employment of surface breaks in the exterior walls to reflect the interior spatial arrangement of the house. The interior plan of the Bendel Residence can almost be read in the exterior elevations of the building. This consistency in plan and elevation was an important element in Beaux-Arts design. Other similarities include the employment of a dominant porte cochere, an axial entry drive, and the use of Renaissance details.

The architect C. P. H. Gilbert was born in New York City and studied architecture and the fine arts in the United States and in Europe. He designed many large houses in New York City, including the Italian Renaissance-styled Otto Kahn Mansion (1918) at One East Ninety-first Street, in association with J. Armstrong Stenhouse (now the Convent of the Sacred Heart); a French Château-styled mansion (1908) for Felix Warburg on Fifth Avenue at Ninety-second Street (now the Jewish Museum); the J. R. De-Lamar Mansion (1905) on Thirty-seventh Street (now the Polish Embassy); and the Harriet V. S. Thorne Residence (1902) on Eighty-fourth Street (now the Marymount School). Gilbert also designed the Cushman Office Building at Broadway and Maiden Lane in New York, and in Glen Cove his credits include the North Country Club development, the Dr. J. C. Ayer Residence, and the J. R. DeLamar Estate.

9

Herbert L. Pratt Estate, The Braes, Glen Cove

James Brite, architect, 1912; James Leal Greenleaf, landscape architect; estate owned by the Webb Institute for Naval Architecture; may be seen from Crescent Beach Road

Herbert Lee Pratt (1871–1945), a graduate of Amherst College, was one of eight children of Charles Pratt, the founder of Charles Pratt and Company, a large crude-oil refining firm in Brooklyn. The elder Pratt was also a partner in Reynolds, Devoe & Pratt, a paint and oil company. In 1874 he became a major executive of Standard Oil, following the merger of his refinery with that firm. In 1887 he founded Pratt Institute, now a well-known art and technical school.

Charles Pratt commissioned the construction of a large city residence for himself and, later, one for each of his sons as wedding presents. Most of these houses were built in the Clinton Hill neighborhood of Brooklyn, where Pratt Institute is located. The Pratt country houses were built in Glen Cove on large adjacent tracts of family-owned property in the area that surrounds the Webb Institute for Naval Architecture.

Pratt's son Herbert, a corporation official, was a director of Charles Pratt and Company and of the Bankers Trust Company. His Glen Cove estate was designed by architect James Brite in 1912 and christened The Braes after a Scottish term for the sloping banks of a hillside leading down to water.

The master plan for The Braes is composed of a series of descending rectangular courts and terraces that lead down toward the waterfront. The house, which sits at the highest level of this composition, was influenced by that seventeenth-century English Renaissance style called Jacobean, after King James I.

This Jacobean influence can be seen in the combination of brick walls with limestone detailing, as in the stone quoins at the corners of the building, in the lintels and mullions of the windows, in the horizontal stringcourses marking the floor lines in the elevations, and in the balustraded parapets at the roof line. Limestone was also used for the classical detailing at the entrances to the house and for the arcades on the waterfront elevation. The spiked, brick chimney tops are typically elongated and grouped in pairs or clusters. Other Jacobean features include the H-shaped plan, with a central entry and two side wings, and a long main hall, or gallery. The same stylistic elements had been employed in James Brite's earlier design for Darlington, the George Crocker Estate in Ramapo Hills, New Jersey, which was constructed between 1904 and 1907.

The composition of the Pratt Estate is so formally organized that initially it gives the appearance of a scholastic

9–1 (right) Site plan and main-floor plan. Drawing by James Brite, architect, 1912

9–2 (below) Entrance or east elevation

9–3 (opposite above) Partial view of waterfront or west elevation

9–4 (opposite below) Waterfront or west elevation. Drawing by James Brite, architect, 1912

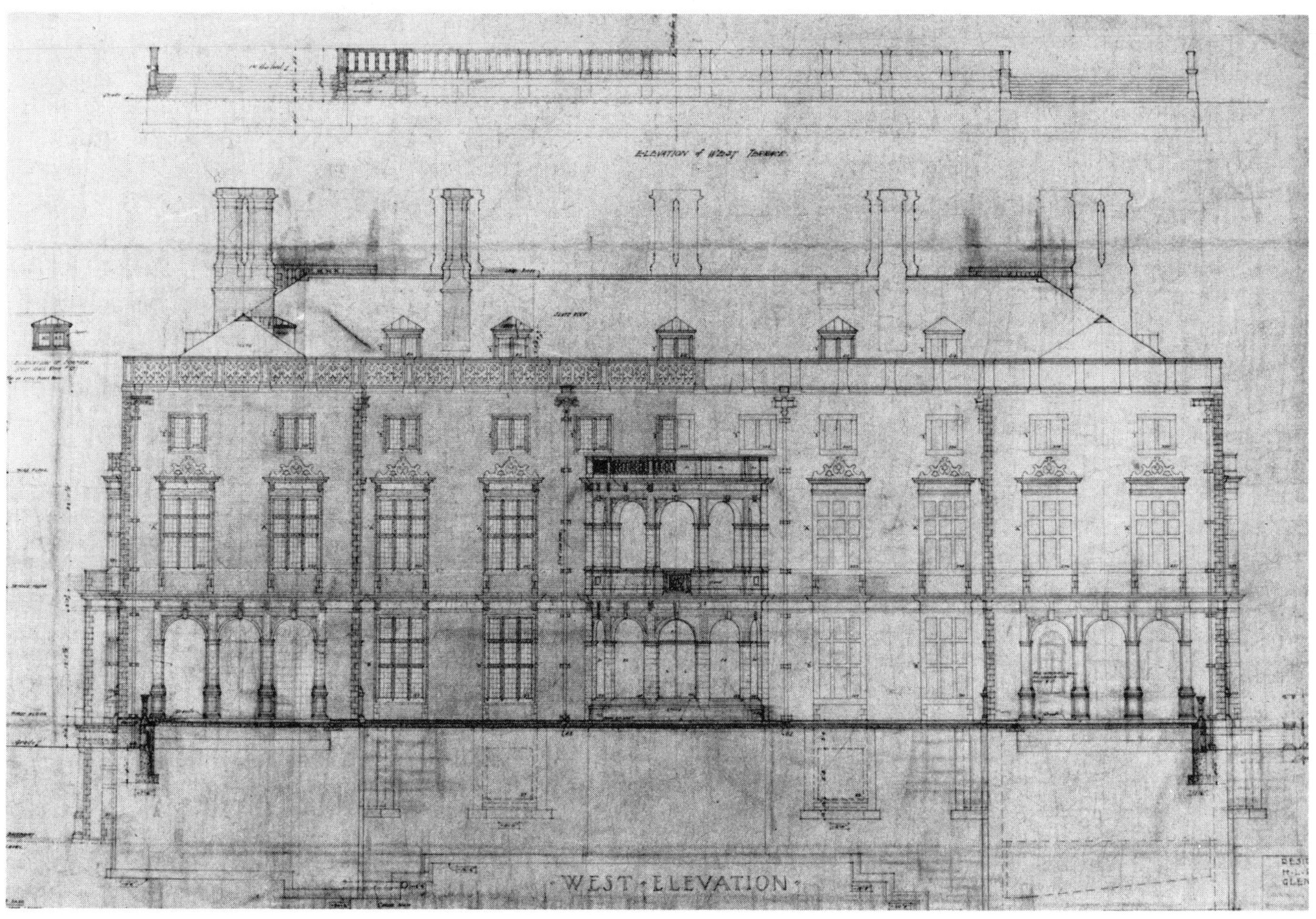
ELEVATION of WEST TERRACE
WEST · ELEVATION

9–5 Living room

drafting exercise. However, upon examination of both the floor plan of the house and the grand plan of the overall site, certain Beaux-Arts spatial elements, in addition to period details, can be identified. The site plan is developed as a moving progression of rectangular spaces. This axial progression, which begins at the entry gates, is elaborated at the rectangular entry, or motor, court and continues through the house itself, encompassing the main hall and drawing room, which are laid out symmetrically on either side of the same axis. At the far side of the house, three levels of open terraces, interconnected by formal double ramps, descend until the lowest one directly overlooks Long Island Sound.

Within the house the feeling of movement between spaces is emphasized by broad openings with sliding doors that interconnect the main living spaces and by a large freestanding double fireplace that separates the drawing room and the dining room. This feeling of open movement is continued in the main hall, where at either end two symmetrical stairs, framed by carved wood screens, lead to the upper floors. The original interior detailing, including elaborate wood wainscot paneling and ornamental plasterwork ceilings, has been well preserved.

On the waterfront elevation, facing north, a large semicircular, glass-enclosed bay projects from the center of the drawing room. From here the viewer can enjoy the expansive vista that continues the axial progression down to the water. At one time symmetrical loggias projected outward from the house and led through open garden pergolas to a teahouse on one side and a children's playhouse on the other.

The terraces are defined by the symmetrical wings of the house as well as by changes in exterior ground levels. Garden pergola structures and formal plantings reinforce the rectangularity of the design. Landscape architect James Leal Greenleaf worked with Brite on the planning of these vast grounds.

At the end of Chestnut Street, not far from the Herbert L. Pratt Residence, is a large stable, garage, and servants' complex known as the Pratt Oval. This group of buildings, constructed about 1904, was the administrative and service center for all of the adjacent Pratt family estates, including The Braes.

The Pratt Oval, designed as a Beaux-Arts version of late-nineteenth-century French architecture, may have been the work of the architectural firm of Babb, Cook & Willard. This office designed several projects for the Pratt family, including the Frederick B. Pratt Residence (1898) and the George D. Pratt Residence (1901), both in Brooklyn, in addition to the Andrew Carnegie Mansion (1901) in New York City.

During World War II, the Oval was converted to industrial uses, and it is now threatened with demolition in order to make way for a new housing development favored by neighborhood groups. However, the existing structures could be converted to new uses, including housing.

The other Pratt family estates built in the area between Pratt Oval and The Braes included the Charles M. Pratt Estate, Seamoor (c. 1926), designed by Peabody, Wilson & Brown (now demolished); the John T. Pratt Estate

(1909), designed by Charles A. Platt (now a private conference center); the Frederick B. Pratt Estate, Poplar Hill (c. 1917), designed by Platt's sons, William and Geoffrey Platt, of the Office of Charles A. Platt (now owned by Glengariff Nursing Home); the George D. Pratt Estate, Killenworth (c. 1914), designed by Trowbridge & Ackerman (now owned by the Soviet Delegation to the United Nations); and the Harold I. Pratt Estate, Welwyn (c. 1906), originally designed by Babb, Cook & Willard and later (c. 1914) altered by Delano & Aldrich (see fig. A–6). The Harold I. Pratt Estate was recently acquired by Nassau County for development as a park and nature preserve. Its grounds were designed by the Olmsted Brothers.

The Braes is occupied by the Webb Institute for Naval Architecture. Several school buildings have been added on the grounds, including a library and gymnasium. In general, these edifices have been designed to blend sympathetically with the original structure.

The Braes's architect, James Brite (1864–1942), began his training as an apprentice in the New York office of McKim, Mead & White. He also studied architecture in Europe and, in 1897, entered into partnership with Henry Bacon, a colleague at McKim, Mead & White and later (1922) the designer of the Lincoln Memorial, Washington, D.C. Together they designed Laurel Hill (1897), a large Georgian Style mansion in Columbia, South Carolina, and worked on the plans for American University (c. 1897) in Washington, D.C. After 1902 Brite practiced independently, designing large country estates, such as Darlington (1904–1907), for George Crocker, in Ramapo Hills, New Jersey. In addition to The Braes, Brite planned Herbert L. Pratt's city residence on Clinton Avenue in Brooklyn.

James Leal Greenleaf (1857–1933), educated at Columbia University as a civil engineer, began his practice as a landscape architect in the late 1890s. Greenleaf worked with Henry Bacon on the landscape design for the Lincoln Memorial, Washington, D.C., and with McKim, Mead & White on the Frederick W. Vanderbilt Estate in Hyde Park, New York. On Long Island he planned the landscape architecture for the George D. Pratt Estate, Killenworth, also in Glen Cove; the George S. Brewster Estate in Brookville; and the Mortimer Schiff Estate in Oyster Bay.

10
Alfred I. Du Pont/ Mrs. Frederick Guest Estate, Templeton, Brookville

Carrère & Hastings, architects, 1916–17; now De Seversky Conference Center of the New York Institute of Technology; estate now used as a conference center (by reservation) for large groups and organizations; may be seen from Northern Boulevard

Alfred I. Du Pont (1864–1935) was the grandson of Eleuthère Irénée Du Pont, the founder of the monolithic Du Pont powder and chemical corporation. The younger Du Pont was educated at Massachusetts Institute of Technology and after graduation entered the family business. Instrumental in securing major defense contracts from the federal government, Alfred became head of E. I. Du Pont and Company in 1902 and remained in that position until 1915. He left the post after a family dispute concerning his divorce from his first wife and his second marriage to Alicia Bradford Maddox.

After moving to New York, Du Pont organized the Nemours Trading Corporation in 1918. Architect Thomas Hastings, of the firm of Carrère & Hastings, designed his new Long Island residence, White Eagle (1916–17). In 1920 Du Pont's wife, Alicia, died, and after marrying again he sold White Eagle and moved to Florida in 1926.

The Du Pont Estate was then purchased by Mrs. Frederick E. Guest. Mrs. Guest (1872–1959), the former Amy Phipps, was the daughter of Henry Phipps, Andrew Carnegie's partner in the Carnegie Steel Company (see page 123). Her husband, Frederick E. Guest (1875–1937), was an English nobleman, the grandson of the seventh duke of Marlborough, and a first cousin of Winston Churchill. He was a member of the House of Commons from 1910 to 1922 and served as Secretary of State for Air under Prime Minister Lloyd George. Guest died in 1937, and his wife maintained the estate, renamed Templeton, until her death in 1959. Her son, Winston Guest, an internationally known polo player, later sold the property to the New York Institute of Technology. Templeton is now used as the De Seversky Conference Center of the institute.

The house can be seen from Northern Boulevard, across a vast meadow and on the far side of a large pond. A sweeping approach drive shows off the design from several vantage points, including a dramatic view of the curved and columned loggia off the great ballroom on the eastern side of the house.

At the main entrance, facing south, one feels that the formal composition of the entrance elevation is somehow unbalanced. Two second-story windows that seem arbitrarily placed disrupt the intended order of windows "in line" over windows. The garden elevation also has some apparently random window additions, one on the second floor above the ballroom, the other a pair of French doors

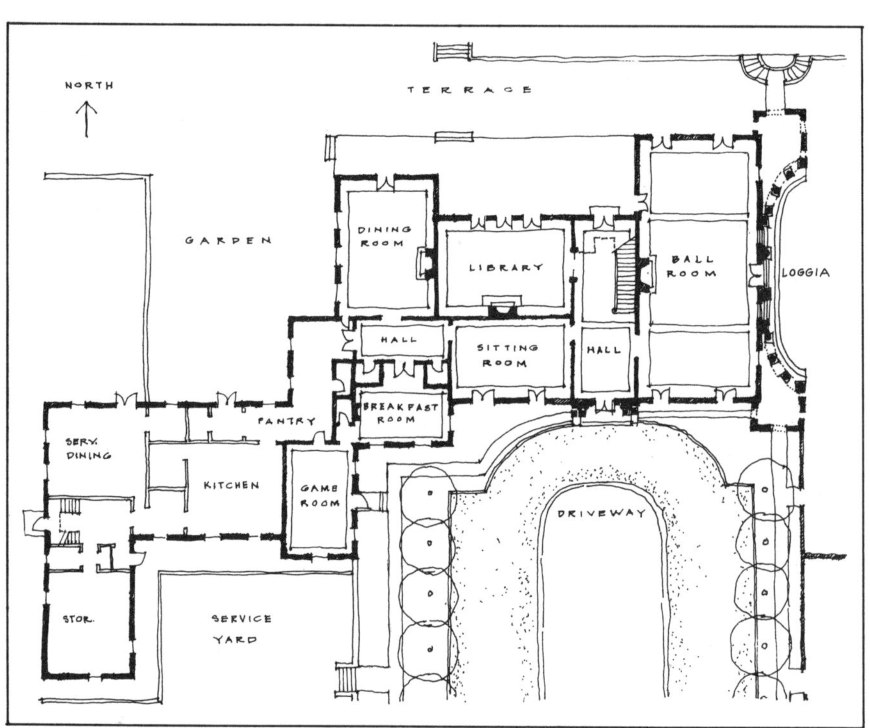

NORTH
TERRACE
GARDEN
DINING ROOM
LIBRARY
BALL ROOM
LOGGIA
HALL
SITTING ROOM
HALL
BREAKFAST ROOM
PANTRY
SERV. DINING
KITCHEN
GAME ROOM
DRIVEWAY
STOR.
SERVICE YARD

with a squared top placed between two arched door openings on the first floor.

The working drawings for the house, now in the Carrère & Hastings Collection at Avery Library, Columbia University, New York, show the original formally organized elevation drawings. Sketched freehand, over the lines of the brickwork on these drawings, are those "afterthought" windows, which may have been added by Mrs. Guest when the house was purchased from Du Pont. This is an alteration that should have been resisted.

The window changes are a reflection of additional alterations that were made in the floor plan of the house. The central hall was originally designed as an unobstructed major space, without stairs, that led directly out to the formal gardens and terraces to the north. The stair hall was originally to the side of this central hall (where the sitting room is now located). During the interior alteration of the central hall, a prominent stair was added, which now obscures the intended grand vista out to the gardens. The original stair-hall space was turned into a sitting room, complicating circulation through the house. One now has to pass through this room in order to reach the dining room and the breakfast area.

Architect Thomas Hastings also planned the original landscape design as a series of defined, exterior terraces and courts that formed an important part of the total master-plan organization. A walled service court separated the kitchen and servants' wing of the house from the main section of the development. Brick garden walls and formally planted rows of trees defined the large motor court

10–1 (opposite above) View of east elevation and terrace

10–2 (opposite below) Main-floor plan

10–3 (above) Original architectural drawing of entrance or south elevation, with later second-story windows drawn in freehand. The service court is to the left

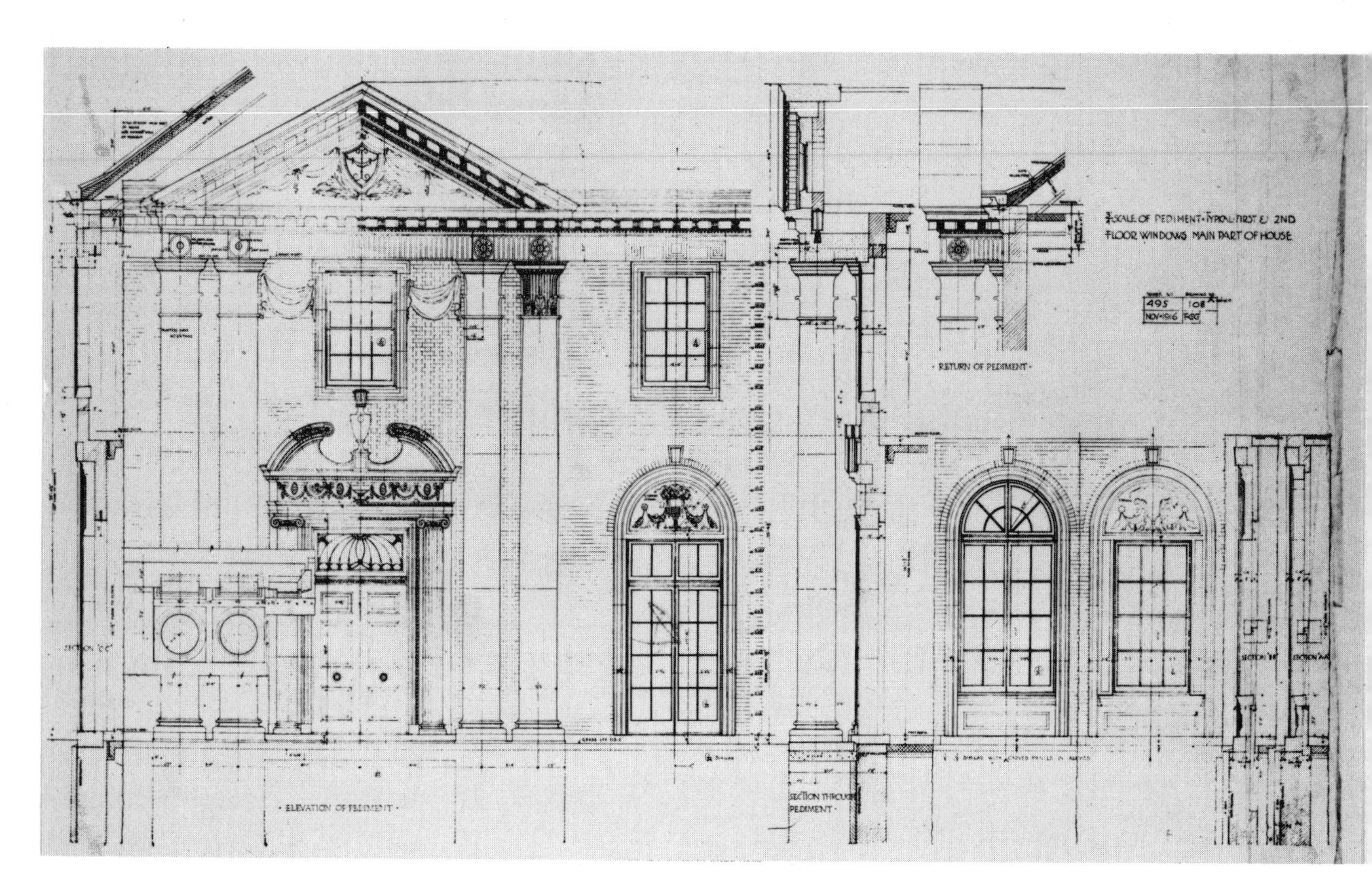
¾ SCALE OF PEDIMENT · TYPICAL FIRST & 2ND
FLOOR WINDOWS MAIN PART OF HOUSE
495
108
NOV·1916
· RETURN OF PEDIMENT ·
· ELEVATION OF PEDIMENT ·
SECTION THROUGH
PEDIMENT ·

and entrance driveway. On the garden side of the house, sloping changes in grade level, combined with balustraded retaining walls, defined the stepped outdoor terraces and formal-garden areas. An elaborate waterworks system was designed to circulate water from the large pond on the site to several levels of fountains, which were approached by a semicircular garden stair. This stair, located off the ballroom loggia, now leads to a swimming pool.

In inspiration Templeton combines Georgian and Adam stylistic influences with Italian Renaissance elements. The smooth brick finish of the exterior walls is punctuated with square-headed windows topped by delicately ornamented, semicircular arched panels. The imposing entrance of very tall double columns, topped by a thin pediment, is a Palladian influence, one reminiscent of the Church of San Giorgio Maggiore in Venice. The impressive elliptical loggia on the ballroom elevation, facing east, is based loosely on the curved court of the Villa Madama in Rome, attributed to Giulio Romano.

The firm of Carrère & Hastings had also designed Alfred I. Du Pont's earlier estate, Nemours (1909), located near Wilmington, Delaware. This prominent New York organization had been founded in 1885, after both John M. Carrère (1858–1911) and Thomas Hastings (1860–1929) had graduated from the Ecole des Beaux-Arts and had served their apprenticeships together with McKim, Mead & White in New York. Their first major commission was for the Ponce de Leon Hotel in St. Augustine, Florida, built for developer Henry M. Flagler in 1887. They later designed other Flagler hotels, as well as his mansion, Whitehall (1901), in Palm Beach, Florida, now open to the public as a museum. Another important early work was the E. C. Benedict Estate, Indian Harbor (c. 1896), in Greenwich, Connecticut.

Many of Carrère & Hastings' largest commissions have become well-known museums and institutions. These include the Daniel Guggenheim (1890) and Murray Guggenheim (1903) residences, both near Elberon, New Jersey, which now form a part of Monmouth College, and the Henry Clay Frick Mansion (1912–14) on Fifth Avenue at Seventieth Street in New York, which now houses the Frick Museum. The firm also designed the Main Building of the New York Public Library (1898–1911) on Fifth Avenue at Forty-second Street and the Senate and House Office buildings (1905–1906) in Washington, D.C.

On Long Island Carrère & Hastings planned estates for Walter Jennings (c. 1905) in Cold Spring Harbor (now

10–4 (opposite above) Architect's drawing of details of entrance or south elevation

10–5 (opposite below) Entrance or south elevation

owned by the Industrial Home for the Blind); for Herman B. Duryea (1903) in Westbury; and for Elihu Root (c. 1905) in Southampton. Other Long Island estates that the firm worked on—including those for W. Deering Howe in Jericho (now owned by Long Island Lutheran High School), for James A. Blair in Oyster Bay, for Charles H. Dana in Roslyn, and for Bradley Martin in Westbury—are recorded in the Carrère & Hastings Collection, which includes the firm's office archives, at Avery Library, Columbia University. Thomas Hastings' own home, built in Westbury (c. 1911), contains many similarities in layout, in use of materials, and in characteristics of style to his later design for the Du Pont Residence.

After Carrère died in 1911, Hastings carried on the firm's work until his death in 1929. Carrère & Hastings gained recognition as one of the outstanding Beaux-Arts firms in the country, and Hastings served as president of the Beaux-Arts Institute of Design in America.

10–6 (opposite above) East elevation showing loggia off the ballroom

10–7 (opposite below) View of north elevation and garden terracing

11
William C. Whitney Racing Stables and Gymnasium, Old Westbury

George A. Freeman, architect, 1898–99; stables now part of the New York Institute of Technology; located off Northern Boulevard

William C. Whitney (1841–1904), born in Conway, Massachusetts, was a descendant of Puritan settlers who came to America in 1635. A graduate of Harvard Law School, Whitney was admitted to the bar in 1865 and then became active in New York City politics. He worked with Samuel J. Tilden in opposing "Boss" Tweed and later supported Grover Cleveland in his campaign for the presidency. In 1885 Whitney was appointed Cleveland's Secretary of the Navy.

Whitney's first wife, Flora, a daughter of the wealthy Payne family, died in 1893. He later married Edith Sibyl Randolph, and shortly thereafter he commissioned architects McKim, Mead & White to design new interiors for his New York City mansion. When Edith died in 1899, Whitney retired from active business life and concentrated on developing his horse-breeding farm in Lexington, Kentucky, and the racing stables on his estate at Old Westbury, Long Island.

The Whitney Residence in Old Westbury, now demolished, was designed by McKim, Mead & White (c. 1902). It was a large, Tudor-influenced, brick-and-shingled structure, with multigabled, high-pitched roofs. When Whitney died in 1904, this residence became the home of his son, Harry Payne.

Harry Payne Whitney (1872–1930) enlarged the stables on the estate and altered portions of the main house (c. 1906). The Whitney Stables reached the peak of their activity between 1924 and 1933, when more than two hundred horses, including Equipoise and Top Flight, were bred and the stables placed first in more than 270 races.

Educated at Yale University and Columbia Law School, Harry Payne Whitney served as the director of the Guggenheim Exploration Company, which controlled mining-development rights throughout the country and abroad (see page 58). He was also a director of several large corporations, including the Guaranty Trust Company. In addition to his racing interests, Whitney was known as an expert polo player and served as captain of the American team that won the International Cup in 1913.

Harry Payne's wife, Gertrude (1875–1942), was an artist and well-known art patron. The daughter of Cornelius Vanderbilt, she married Whitney in 1896. After studying sculpture at the Art Students League in New York and in Paris, Gertrude Vanderbilt Whitney established her own art studio in Greenwich Village in 1907. She became an important patron of "The Eight," a group of modern American artists that included Robert Henri, Maurice Prendergast, and William Glackens, and in 1918 she or-

11-1 (opposite above) Sketch of the main house, William C. Whitney Estate, designed by McKim, Mead & White, c. 1902. Cornelius Vanderbilt Whitney had the house demolished in 1942

11-2 (opposite below) Whitney Racing Stables, seen from the southwest

Front Elevation
Gymnasium and Squash Racket Court,
for
The Hon. W. C. Whitney.
Westbury — L. I.

ganized the Whitney Studio Club as both a gallery and a meeting place for young artists. This organization was the forerunner of the Whitney Museum of American Art, established in 1931 in New York City.

Gertrude Vanderbilt Whitney's designs for public sculptures were erected in Washington, D.C., New York, and San Francisco, and abroad in Spain and France. Her sculptures are also in museum collections, including those of the Metropolitan Museum of Art, New York, and the Art Institute of Chicago.

Harry and Gertrude's son, Cornelius Vanderbilt Whitney, inherited the estate. In 1942 he demolished the original main residence and erected a new house on the site. This building is now the Old Westbury Golf and Country Club. The estate's large indoor tennis-court structure and a tall, shingled windmill tower, originally a water tower, are now on the grounds of the country club. A studio for Gertrude Vanderbilt Whitney, designed as a small Palladian-style temple (c. 1913) by Delano & Aldrich, is still privately owned. The William C. Whitney Racing Stables and Gymnasium now form a part of the New York Institute of Technology. The stables serve as the main Education Building, containing the School of Architecture, and the gymnasium houses the School of Fine Arts.

The Whitney Stables, as well as the nearby Gymnasium, were designed by architect George A. Freeman and built about 1898–99. Prominently sited at the top of a broad sloping hill, the stables can be seen most clearly from Wheatley Road.

Many Long Island estate owners maintained stables to keep horses for racing and polo, as well as for transportation, and these structures were an important consideration in the master planning of many estates. The layout, or parti, of the stable plans and the spatial and surface designs of these buildings displayed as many variations as the main houses.

The William C. Whitney Racing Stables were organized along a linear parti, as opposed to the courtyard parti of the F. Ambrose Clark Racing Stables (1912) at Old Westbury (see page 131), designed by Rogers & Zogbaum, and the Marshall Field III Polo Stables (c. 1925) at Caumsett, his estate at Lloyd Neck (see page 170), planned by Alfred Hopkins and John Russell Pope. The tremendously long building relies on the careful modulation of gables and dormers for visual relief. The Tudor-styled, half-timbered patterns of the elevations help to control the

11–3 (opposite above) Whitney Gymnasium. Drawing of the entrance or south elevation by George A. Freeman, architect, 1899

11–4 (opposite below) Whitney Gymnasium, entrance or south elevation

scale of the huge complex and blend with the Tudor-influenced design of the main house.

Numerous skylights and grouped door and window openings allowed natural light and ventilation into the interior stalls, and the doors gave direct access from the stalls to the exercise fields, which were originally located on the meadow in front of the stables. The exterior architectural details, including a large ornamental clock, have been preserved by the institute, while the interiors have been completely renovated and converted into classrooms, drafting studios, and offices.

The Whitney Gymnasium, reminiscent of a Tudor hunting lodge, retains many of the characteristics of the original interior, as well as exterior, design. The focus of the building is a great, two-story-high central space with a massive brick fireplace and open balconies on the upper floor. This great hall area originally led to the exercise rooms, squash courts, and bowling alleys, which are used today as painting studios. This major space now functions as an exhibition hall and is surrounded by studios on both levels.

11–5 Whitney Gymnasium, bay windows above the entrance porch

The central hall can be identified on the exterior of the building by three interconnected, high-pitched roof gables, each of which has a delicate, Queen Anne-styled curved bay window. A broad entrance veranda, recessed under the projecting bays, extends out over the entry drive with a gracefully arching porte cochere.

Rubblestone base walls and small ornamental pebbles set into the stuccoed surfaces between the half-timbers give the building a handcrafted look. Ornamental pebblework was also employed in many of Stanford White's early designs.

Architect George A. Freeman (1859–1934) was born in New York City and educated at Massachusetts Institute of Technology. Freeman practiced both in Stamford, Connecticut, and in New York City, designing many estates and country homes in the area. His work on Long Island includes the William Erhart Residence (c. 1904) in Cedarhurst and the Foxhall Keene/William Grace Holloway Estate (c. 1904) in Old Westbury (see page 118), both planned in association with architect Francis G. Hasselman. The nearby Keene/Holloway Estate also now forms a part of the New York Institute of Technology.

In 1882 Freeman associated with the well-known architect Bruce Price on the design for Seacroft, a large estate in Seabright, New Jersey. His later projects include the Charles H. Mellon Estate (c. 1908) in Morristown, New Jersey; the Matthews Residence (c. 1888) in Narragansett, Rhode Island; and the Bridgeport Trust Company (c. 1910) in Bridgeport, Connecticut. One of his largest projects was the Rumson Country Club and Park development (c. 1910) in Rumson, New Jersey, which was planned with landscape architect Charles W. Leavitt (see page 52).

12 Mr. and Mrs. Roderick Tower Residence, Old Westbury

Delano & Aldrich, architects, 1924; residence now part of the New York Institute of Technology; located off Northern Boulevard

12–1 (opposite above) View from southeast of garden elevation with polygonal bay

12–2 (opposite below) Main-floor plan

Flora Payne Whitney, the daughter of Harry Payne and Gertrude Vanderbilt Whitney, was married to Roderick Tower in 1920. Tower was the son of Charlemagne Tower, a former U.S. Ambassador to Russia and to Germany. He was a graduate of Harvard University (1915), served as an Air Force captain during World War I, and later became a member of the New York Stock Exchange. The Towers' Norman-styled country home, designed by architects Delano & Aldrich, was built on a portion of the Harry Payne Whitney Estate property in 1924 (see page 109).

Flora Whitney shared her mother's interest in art, and she served as head of the Whitney Museum of American Art in New York City. After her divorce from Roderick Tower, she married an architect, George MacCulloch Miller, the son of a prominent corporate lawyer.

The Roderick Tower Residence, which then became known as the George MacCulloch Miller Residence, was eventually acquired by the New York Institute of Technology, which purchased a large portion of the former Whitney Estate in 1963 from a developer who had bought the property in 1959. The building presently houses faculty and administrative offices on the campus. The exterior of the house still retains the character of the original design with one exception. The shutters that formerly were located at the window and door openings have been removed, which gives the house a harsher, somewhat more severe appearance.

Known on the Institute campus as the French Château, the Tower/Miller Residence is located on a heavily wooded hill and resembles a modest, secluded, Norman country manor more than an elaborate Loire Valley château. The walls are built of bricks laid with "rough-set" mortar joints and accented by dressed stone quoining at the corners and window openings. The floor plan of the house is L-shaped, with brick wall extensions defining an enclosed, cobblestoned entry, or motor, court. A round, conically roofed tower in the corner of the motor court marks the entrance to the house. Inside this tower is a vestibule level, slightly lower than the main floor, which contains a semicircular main stair hall.

A glass-enclosed porch on the opposite side of the house projects out into the garden as a polygonal bay with a high-pitched roof, recalling the projecting tower form in the entrance courtyard. The living and dining rooms of the house originally opened onto the sides of this porch, as well as out onto the lawn and the gardens. The master-

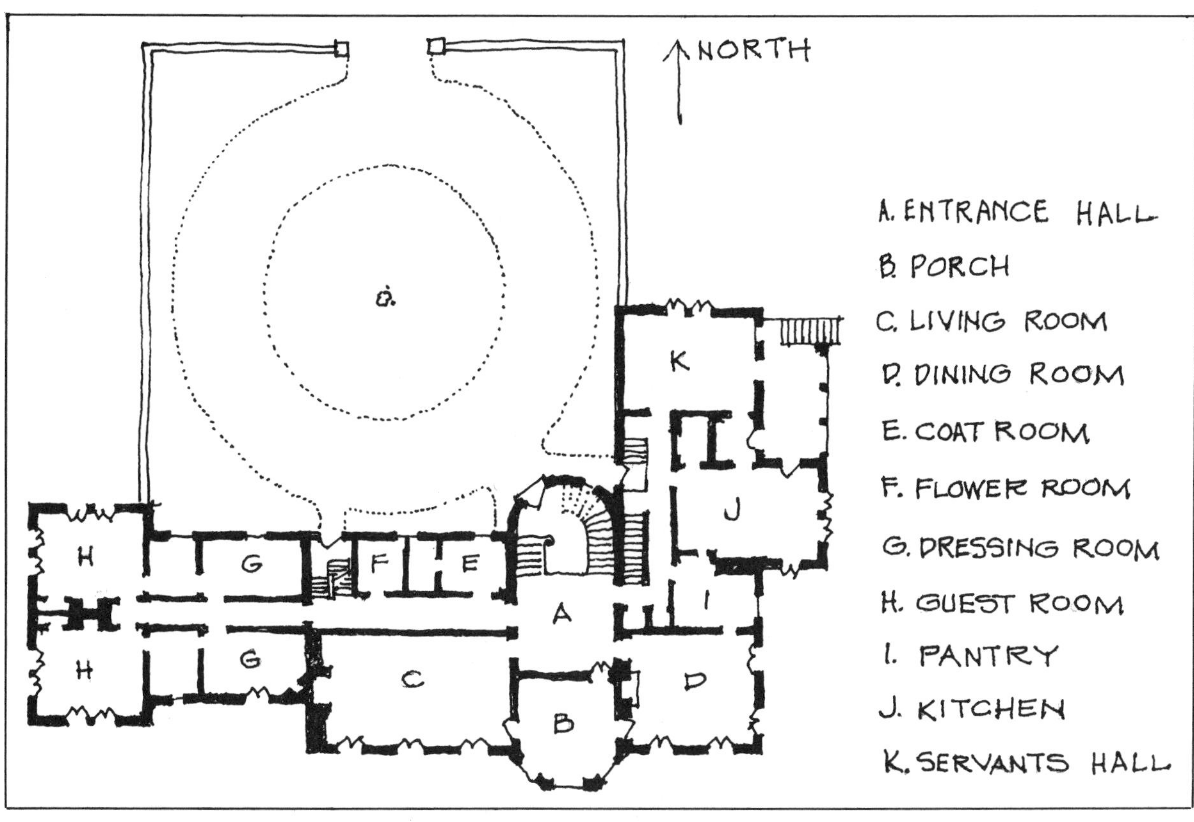
NORTH
A. ENTRANCE HALL
B. PORCH
C. LIVING ROOM
D. DINING ROOM
E. COAT ROOM
F. FLOWER ROOM
G. DRESSING ROOM
H. GUEST ROOM
I. PANTRY
J. KITCHEN
K. SERVANTS HALL
A
B
C
D
E
F
G
G
H
H
I
J
K

bedroom suite on the second floor also extended out over the porch to continue the polygonal form up to the roof line. The entrance to this suite is raised slightly above the interior second-floor level and overlooks the semicircular stair hall and corridor space within from an open interior balcony level.

The Tower house was designed with a private, almost intimate character that was carefully composed both in plan and in section. This intimacy was achieved by the intentionally small scale of the interior spaces, by the vertical level changes that separated and defined these spaces, and by the private garden and courtyard walls that secluded the house from other nearby buildings on the Whitney Estate.

12–3 Drawing of entrance or north elevation and entrance court

The office of Delano & Aldrich was one of the most prolific Beaux-Arts architectural firms in New York City. William A. Delano (1874–1960) was born in New York and educated at Yale University. His partner, Chester H. Aldrich (1871–1940), a native of Providence, Rhode Island, was educated at Columbia University. Both served their apprenticeships in the office of Carrère & Hastings (see page 105), and both studied architecture at the Ecole des Beaux-Arts. They established their own office in 1903.

One of the firm's early commissions on Long Island was the Federal-styled Egerton L. Winthrop, Jr., Estate (1903–1904) in Syosset (see page 149), now owned by the Nassau County Museum and used as an administration center. Another early project was the now-demolished Château des Beaux-Arts Casino (1905) in Huntington, a waterfront club and casino designed in a Beaux-Arts version of the French Renaissance Style.

The firm later planned several large estates on Long Island in the style of French Renaissance country manors, all with high, steeply pitched mansard or hipped roofs. These included the Otto Kahn Estate (c. 1923) in Woodbury (now Eastern Military Academy); the Vincent Astor Estate (c. 1926) in Port Washington; and the Benjamin Moore Estate in Syosset. Other commissions were the Italian Renaissance-styled Bertram G. Work Estate in Oyster Bay, Gertrude Vanderbilt Whitney's Palladian studio (c. 1913) on the William C. Whitney Estate in Old Westbury (see page 111), and the Eberstard Estate (c. 1937) in Lloyd Harbor, which now forms part of the "Target Rock" U.S. Fish and Wildlife Preserve.

In New York City, the firm planned many private town houses and large clubs. Several of these were designed in the Georgian and Federal styles, including the Willard Straight Residence (1914) at Ninety-fourth Street and

Fifth Avenue (now the International Center for Photography) and the Colony Club (1924) at Park Avenue and Sixty-second Street. The Union Club (1932) on Sixty-ninth Street and the Harold I. Pratt Residence (1920) at Sixty-eighth Street and Park Avenue (the latter now the Council on Foreign Relations) were influenced by Italian and English Renaissance prototypes. Other important projects by Delano & Aldrich include the American Embassy (1933) in Paris, the Japanese Embassy (c. 1931) in Washington, D.C., and the U.S. Post Office (1934) in Washington, D.C.

Both members of the firm were also active in architectural education. Delano was a professor of architecture at Columbia University from 1903 to 1910, and he also served as the president of the Beaux-Arts Institute of Design in America from 1927 to 1929. Aldrich served as the director of the American Academy in Rome from 1935 to 1940. An additional discussion of the firm is contained in the article on the Egerton L. Winthrop, Jr., Estate at Syosset (see page 149).

12–4 View from northeast with entrance court to right

13
Foxhall Keene/ William Grace Holloway Estate, Old Westbury

George A. Freeman and Francis G. Hasselman, architects, c. 1904; Charles W. Leavitt, landscape architect; estate now owned by the New York Institute of Technology; not open to the public; property under development; located off Wheatley Road

Foxhall Keene (1870–1941) was the son of New York financier and sportsman James R. Keene. Educated at Harvard University, Keene joined his father in operating the family's racing stables and their horse-breeding farm, Castleton, in Kentucky. The Keene Racing Stables raised many prize-winning horses at the turn of the century, including Commando and Sysonby, and in 1907 earned more than $400,000 in prize money. Along with Harry Payne Whitney, Foxhall Keene was a well-known polo player and served as a member of the American International Polo Team in 1913. He was also an early automobile enthusiast and participated in the Vanderbilt Cup Automobile Races (see page 185) on Long Island.

The Foxhall Keene Residence, Rosemary Hall, was located near the William C. Whitney Estate at Old Westbury (see page 109), off Wheatley Road, and was designed about 1904 by architects George A. Freeman and Francis G. Hasselman. This property was later purchased by William Grace Holloway, who renamed the estate Foxhurst. Holloway (1886–1959), a member of the Grace shipping line family, was also a graduate of Harvard University. He began working at William R. Grace and Company in 1908, later becoming director and chairman of the board. Holloway married Hilda Holmes in 1918. Some years after his death in 1959, Mrs. Holloway sold the estate to the New York Institute of Technology for development as a future campus facility.

The Keene/Holloway Residence is a good example of a traditional or Colonial central-hall plan reinterpreted and elaborated with the use of Beaux-Arts principles. Its central, pedimented portico with two-story-high Corinthian columns gives the residence the character of a Palladian villa. This portico, which is approached by a broad flight of stairs, marks the entrance into the central hall.

The rear elevation also has a central, pedimented bay. This elevation is treated in a more severe fashion, with plain, stuccoed surfaces punctuated by small, sparsely placed openings. The stark, unrelieved geometry recalls the design of Tuscan villas, while the use of small circular windows is characteristic of Georgian Colonial and Federal period houses. The hipped roof has round-topped dormers, another feature found in Georgian Colonial designs.

The central hall is the major interior space of the house and employs grandiose proportions. It is a rectangular space terminating in a grand stair that was, originally, also rectangular in shape but that was later altered into an elliptical form. Two pairs of large, formally designed liv-

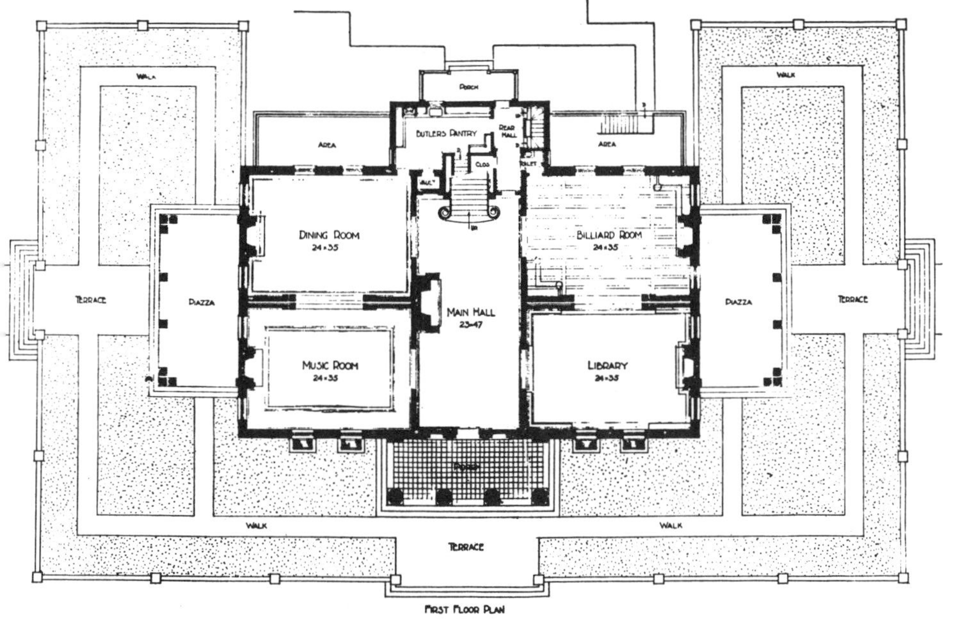

13–1 (left) Main-floor plan

13–2 (below) Entrance or south elevation

ing spaces open symmetrically onto either side of the hall. These rooms also open into each other, through broad pairs of sliding pocket doors, thus forming secondary, parallel, and cross axes of movement in relation to the main central-hall axis. The living spaces in turn open onto covered outdoor piazzas, or porches, located at both ends of the house.

A butler's pantry, behind the grand stair, is the receiving point for food prepared in the central kitchen, which is located on the floor below. By reducing the service area on the main floor, the simplicity and airiness of an "open" plan was maintained. In addition, the interconnected openings between the various spaces make the normally simple but static Colonial central-hall plan more fluid and dynamic.

The house sits on a raised terrace platform located at the crest of a broad, sloping meadow running south down to the Long Island Expressway. Gardens were originally developed off the piazzas on either side of the house, and they were planned by landscape architect Charles W. Leavitt.

Architect George A. Freeman also designed several of the buildings on the nearby William C. Whitney Estate, including the Whitney Racing Stables (see page 109). He later collaborated with architect Francis G. Hasselman on the design of many projects in the New York area.

Freeman & Hasselman designed several country houses with the same parti as that of the Foxhall Keene Residence. Although different in exterior design, each was characterized by a main-floor layout almost completely open in plan and with broad sliding doors interconnecting all the main living spaces. The Charles H. Mellon Residence (c. 1904) in Rye, New York, is one example of the variations on this theme. Freeman & Hasselman also designed the William Erhart Residence (c. 1904) in Cedarhurst and the Rumson Country Club and Park development (c. 1910) in Rumson, New Jersey. An additional discussion of their work is contained in the article on the William C. Whitney Racing Stables and Gymnasium at Old Westbury (see page 109).

Landscape architect Charles W. Leavitt also planned the grounds of the Henri Bendel/Walter P. Chrysler Estate (c. 1929) at Kings Point (see page 51). In addition, he collaborated with Freeman & Hasselman on the Rumson Country Club and Park development (c. 1910) in Rumson, New Jersey. Additional discussions of his work are contained in the articles on the Henri Bendel/Walter P. Chrysler Estate at Kings Point (see page 51), and the William C. Whitney Racing Stables and Gymnasium at Old Westbury (see page 109).

13–3 Garden or north elevation

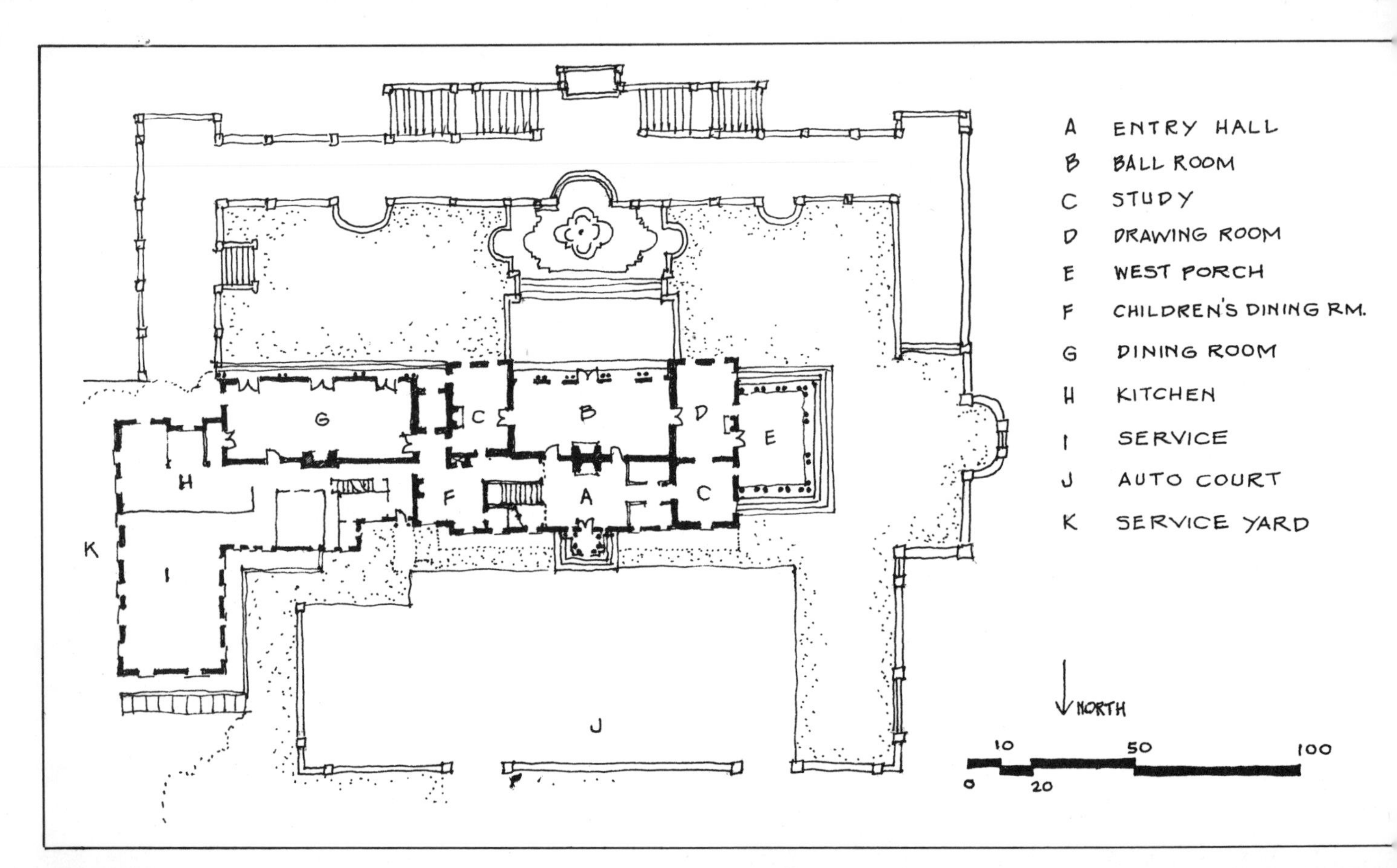
A ENTRY HALL
B BALL ROOM
C STUDY
D DRAWING ROOM
E WEST PORCH
F CHILDREN'S DINING RM.
G DINING ROOM
H KITCHEN
I SERVICE
J AUTO COURT
K SERVICE YARD
NORTH
0 10 20 50 100

14
John S. Phipps Estate, Westbury House, Old Westbury

George Crawley, architect, 1906–24; Alfred C. Bossom and Edward Hinkle, associates; 1911 addition, Horace Trumbauer, architect; landscape consultant, Jacques Gréber; estate now owned by the Old Westbury Gardens Foundation; open to the public; located off Old Westbury Road

John S. Phipps (1874–1958) was the son of Henry Phipps, a financier and partner of Andrew Carnegie in the Carnegie Steel Company. The younger Phipps was a graduate of Yale College and Harvard University (1899), and he married an Englishwoman, Margarita Celia Grace, of the Grace shipping line family in 1903. He served as a director of the United States Steel Corporation, the Grace Steamship Lines, and the Guaranty Trust Company.

The Phipps residence, Westbury House, was planned in 1906 by the London designer George Crawley. Located in Old Westbury, the estate originally included polo fields to the south and a large stable group to the north, in addition to a dairy farm, an orchard, a golf course, and indoor tennis courts. After Phipps died in 1958, Old Westbury Gardens was established as an arboretum and horticultural center. The property is now administered by the Old Westbury Gardens Foundation, and the main house and grounds are open to the public.

Westbury House was designed by George Crawley in the style of a Charles II country manor. The reign of Charles II (1660–85) occurred toward the middle of the Stuart period (1603–1714) of English Renaissance architecture, a period that was characterized by the design influences of Inigo Jones (1573–1652), Sir Christopher Wren (1632–1723), and their contemporaries. Inigo Jones first popularized the work of Andrea Palladio (1518–1580) in England after studying and traveling in Italy, and Wren's designs showed the influence of the court of Louis XIV and of French architects and planners, including Jules Hardouin Mansart and Louis Le Vau.

Stuart period houses, such as Westbury House, were usually symmetrical in layout, with a rectangular plan divided into three parts, the center third containing the hall and main salon. Other characteristics of this style that appear in Westbury House are the use of brick walls with classical detailing in dressed or carved stone; a prominent, horizontal, denticulated cornice at the roof line; and hipped roofs with dormers (as opposed to gables).

The house is set on the crest of a hill, with landscaped terraces stepping down to a great lawn and elaborate gardens to the south. The master plan for the estate grounds was developed along a major axis running from north to south, lined with grand allées of beech and linden trees, respectively. A minor axis running from east to west ends in landscaped ponds. The house is placed at the intersec-

14–1 (opposite above) Main-floor plan

14–2 (opposite below) Entrance or north elevation

14–3 (overleaf) Garden or south elevation

tion of these axes and commands dramatic elongated views in each direction.

Westbury House is approached through an entry, or motor, court defined by low, brick garden walls. The entrance elevation, articulated into three sections, is characterized by formal, high windows, symmetrically placed about a tripartite, Ionic-columned entrance vestibule. This vestibule lights the main entry hall on the first floor. Above it, the second floor hall is lighted by elliptical windows on either side of a segmentally arched opening. At the roof level a large, round-headed dormer with a Palladian window completes the exterior vertical expression of the main interior circulation spaces. The dormer is also aligned with the four-part chimney projection above. This achieves a central hierarchy in the composition of the front elevation while maintaining an overall symmetrical arrangement.

The interior of the entry hall is defined and separated from the adjacent grand staircase by an open, carved wood screen of fluted Corinthian columns. The entry hall leads into the large living hall, or ballroom, through doors on either side of a double fireplace. Following an axial progression, the ballroom leads out through French doors to the formal garden terraces that overlook the great lawn and grand allée of linden trees.

Located to one side of the ballroom is a formal drawing room with a colonnaded, glass-enclosed sun porch beyond. On the other side is the study, which originally was probably the dining room, with later dining- and service-wing additions beyond. The service wing was added in 1911 by Philadelphia architect Horace Trumbauer, who was also commissioned to plan Henry Phipps's Estate, Bonnie Blink, in Great Neck, now the administration center of the Great Neck Board of Education.

George Crawley designed two of the later additions to the house—the dining room in 1915 and the sun porch in 1924. In the latter, large glass sheets span the distance between the double, Ionic columns that support the porch roof beams. These windows can be lowered directly into the ground, transforming the sun room into an outdoor covered veranda.

The garden elevation of the house was carefully composed by Crawley, both in the original central block of the house and in the later additions on either side. A superimposed Ionic colonnade identifies the ballroom in the central bay of the exterior. Breaks in the wall planes, along with projecting, hipped roofs and round-headed dormers, define the two exterior side bays containing the study and

14–4 (opposite) Drawing room

14–5 *Drawing of entrance or north elevation*

the drawing room. The one-story additions of the sun porch to the west and the dining room to the east repeat the rhythm of the original double columns and achieve a symmetrical balance in the elevation. The consistent line balances the strong diagonals of the terrace stairs and the lower horizontal level of the great lawn.

The landscaping at Westbury House is a good illustration of the academic Beaux-Arts concept of the grand plan, using major and minor axes and extended vistas. In addition to Crawley's work on the landscaping, the French landscape architect and planner Jacques Gréber was a consultant on the design of the gardens. Four sketches of plans by Gréber for the gardens are on exhibit in the house. The master plan includes both formal elements of French Renaissance landscape architecture and informal elements of English Romantic, or "picturesque," landscaping. The formal elements include the grand allées of trees that create axial vistas to the north and south and the great south lawn, which is defined by a series of retaining walls, garden terraces, symmetrical exterior grand stairs, and geometrically aligned plantings. Period gardens, including a walled Italian garden, an English rose garden, and a boxwood garden, create a variety of sequential outdoor spaces. Carved sculptures and ornamental wrought-iron gates, in addition to brick garden walls and stone balustrades, are employed to further articulate these areas. Picturesque elements of the landscape design include the duck pond, to the west of the house, and the lake with its naturalistic woodland walk and romantically sited Temple of Love to the east.

The interior detailing of the Phipps house and many of the antique furnishings have been preserved and maintained in their original condition. The Phipps family collection of paintings has also been retained, and it includes landscapes and portraits by Sir Joshua Reynolds, Thomas Gainsborough, John Constable, and John Singer Sargent, among others.

George Crawley (1864–1926), born in London, was the son of an English lawyer and railroad contractor. He was educated at Trinity College and first became involved in architectural design through Henry Phipps, whose family owned a residence adjacent to his in England. Crawley became a family friend, and in 1903 he was commissioned to design the interiors of Henry Phipps's town house in New York City. In 1906 he opened a New York office in the Flat Iron Building with two associates, architects Alfred C. Bossom, also English, and Edward Hinkle, an American. Both designers worked with Crawley on the drawings and on the execution of Westbury House.

Crawley was a contemporary of the noted English architect Sir Edwin Lutyens (1869–1944), and may have been influenced by some of his work, including Heathcote, at Ilkley, England, built in the same year as Westbury House. It shows a similar dramatic massing above high garden terrace walls and a similar use of prominent hipped roofs. However, Crawley's work was much more scholastic than Lutyens' and was influenced by historic Stuart period prototypes, such as Honington Hall (c. 1685) in Warwickshire, which has an exterior composition similar in character to Westbury House; Belton House (1685–88) at Grantham, whose interior detailing resembles Crawley's designs; and Ashburnham House (c. 1662) at Westminster.

Crawley was also influenced by the English architect Richard Norman Shaw (1831–1912), whose 1888 design for the house at 170 Queen's Gate in London includes a round-topped dormer window, a characteristic of the English Queen Anne Style. Westbury House also recalls certain English Colonial prototypes in the United States, such as Stratford Hall (c. 1725), the Lee homestead on the Potomac River, which has a similar four-part, interconnected chimney with arched penetrations. Stratford Hall also shows the same type of high-pitched roofs and hip-roof bays as those in the Phipps Residence.

Crawley later returned to practice in England, and his work there includes the Stanley Brotherwood House at Thornhaugh; Peterborough, the Cuthbert Heath House on Park Lane, London; and the Blake Residence at Sunningdale in Berkshire. Between 1912 and 1928 he also designed the interiors of several ships for the Grace Steamship Lines.

Crawley's early associate, architect Alfred C. Bossom, later went on to plan other large country houses on Long Island, including the J. W. Harriman Estate (c. 1918) in Brookville and the Henry Whiton Residence (c. 1923) in Hewlett. He also designed the Seaboard National Bank Building (c. 1922) in New York City.

Horace Trumbauer (1868–1938) became famous for the large estates that he planned outside Philadelphia and at Newport, Rhode Island (see page 15). On Long Island he later designed the Howard Brokaw Estate (c. 1918) in Brookville.

The French landscape architect and planner Jacques Gréber (1882–1962) is best known in the United States for his master plan for the Benjamin Franklin Parkway (c. 1917) in Philadelphia, designed in the tradition of Baron Georges Haussmann's plans for Paris. Gréber laid out a grand boulevard lined with trees, similar to the Champs-Elysées in Paris, with an axial vista leading from Fairmount Park and the Philadelphia Museum of Art, through Logan Circle (modeled after the Place de la Concorde), and ending in the urban center at City Hall. Between 1917 and 1929 he also collaborated with the famous Beaux-Arts architect and critic Paul P. Cret on several buildings in the Philadelphia master plan, including the Rodin Museum, the Franklin Institute Science Museum, the Philadelphia County Court House, and the Free Library of Philadelphia.

Gréber, who graduated in architecture from the Ecole des Beaux-Arts (1908), designed the landscaping and master plans for several country homes outside Philadelphia, including the Edward T. Stotesbury Estate, Whitemarsh Hall (1915–21), in Chestnut Hill, in association with architect Horace Trumbauer. He also planned the grounds and landscaping about 1910 for the Clarence H. Mackay Estate, Harbor Hill (1902–1905), in Roslyn, Long Island, with McKim, Mead & White (see fig. I–26), and he designed many estates in France, one of the largest being Villa Altona in Antibes, which has a site plan similar to that of Westbury House. This plan shows the same strong axes and vistas and a similar use of grand allées with an extensive system of terraces, retaining walls, and double grand stairs leading down to the gardens.

15
F. Ambrose Clark Racing Stables, Old Westbury

Rogers & Zogbaum, architects, 1912; stables now owned by the State University of New York, College at Old Westbury; used as a training center by the Board of Cooperative Educational Services; located off the Long Island Expressway Service Road

F. Ambrose Clark (1881–1964) was a well-known sportsman and a leading figure in horse racing. An heir of the former president of the Singer Sewing Machine Company, Edward Clark (1811–82), F. Ambrose Clark commissioned the design of his four-hundred-acre estate, Broad Hollow, in 1912. The main house, designed by the New York firm of Rogers & Zogbaum, was destroyed by fire in 1968, shortly after the property was purchased by the State University of New York, College at Old Westbury. The remaining buildings on the university campus that survive from the original estate include the F. Ambrose Clark Racing Stables, now a Board of Cooperative Educational Services (B.O.C.E.S.) agricultural school, the horse trainer's residence, a Colonial-styled structure now used by Empire State College, and a large service building that originally housed the laundry and the servants' quarters.

Harry St. Clair Zogbaum's design for Broad Hollow combined formal Georgian and Palladian prototypes with the informality and airiness of an American central-hall parti. The plan included a series of open loggias and arcades projecting off the main entrance as well as off the dining and living areas. In addition, a gallery located off the main stair and within the central hall was open to the second floor above, creating breezy cross-ventilation between the hall and the porches during the summer months.

The racing stables were designed with Georgian and Dutch Colonial Revival elements and show the same attention to detail as the design for the original main house. A large gambrel-roofed structure surrounded by broad meadows, the stable complex remains an impressive symbol of a man who was a leader in the racing field for more than sixty years. Clark's prize-winning horses, including Kellsboro Jack and Teamaker, earned more than $200,000. This was also the site of the Meadow Brook Cup Race, the oldest point-to-point horse race in the United States.

The large field between the horse stables and the head trainer's house is divided by stone walls and wood fences into formal equestrian rectangles. The pattern thereby created is as organized and sophisticated as a formal garden arrangement. The stables themselves are also formally organized into a courtyard parti. Access to the court is through symmetrically placed arched openings within two-story-high, gambrel-roofed entrance pavilions. The open court, used for grooming and watering the horses, is surrounded by a covered promenade or walkway that connected all the stalls located on the outer perimeter of the

building. The exterior walls of the stables are brick at the first-floor level, with shingled surfaces and sloping dormers above. Within the courtyard, the brick is carried up to the gambrel roofs, with formal Palladian windows above the entry arches.

The F. Ambrose Clark Racing Stables can be compared to some of the other estate stables discussed in this guide. The Marshall Field III Polo Stables at his estate, Caumsett, in Lloyd Neck (see page 170) show a similar Georgian influence, with Flemish detailing, and are arranged in a U-shaped parti with stalls on both sides of a central corridor. The William C. Whitney Racing Stables in Old Westbury (see page 109) are arranged in a linear parti in which the stall areas open directly onto the outdoor exercise fields. The Foxhall Keene Racing Stables, also in Old Westbury (see page 118), have an L-shaped parti with a walled entry court. Both the Marshall Field III and the Foxhall Keene stables are unused and unoccupied at present, but they both possess a potential for adaptation and reuse following the example of the F. Ambrose Clark and the William C. Whitney stables, both of which are now educational facilities.

15–1 (opposite above) Main house, entrance or south elevation. Designed by Rogers & Zogbaum, 1912, the house was destroyed by fire in 1968

15–2 (opposite below) Stables, view of the exercise fields to the south

15–3 (left) Stables, view of the courtyard with detail of roof gable

15–4 *Stables, view of the south elevation*

Broad Hollow was designed by architect Harry St. Clair Zogbaum (1885–1954), of the firm of Rogers & Zogbaum. Born in New York, Zogbaum was the son of a naval architect and illustrator. He was educated at Columbia University and apprenticed in the New York office of McKim, Mead & White, working there from 1906 through 1909. Zogbaum later designed buildings in Westchester County and in New York City as well as on Long Island. He was a resident of Cooperstown, New York, and worked on the design of several buildings there, including the National Baseball Hall of Fame and the New York State Historical Society. Zogbaum was noted for his many projects in Colonial Revival styles, and his work often featured the use of native or local building materials.

Separate from the Clark stables and at the opposite end of the site, now the Old Westbury campus of the State University of New York, lies Academic Village A, designed in 1965 by architects Alexander Kouzmanoff, Victor Christ-Janer, and John Johansen. This project attempts to simulate the character of an Italian hilltown, with an intricate, multilevel design combining classrooms, offices, dormitory rooms, social spaces, and roof-top terraces. However, the master-plan relationship of the new academic village to the original estate buildings on the campus remains unclear. The creative reuse of the existing estate structures and their relationship to any new construction or future site planning must be carefully considered.

16
J. Randolph Robinson Residence, Brookville

William L. Bottomley, architect, 1927–28; residence now the Long Island University Administration Center; located off Northern Boulevard

J. Randolph Robinson (1879–1933), born in Baltimore, was a member of a prominent and wealthy Maryland family. Robinson graduated from Yale University in 1903 and became the New York representative of Harbison, Walker and Company, a Pittsburgh manufacturer of bricks and of refractories used in construction and in industrial production.

Robinson originally lived in Brookville in a house designed about 1917 by John Russell Pope, which was first purchased by Philip Gossler and later by Edward F. Hutton. It now serves as the Fine Arts Center of C. W. Post College of Long Island University (see page 144). In 1927 architect William L. Bottomley was commissioned to design a new Brookville residence for Robinson. It later became the Daniel G. Tenney Residence and is now used as the Administration Center of Long Island University.

Bottomley's design for the house was based on Georgian Colonial prototypes. The parti, or layout, of a central block with interconnected side pavilions is found in many Palladian-influenced Georgian Colonial manor houses located in the South. One of the most famous examples is Westover (c. 1735), the Byrd Residence in Charles City County, Virginia. This parti may also be seen in the Lloyd Bryce/Childs Frick Estate, Clayton (1895), at Roslyn Harbor (see page 83), designed by Ogden Codman, Jr.

The Robinson house has a symmetrical composition consisting of a two-story, hip-roofed central block with two gable-roofed side pavilions reached by low, one-story links. The south pavilion, or wing, contains the kitchen and service areas of the house, and the north pavilion is designed as a formal living space. These wings are further articulated by their high-pitched roofs set perpendicularly to the roof line of the main block.

Inside the rectangular central section of the house, an elliptically shaped entrance hall contains a delicate, curving stair leading up to the second floor, a design device that was also used by Henry Hornbostel in his plans for the Robin/Wagg/Meyer Residence, Driftwood Manor (1906–1908) at Baiting Hollow (see page 216). The other interior spaces of the Robinson home were altered during the building's conversion into an administration center, which makes it difficult to recognize now the original functions of the various areas. The entrance hall originally led to the dining room and sitting room and to the library or study. A hall led past these areas to the main drawing room, or music room, pavilion. This space was designed

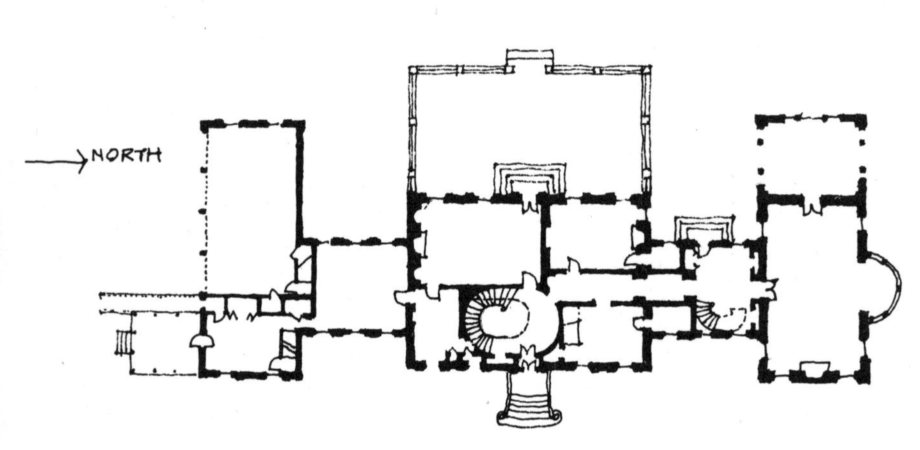

with a large projecting bay window and an enclosed sun porch overlooking the gardens.

The garden terrace has been filled in to create a large administration-office addition, a change that obscures the original garden elevation. However, the entrance elevation has been well preserved. Here one can see Bottomley's attention to historical detail in the broken-segmental pediment and fanlight over the entrance door and in the finely detailed circular windows that appear both on the second floor above the entry and on the first floor in the connecting links to each of the side wings. The overall scale of the house is small, and the interior spaces are intimate with little of the exaggerated detail and building scale sometimes seen in other Beaux-Arts interpretations of Georgian Style residences.

William L. Bottomley (1883–1951), a native New Yorker, was a graduate of Columbia University and won the Rome Prize in architecture in 1906. He studied at the American Academy in Rome and at the Ecole des Beaux-Arts in Paris (1907–1909). In 1912 he began his practice as a partner in the New York firm of Hewlett & Bottomley, and after 1919 he practiced independently.

Bottomley lived in Glen Head and designed many estates and country homes on Long Island. These include the Norman Whitehouse Estate in Old Brookville; the

16–1 (above left) Main-floor plan

16–2 (above right) Entrance or west elevation

Westbury residences of Cornelius J. Rathborne, Richard Trimble, Jr., and Robert Strawbridge, Jr.; and the Ernest P. Davies Residence in Roslyn. He was also the architect of Canoe Place Inn (c. 1921), a landmark for tourists on the South Shore near Southampton, as well as of Southampton High School (c. 1914). In New York—then in association with the firm of Bottomley, Wagner & White—he planned River House, a major apartment-house complex built in 1931 on East Fifty-second Street, overlooking the East River. He also designed several country houses in the South, including three Virginia homes—the William Ziegler, Jr., Residence in Middleburg and homes for Amory S. Carhart in Warrenton and for R. G. Cabell in Richmond.

A noted architectural critic and author in addition to being a practicing architect, Bottomley was an authority on the Georgian Colonial period and edited a survey of these residences, *Great Georgian Houses of America*, for the United States government. This work, which was completed in 1937, involved the documentation and preparation of detailed plans, elevations, and renderings of historic Georgian Colonial houses located throughout the northern and southern United States. Bottomley was also an active member of the Beaux-Arts Institute of Design in New York and served on its board of trustees (1912–20).

17 Marjorie Merriweather Post/ Edward F. Hutton Estate, Hillwood, Brookville

Hart & Shape, architects, 1921; Marian C. Coffin, landscape architect; estate now the Administration Center of C. W. Post College, Long Island University; located off Northern Boulevard

17–1 (opposite above) Garden or south elevation

17–2 (opposite below) Main-floor plan

Marjorie Merriweather Post (1887–1973) was the daughter of Charles W. Post, the founder of the Postum Cereal Company, a firm that she inherited in 1914 following her father's death. In 1920 she married Edward F. Hutton, a New York stockbroker and the founder of the Wall Street firm of E. F. Hutton and Company. Together they began to merge the Postum Cereal Company with firms that produced other well-known brand-name foods, including Jell-O, Maxwell House coffee, Sanka, and Birdseye frozen foods, eventually creating the General Foods Corporation.

After their marriage, the Huttons began making plans for a Brookville estate, which they christened Hillwood. They commissioned architect Charles M. Hart of the New York firm of Hart & Shape to design a Tudor-styled, half-timbered residence on the site of an older, existing frame house. The new building was constructed in 1921 by E. W. Howell and Company of Babylon, Long Island. In addition to the main house, the estate included a large garage and servants' quarters and a horse farm. Adjacent to the main house, a smaller residence, also designed in the Tudor Style, with an octagonal observation tower was built for one of Mrs. Post's daughters, Eleanore Close Riggs. Nearby was a playhouse, originally a thatched cottage, built for Mrs. Post's youngest daughter, Nedenia, who later changed her name to Dina Merrill and pursued a career as an actress.

The Huttons were divorced in 1935, and some time later Edward F. Hutton purchased the Philip Gossler residence, also in Brookville. Both Hillwood and the Robinson/Gossler/Hutton Residence (see page 144) now form part of C. W. Post College. The Robinson/Gossler/Hutton Residence is the college's fine arts center, and Hillwood serves as the college's administration center.

Marjorie remarried several times, but in 1958, after her fourth divorce, she resumed her maiden name and thereafter was known as "Mrs." Marjorie Merriweather Post. Hillwood was acquired by Long Island University and became the college center in the 1950s. The center was later renamed C. W. Post College in memory of Mrs. Post's father. The main house, as pointed out, is now the administrative center, and the garage and servants' quarters have been transformed into a student-services building. The horse farm continues as an equestrian center, and Eleanore's house is now a graduate center and admissions building.

Mrs. Post owned several other large estates that have also been converted to public use. Her Washington, D.C.,

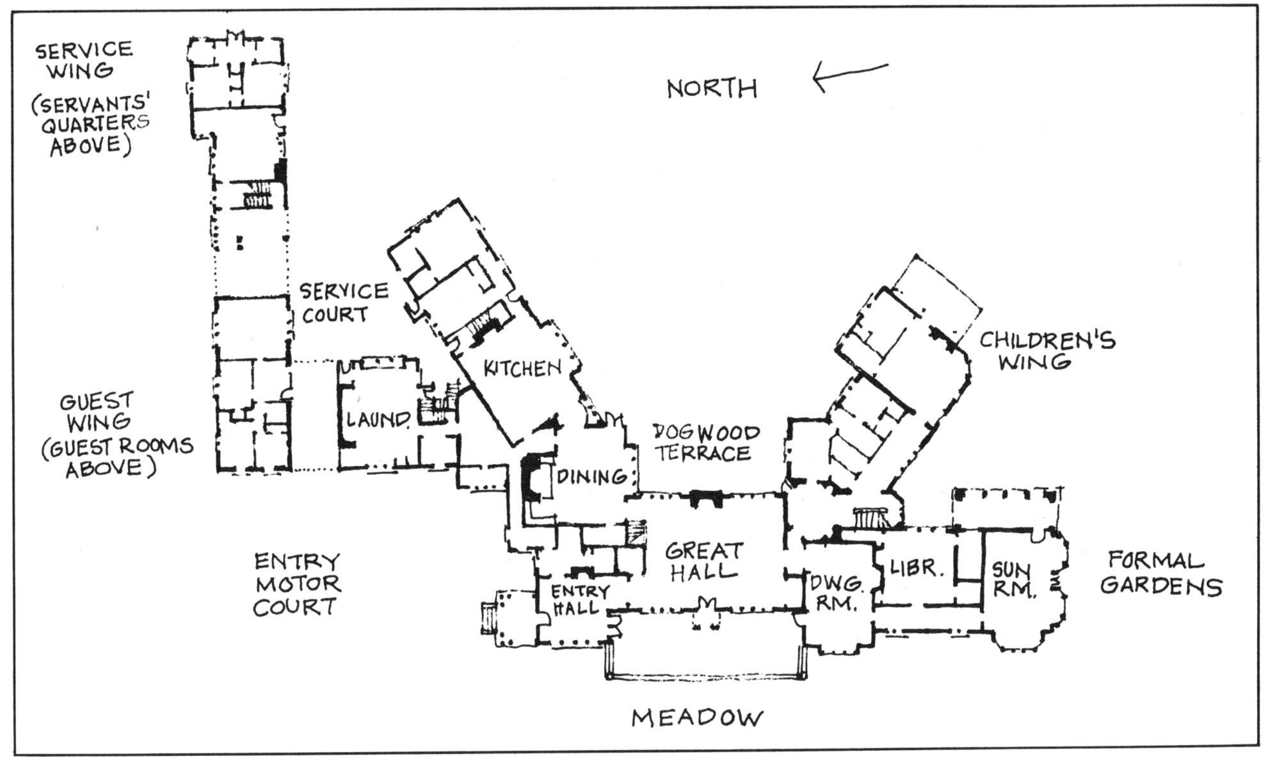

SERVICE WING
(SERVANTS' QUARTERS ABOVE)
NORTH
SERVICE COURT
KITCHEN
CHILDREN'S WING
GUEST WING
(GUEST ROOMS ABOVE)
LAUND.
DOGWOOD TERRACE
DINING
GREAT HALL
ENTRY MOTOR COURT
ENTRY HALL
DWG. RM.
LIBR.
SUN RM.
FORMAL GARDENS
MEADOW

17–3 West elevation

home, also called Hillwood, was given to the Smithsonian Institution; her summer retreat, Topridge, in the Adirondacks near Saranac Lake, was willed to C. W. Post College in 1973 and is now a part of the Adirondack State Forest Preserve; and her Palm Beach estate, Mar-A-Lago, was given to the United States government for use as a presidential retreat.

At the Brookville Hillwood, the seventy-room main house is so large that it resembles a small English country village rather than a single building. Several wings intersect at irregular angles to create small courtyards, some paved as entry or service courts, others landscaped as gardens. The projecting wings break up the tremendous length of the building, and its relatively low height gives a domestic scale to an unusually large floor plan.

The original approach to Hillwood was from the northwest, where a broad, gently sloping meadow allowed a dramatic view of the full length of the house. A porch located off the motor, or entry, court leads into a low-ceilinged entry hall and then into the two-story-high great hall, which spans the full width of the house from the sheltered garden, or dogwood terrace, to the east to the expansive, open hillside to the west.

On the north side of the great hall were located the dining room, which opened onto the dogwood terrace, and the kitchen and service wing, which were placed diagonally to the main section of the house. The south side of the great hall led to the drawing room, study, and sun room, the latter of which had an entrance out to the elaborate formal gardens. The children's wing also projects out from this side of the great hall. It is set at a diagonal angle to the main house and forms an end of the dogwood terrace.

To the north two later additions to the house provided more service space and several extra guest bedrooms. These wings were connected to the main portion of the house by bridged overpasses that were open on the ground floor, with the second floor and roofs running continuously above. The arrangement created a semienclosed service court, visually separated from the entrance court and the landscaped gardens.

Most of the interior spaces of the house have since been altered for use as administrative-office space, but the original character of the great hall has been preserved. It is reminiscent of a medieval Tudor hunting lodge, with exposed heavy-timber trusswork, a variation on the English "King Post" truss, and with mounted animal heads decorating the walls and balustraded mezzanine. This open mezzanine connects the separate wings of the upper floors.

The exterior of the house is detailed with roughhewn, half-timbered patterns and also recalls English Tudor and medieval period designs. A bay window in the nursery wing has a curved underpanel, or soffit, ornamented with the carved silhouettes of medieval fairy-tale characters, and the south elevation, facing the gardens, is ornamented with heraldic floral patterns.

Although the configuration of Hillwood is asymmetrical, its physical masses radiate from the great hall, which functions as the focal point of the house. This space is not visibly expressed on the western exterior elevation, since the hall is horizontally divided by an upper mezzanine at that point. On the east, however, the diagonal lines of the projecting side wings lead toward the great hall and reinforce the dramatic two-story-high space within.

The garden landscape surrounding the main house was designed for the Huttons by Marian C. Coffin, whose site plan included both formal and naturalistic, or Romantic, elements. A major axis extended from the southern end of the house, leading through a covered arbor and a formal flower garden to a circular putting green. This axis continued into the distance along a woodland walk. A cross-axis incorporated a brick-arched promenade, designed as a rose arbor, which stretched from the putting green to a circular rose garden. A separate magnolia garden led back

17–4 (above) Decorated soffit of a bay window projecting from the children's wing

17–5 (right) Great hall

toward the house to the sheltered dogwood terrace. A tennis court and topiary garden were also included in the overall plan. Many elements of the original landscape design may still be recognized in the gardens located to the south of the main house.

Charles Mansfield Hart (1886–1968) was born in New York and educated at the Pratt Institute School of Architecture. After graduating in 1905, he traveled through England and France, and on returning to New York he practiced as a partner in the architectural firm of Hart & Shape. This office planned several country residences in the New York area and redesigned the Timber Point Yacht Club (c. 1924) in Great River, Long Island. Hart also served as consulting architect on the design of the Exeter Inn (1930) in Exeter, New Hampshire, and the Williamsburg Inn (1934) in Williamsburg, Virginia. Hart was later the senior partner in the firms of Hart, Jerman & Associates and Hart, Benvenga & Associates, the architects of the Williamsburg Savings Bank in Brooklyn and the Suffolk County Office Building in Bay Shore, Long Island.

Marian Cruger Coffin (1872–1957), a grandniece of the well-known American artist John Trumbull, was a painter as well as a landscape architect. Along with landscape designer Ellen B. Shipman (see page 148) and architects Theodate Pope and Julia Morgan (see page 18), Mrs. Coffin was one of the most famous women designers who practiced during the Beaux-Arts period.

In addition to the site plan for Hillwood, Mrs. Coffin worked on the gardens for the Lloyd Bryce/Childs Frick Estate, Clayton, in Roslyn Harbor (see page 83) and on the Marshall Field III Estate, Caumsett, at Lloyd Neck (see page 170). She also designed the landscaping for the Charles H. Sabin Estate in Southampton and for the Irving Brokaw Estate in Mill Neck, both on Long Island, and she planned many large gardens in Connecticut and in other New England states.

18
The Robinson/Gossler/Hutton Residence, Brookville

John Russell Pope, architect, c. 1917, 1926; Ellen B. Shipman, landscape architect, c. 1926; residence now the Fine Arts Center of C. W. Post College, Long Island University; located off Northern Boulevard

18–1 *(opposite above) Garden or north elevation*

18–2 *(opposite below) Entrance or south elevation*

This residence was originally designed by architect John Russell Pope for J. Randolph Robinson (1879–1933), a wealthy businessman and manufacturer's representative (see page 135). In the mid-1920s, when the property was purchased by Philip Gossler (1870–1945), Pope designed some alterations to the house and additions to the estate and to the landscaping. Gossler was the chairman of the board and the president of Columbia Gas and Electricity Company from 1909 to 1936. He was also a director of the Guaranty Trust Company of New York. Edward F. Hutton purchased Gossler's house after his divorce from Marjorie Merriweather Post (see page 138). Since then, it has become the fine arts center of C. W. Post College, Long Island University. A large classroom addition has been added to one side of the building, adjacent to the former service area. The original stables are now used as sculpture and painting studios.

Pope's design was praised by his contemporaries as an excellent adaptation of the Georgian Colonial Revival Style to the needs of the "smaller country estate." Situated on the crest of a steep hill, the house overlooks a valley and a horse farm surrounded by broad meadows. The original approach to the site was from the south, along a wooded entry drive. The high elevation of the property was not apparent until one entered the house and first saw the view to the north of terraced gardens and retaining walls stepping down the hillside into the valley.

A brick-paved entry portico with two-story-high Doric columns originally ran the full length of the house, but two of the bays have since been enclosed. The roof of the portico, slightly lower in elevation than the main roof, articulated the transition between exterior and interior spaces. A Palladian window treatment above the entry door is repeated on the opposite, or garden, elevation above the terrace door. These two entrances are connected inside the house by the central hall.

The house is symmetrically laid out around the hall, with the major or central axis leading outside to the extended vista overlooking gardens and valley. Inside, the hall interconnects the major living spaces on the ground floor. To the west were the original smoking room, or study, and the living room, which opened onto the gardens. This space was designed with a projecting bay window and an outdoor covered porch, which was originally rectangular in shape but was later altered into a semicircular projection. The eastern side of the hall led to the dining room and kitchen and to a service area, which was later extended

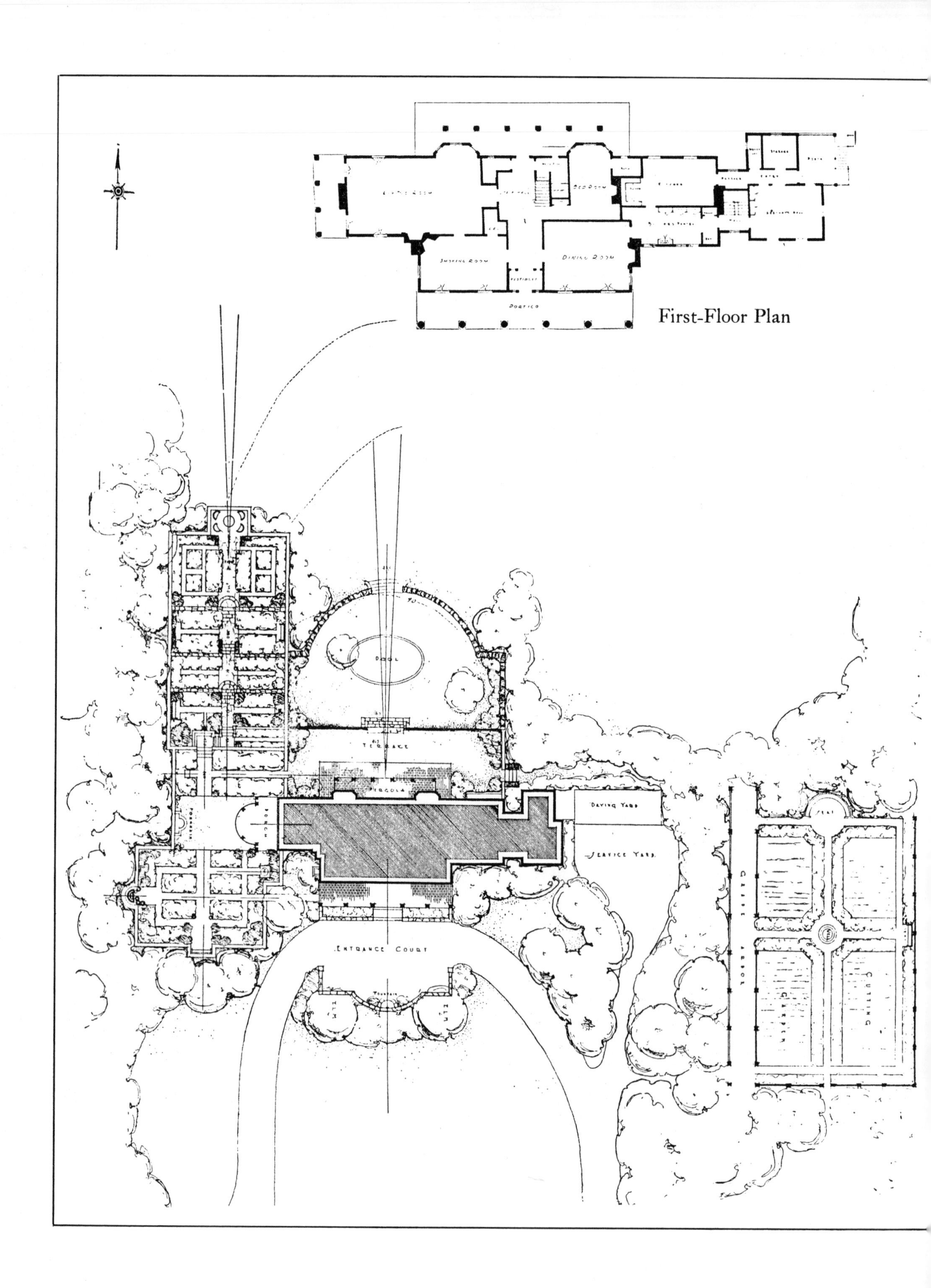

First-Floor Plan

by a children's wing added to the eastern end of the house.

The central-hall space widens at the northern end of the house to include the main stair hall before leading out to the garden. The shingled walls of the garden elevation were designed with symmetrical projecting bay windows, which give the wall surface an undulating character. A delicate one-story pergola, supported by Doric columns, runs in front of the façade to provide a shaded sitting area on the brick-paved terrace. This elevation still appears almost exactly as it was originally designed about 1917.

When Gossler purchased the estate, he commissioned Pope to design a semicircular porch off the living room and to make additions to the service and children's wing. At the same time a stable and garage complex was built, and a more extensive garden and site plan was designed in association with landscape architect Ellen B. Shipman.

The overall plan was an unusually intimate one for Pope, who was often associated with more formal or large-scale designs, such as that for the Marshall Field III Estate, Caumsett, in Lloyd Neck (see page 170). The site development around the Robinson/Gossler/Hutton Residence reinforces a sense of intimacy by concealing portions of the house with landscaping and with garden or retaining walls, thus keeping the views close to the building and opening them up only along the expansive north-south vistas.

Ellen B. Shipman's design for the gardens (c. 1926) was based on a series of descending rectangular terraces connected by geometrically organized plantings and stairs. An opening in the retaining wall of the centrally located, semicircular lawn terrace to the north of the house is aligned with the view from the house and reinforces the axial alignment of the plan.

The house underwent additional alterations after it was purchased by Edward F. Hutton. Two bays of the entry portico were enclosed; a projecting bay window was built overlooking the portico from the dining area; and an enclosed, semicircular projection was added on the second floor above the western porch.

Another building on the C. W. Post College campus was formerly the home of W. E. Hutton, Edward's brother. Mariemount was originally built for H. W. Lowe and was designed, c. 1927, by the office of John Russell Pope. It has since been extensively altered and is now used as the Roth Graduate School of Business Administration.

The architect John Russell Pope (1874–1937) was the son of a portrait painter and a descendant of English set-

18–3 (opposite) Site plan, showing main-floor plan of the house, and the layout of the gardens, designed by Ellen B. Shipman, landscape architect

tlers who had come to America in 1630. Born in New York City, he was educated at Columbia University and, in 1895, won the Rome Prize in architecture, enabling him to enter the American Academy in Rome. He also studied architecture at the Ecole des Beaux-Arts in Paris (1898–1900). When he returned to the United States, he worked in the New York office of Bruce Price and, in 1903, opened his own office.

Pope became one of the most famous Beaux-Arts architects in America, designing buildings throughout the United States and abroad. His early projects on Long Island include the Italian Renaissance-styled W. L. Stowe Residence (1906) in Roslyn and the French Renaissance-influenced Charles R. Gould Residence (1911) in Greenlawn. He also planned during the 1920s the Ogden L. Mills Estate in Woodbury and the Arthur S. Burden Residence in Jericho, both of which were designed in the Federal Style. One of his largest residential commissions was the Marshall Field III estate, Caumsett (c. 1925), in Lloyd Neck (see page 170).

In New York City Pope designed the Mrs. Graham Fair Vanderbilt Residence (1930) on East Ninety-third Street, as well as a major addition to the Museum of Natural History—the Roosevelt Building (1936). Pope is most remembered for his monumental buildings and museums. They include additions to the British Museum and to the Tate Gallery, both in London, and the designs for the National Gallery (completed in 1941) and the Jefferson Memorial (1934–43), both in Washington, D.C.

Ellen Biddle Shipman (1870–1950) was a prominent landscape architect who had studied under Charles Adams Platt (see page 100) and who, like Platt, lived in Cornish, New Hampshire. Mrs. Shipman designed the landscaping for many estates and country homes in the Northeast and worked on the master plans for several large-scale projects, including the Bronx Botanical Gardens, New York; Duke University, Durham, North Carolina; and Longue Vue Gardens, New Orleans, Louisiana. On Long Island she also designed the landscaping for the Samuel A. Salvage Estate, Rynwood, at Glen Head (see fig. A–8).

19

Egerton L. Winthrop, Jr., Estate, Syosset

Delano & Aldrich, architects, 1903–1904; estate now known as Nassau Hall, the Nassau County Museum Administration Center; grounds open on a limited basis as part of the Muttontown Nature Preserve; building undergoing restoration; located off Muttontown Road

Egerton L. Winthrop, Jr. (1861–1926), was a lawyer, an administrator, and a prominent member of New York society at the turn of the century. Born in France, he was educated at Harvard University and at Columbia University Law School. After admission to the New York bar, he became a partner in the Wall Street law firm of Winthrop and Stimson, along with his brother, Bronson. Also associated with this firm were former Secretary of War Henry L. Stimson and former Secretary of State Elihu Root.

Winthrop was married to Emeline Hecksher in 1890. They were known for their patronage of the arts and of literature and for their philanthropies. Novelist Edith Wharton was a good friend of the family, as was the architect Charles Follen McKim. Winthrop's father, along with McKim, had been one of the initial sponsors of the American Academy in Rome in 1898, an institution that was organized to provide graduate fellowships to Americans in architecture, painting, and sculpture.

In addition to his law practice, Winthrop served as president of the New York City Board of Education from 1906 to 1913, and he was the legal guardian of John Jacob Astor, Jr., whose father had died in the *Titanic* disaster.

Winthrop's country estate, designed by the young architects Delano & Aldrich in 1903–1904, was originally built for his brother Bronson, but it became Egerton's home when Bronson commissioned Delano & Aldrich to design a larger house for him on an adjoining property. Bronson's house has since been demolished, and the property on which it stood now forms part of the Muttontown Nature Preserve.

After Egerton's death, his estate was sold to Elisha Walker, an investment banker and a partner in the firm of Kuhn, Loeb and Company. In 1953 the property was purchased by Lansdell Christie, a mining industrialist and the developer of iron-ore deposits in Liberia. Nassau County acquired the land in 1969 for use as a county park and nature preserve, and the house, now known as Nassau Hall, is currently being converted into a museum and administration center.

The Winthrop house was designed in the style of a Federal period country seat and is reminiscent of George Washington's Mount Vernon and other Southern wood-frame manors. This influence can be seen in the overall scale of the house and in such details as the wood siding, which has been carved to simulate the rusticated quoins and

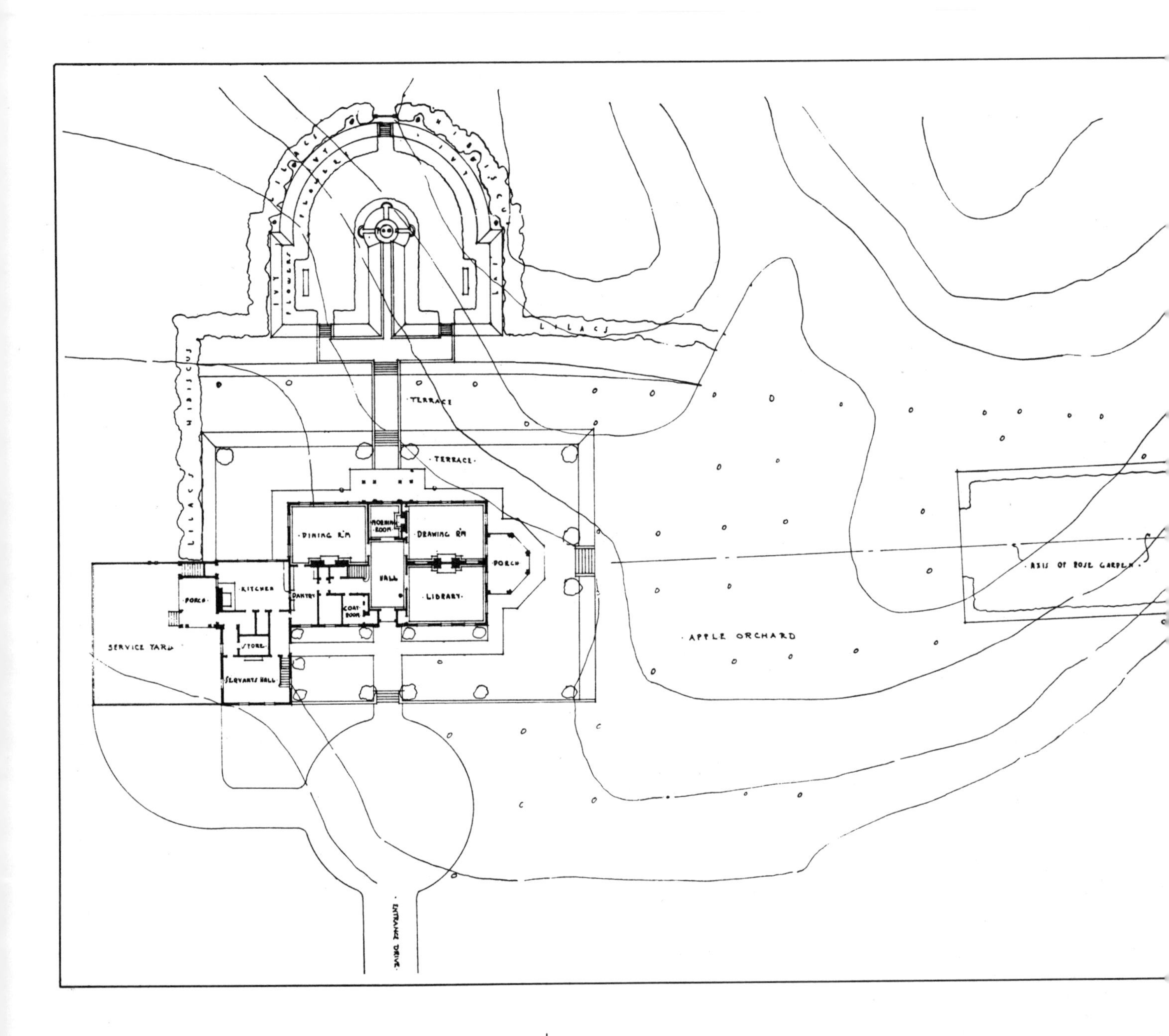

19–1 (above) Site plan, showing main-floor plan and terraces

19–2 (opposite above) Garden or south elevation

19–3 (opposite below) West elevation, as seen from the rose garden

NO
TRESPASSING

points of stone construction. Other similarities include the treatment of the door and window openings and the central lantern skylight that projects from the roof in the entrance elevation. The design of the glass-enclosed sun porch on the west recalls the detailing of the open, semicircular arcades on either side of the central section of Mount Vernon, and the broad gable at the end of the house resembles the proportions of an old New England meeting hall.

The house sits on a brick-paved platform or terrace that overlooks an entrance court to the north and terraced gardens to the south and west. From the central hall of the house, the library and drawing room to the west lead out to the polygonal sun porch, and to the east lie the dining room and service areas. In addition, a servants' hall was designed as a projecting wing adjacent to the kitchen, shielding the service yard from the entry terrace.

Both the floor plan of the house and the master plan for the site are carefully coordinated. The central hall lies on a major axis that begins with the long entrance drive, continues inside through the hall and morning room, and extends out again to a series of rectangular terraces that step down into semicircular gardens. The vista continues past the gardens, through an opening in the landscaping, along the same axis. A minor axis to the west is developed from the sun porch and extends out to a landscaped vista defined by formal gardens, fountains, and outdoor sculpture. On the southern or garden elevation, high, narrow French doors open off the main living spaces and onto the raised brick terrace. The entrance to this terrace from the central hall and morning room is articulated with a delicate, arching trellis.

The interiors of the house include a delicately scaled group of period rooms that are being restored to serve as a museum. The second-floor hall, which now leads to the museum offices, is a generous two-story-high space with an open balcony at the upper or attic level lighted by a skylight. The roof lantern that provides the natural light is a prominent part of the exterior roof profile.

The master plan for the estate included a small farm designed to resemble Colonial and Federal period service buildings, such as those at Williamsburg, Virginia. A large stable and servants' quarters were designed as a U-shaped structure with an access roadway passing through the building. A lowered, sloping roof line with an eyebrow-dormer window above the bridged overpass creates a covered entrance frame between the estate and the main road.

19–4 (opposite above) Stable and service complex

19–5 (opposite below) Entry drive and entrance or north elevation

19–6 *Drawing room, c. 1920*

William A. Delano (1874–1960) and Chester H. Aldrich (1871–1940) were both graduates of the Ecole des Beaux-Arts in Paris. They trained in the New York office of Carrère & Hastings before establishing their own firm in 1903. The Winthrop house was one of their earliest commissions. They designed several other estates in the Syosset area, including the James A. Burden Estate (c. 1916), now the Woodcrest Country Club; the Benjamin Moore Estate, still privately owned; and William A. Delano's own residence. Other well-known projects by this prolific firm are described in the article on the Mr. and Mrs. Roderick Tower Residence at Old Westbury (see page 114). Delano served as the president of the Beaux-Arts Institute of Design in America, and Aldrich was the director of the American Academy in Rome.

20
William R. Coe Estate, Planting Fields, Upper Brookville

Walker & Gillette, architects, 1919; Olmsted Brothers, landscape architects; estate now Planting Fields Arboretum, administered by the Long Island State Park Commission; arboretum grounds open to the public; house open for scheduled events; located off Planting Fields Road

William R. Coe (1869–1955), a native of England, emigrated with his family to the United States in 1883. Coe worked for the Philadelphia insurance brokers Johnson and Higgins, and after first managing their New York office, he became president of the company in 1910 and chairman of the board in 1916, a position he held until 1943. He was also a director of the Brooklyn Union Gas Company and of the Wyoming Land Company. In 1910 Coe purchased the 200,000-acre ranch of William ("Buffalo Bill") Cody in Cody, Wyoming. He developed a strong interest in the history of the American West, collecting many original documents, books, and materials on its development and later sponsoring American Studies Programs at Yale University and at the University of Wyoming.

In 1919 Coe commissioned the architectural firm of Walker & Gillette to plan his Long Island residence on the site of an older house that had been destroyed by fire. The design is a combination of English medieval and Elizabethan elements, constructed in a pale Indiana limestone. The name of the estate, Planting Fields, was the original Indian name for the property.

Planting Fields was donated by Coe to the State of New York in 1949, and its administration was taken over by the Long Island State Park Commission in 1971. The grounds are now open to the public as Planting Fields Arboretum, and the house is open for specially scheduled events.

The overall design of Planting Fields, as well as its interiors and details, reflects Coe's distinctive personality. His fondness for his native country is seen in the English medieval style of the building and in the Romantic or picturesque landscaping of the great lawns and gardens surrounding the house. His interest in American history, reflected in his collection of rare books and documents, is also seen in some of the details and ornamentation within the house. The Buffalo Room, or breakfast room, was decorated with large buffalo wall murals painted by Robert W. Chanler about 1920. Other American motifs appear in the exterior architectural ornamentation, such as the sculpted rabbit heads and corn husks at the main entrance to the house.

The plan of the house is asymmetrical. It was designed as a linear sequence or progression of spaces. The entrance vestibule, located on the eastern side of the house, leads the visitor into a generous, two-story-high entry hall. The vestibule and hall form the beginning of an east-west axis

20–1 (overleaf) Lawn or north elevation

that connects all the major spaces of the house, from the hall, through the main stair hall, and into a grand, two-story-high gallery, or living hall, which looks out over the broad, landscaped great lawn to the north. The axial progression of spaces ends at the formal drawing room, which opens onto an arcaded pavilion, or sun porch, and from there to a garden terrace. A vaulted, glass-enclosed cloister, which skirts one side of the gallery, frees the general circulation through the house from dependence on the gallery. From this cloister a garden vista extends to the south, and it serves as a perpendicular cross-axis in plan, beginning with a terraced courtyard defined by the irregular projecting forms of the house and continuing through a series of elaborate gardens.

The intentional use of organizing major axes and minor, or perpendicular, cross-axes was an important principle of Beaux-Arts design at that time (see page 39), and its employment differentiated the Coe house from actual medieval-period houses in which the rooms were much more static in layout and did not have the sense of spatial progression that the Beaux-Arts system demanded. Another Beaux-Arts characteristic of the design is the articulated circulation in the plan, which acts to separate the service and social functions within the house. To the south of the entry hall is the dining room, with the kitchen and a large service-wing projection beyond. The service wing is designed as a separate functional element in plan, and it is set at an irregular angle to the main section of the house. It is also differentiated in the exterior design by the use of a rough, half-timbered surface, which contrasts with the formal, dressed stonework covering the rest of the building.

Inside the house, adjacent to the entry hall, the main circular stair is set in a polygonal, projecting bay and separated from the hall by a carved wood screen. On the south side of the hall a corresponding octagonal reception room overlooks the cloistered garden terrace and recalls the polygonal stair hall. This consistency of configuration in plan is carried out in the elevation of the house as well, where a series of projecting, polygonal bay windows on the north gives the exterior wall surface an undulating character. The polygonal projections and indentations articulate the different interior spaces on the exterior of the house.

The English medieval character of the design is carried out in the interiors of the house and in its architectural details and ornamentation. The interiors were designed with medieval tapestries and murals, tiled floors, and

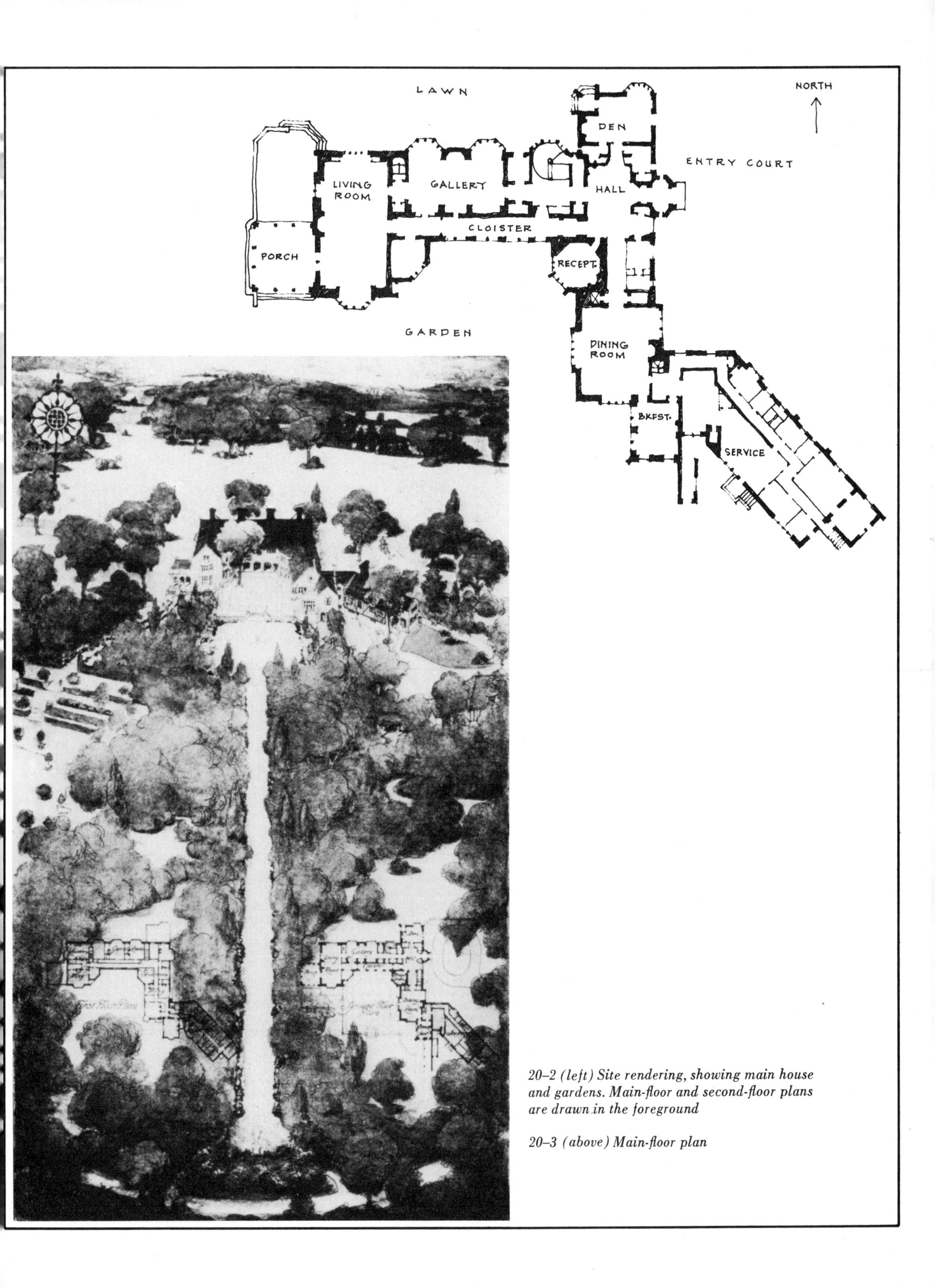

20–2 (left) Site rendering, showing main house and gardens. Main-floor and second-floor plans are drawn in the foreground

20–3 (above) Main-floor plan

carved stone fireplaces. In the gallery these elements were combined with an exposed beamed ceiling, mounted animal heads, and carved wood screens set into the arched stone entryways. Ribbed cross vaulting spans the ceiling in the cloister area. The Elizabethan character of the exterior was based on English prototypes of the late sixteenth and the early seventeenth century. The elaborate exterior detailing includes carved ornamentation and Baroque twisted columns at the main entrance and tall brick chimneys that punctuate the roof line.

The landscaping for the site, planned by the Olmsted Brothers, has a naturalistic or English Romantic character that is combined with several formal or geometrically organized elements. The great lawns to the north and east of the house are designed with large English hollies, beeches, and linden trees. The gardens to the south are laid out axially; this axis leads from the cloister of the house and passes through a series of gardens that incorporate a picturesque cottage, outdoor garden sculptures, an elaborate rose arbor, and an azalea walk. The large, Georgian-styled greenhouses nearby are surrounded by specimen rhododendron beds. Another formal element in the landscape is the Carshalton Gate, a delicate wrought-iron structure dating from 1723 and imported from England. This gate originally served as the entrance to the estate; however, the park administration now uses an entrance to the northeast of the house for public access to the property.

A. Stewart Walker (1880–1952) and Leon Gillette (1878–1945) began their architectural partnership in 1906. Walker was a graduate of Harvard University, and Gillette studied at the Ecole des Beaux-Arts in Paris, graduating in 1906. Gillette had also served an apprenticeship with the prominent firm of Babb, Cook & Willard.

The office of Walker & Gillette was active in New York for more than forty years and was well known for its many designs for large residences and commercial buildings. In addition to Planting Fields, the firm designed Coe's ranch home in Wyoming. Other projects on Long Island include the H. H. Rogers Residence (c. 1916) in Southampton, the Francis L. Hines Estate (c. 1918) in Glen Cove, and the H. F. Godfrey Estate (c. 1912) in Roslyn. Walker & Gillette also designed the Creek Club (c. 1924) in Locust Valley.

In New York City, the firm planned the Henry P. Davison Residence (1917) on Park Avenue (now the Italian Consulate), the Thomas W. Lamont Residence (1921) on

20–4 (opposite above) Garden court or south elevation

20–5 (opposite below) West porch

East Seventieth Street (now owned by the Visiting Nurse Service), and the William Goodby Loew Mansion (1931) on East Ninety-third Street (later the Billy Rose Mansion and now owned by Roosevelt Hospital). The firm's most famous commercial project was the Fuller Office Building (1928–29) on East Fifty-seventh Street, an important example of Art Deco Style architecture in New York. Walker & Gillette also planned the First National Bank Building at One Wall Street and fifteen of First National's branch banking offices in New York.

Frederick Law Olmsted (1822–1903), America's most famous landscape architect (see page 23 and page 196), taught his skills to his stepson John Charles Olmsted (1852–1920) and to his son Frederick Law Olmsted, Jr. (1870–1957). John graduated from Yale University in 1875 and became his stepfather's associate, and Frederick, Jr., was educated at Harvard University and joined the firm in 1895. After Olmsted's death in 1903, John and Frederick, Jr., continued the firm, working together as Olmsted Brothers of Brookline, Massachusetts.

The Olmsted office participated in planning many large-scale master plans throughout the country, including those for the Boston and Chicago municipal parks systems (1886–87), for Chicago's World's Columbian Exposition (1891–93), and for Forest Hills Gardens (1913) in Queens, New York. It also designed many residential parks and gardens, including those for the Francis L. Hines Estate (c. 1918) in Glen Cove, with Walker & Gillette; for the Harold I. Pratt Estate, Welwyn (c. 1906), also in Glen Cove, now owned by Nassau County Museum (see fig. A–6); for the James A. Burden Estate (c. 1916) in Syosset (now the Woodcrest Country Club); and the J. W. Harriman Estate (c. 1918) in Brookville.

20–6 Great hall or gallery, c. 1921

21 Theodore Roosevelt Residence, Sagamore Hill, Oyster Bay

Lamb & Rich, architects, 1884–86; 1905 addition, C. Grant La Farge, architect; residence now administered by the National Park Service as a National Historic Site; house and grounds open to the public; located off Cove Neck Road

Theodore Roosevelt (1858–1919), twenty-sixth president of the United States, holding that office from 1901 to 1909, was a native of New York City. He graduated from Harvard University in 1880 and first entered politics on his return to New York from Cambridge. Roosevelt was elected to the New York state legislature in 1882, and in 1884 he commissioned architects Lamb & Rich to design his country home, Sagamore Hill, in Oyster Bay. The name of his estate was derived from the name of the Indian chief Sagamore, who had originally governed that area of Long Island. After his first wife, Alice, died before construction of the house had even begun, Roosevelt left New York and lived in North Dakota for two years. The house was completed in his absence, and after his return Roosevelt married Edith Kermit Carow. The Roosevelts lived at Sagamore Hill for the next thirty years, raising six children there.

During Roosevelt's presidency, Sagamore Hill functioned as the Summer White House. In 1905 Roosevelt added the large north room or trophy room addition to the house to serve as a presidential reception room. Designed by architect C. Grant La Farge, the north room was used for official ceremonies and for meetings with heads of state and visiting dignitaries. Filled with trophies from Roosevelt's famous hunting expeditions, this great room evokes Teddy's distinctive personality. It now displays awards and personal memorabilia from throughout his entire career.

The appearance of Sagamore Hill has remained relatively unchanged since Theodore Roosevelt lived there. Many of the original interiors have been preserved, and some exhibits have been added on the upper floors. The house is open to the public as a National Historic Site and is administered by the National Park Service. Nearby on the same property is Old Orchard, the estate of Theodore Roosevelt, Jr., which was designed in 1937 by architect R. E. Lee. This building is also open to the public as an exhibition and audio-visual center that relates the history of the Roosevelt family and its role in American life.

The design of Sagamore Hill is a combination of early Queen Anne and later Shingle Style elements. It is included in this discussion of Beaux-Arts architecture on Long Island because of the influence that the domestic Queen Anne Style exerted on Beaux-Arts architects during the period in which Sagamore Hill was built and because of the reciprocal influence that the Beaux-Arts training of these architects exerted on the final development of the Shingle

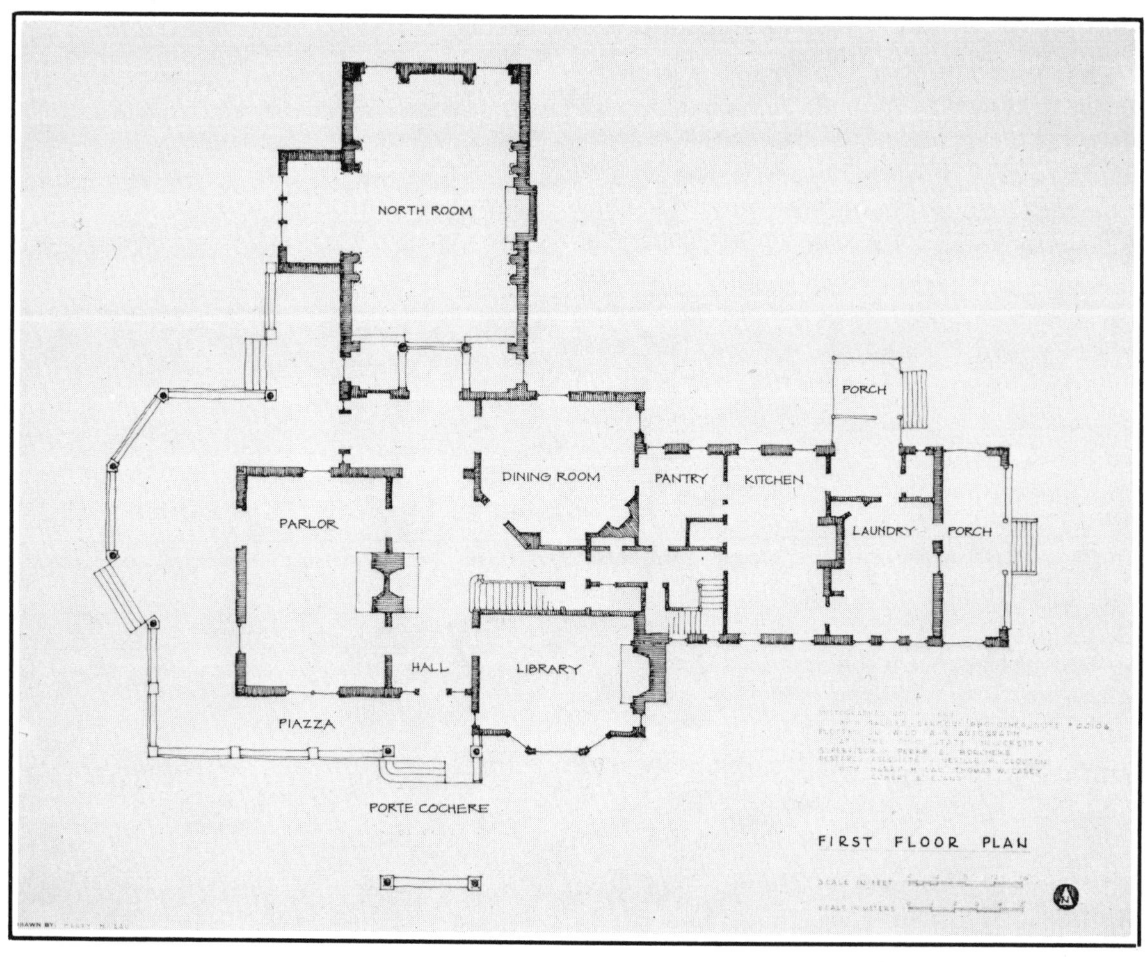

NORTH ROOM
PORCH
DINING ROOM
PANTRY
KITCHEN
PARLOR
LAUNDRY
PORCH
HALL
LIBRARY
PIAZZA
PORTE COCHERE
FIRST FLOOR PLAN

Style. Sagamore Hill is related to houses designed by many early American graduates of the Ecole, including H. H. Richardson, Robert Swain Peabody, and Charles Follen McKim. McKim, Mead & White gained its initial reputation by mastering this shingled genre, as in the Association Houses (1882–84) at Montauk Point (see page 237). While working in this style, these architects imposed their own interpretation of Beaux-Arts spatial principles on the more vernacular, or domestic, design forms.

The influence of Ecole training can often be discerned in the organization of the floor plan and in the spatial development of the interior—for example, in the double-height entry and stair halls developed as a major circulation space and in the changes in levels that define these spaces. Another important characteristic is the generosity and alignment of the openings between rooms, which allowed expanded vistas and achieved the sense of spatial movement as taught at the Ecole. The interior spaces were made apparent on the exterior of the building by the controlled inventiveness of the surface ornamentation and by grouped window openings.

Of great importance in the development of the Shingle Style was the emphasis placed on covered verandas. Long a part of American domestic architecture, verandas were used in Sagamore Hill to move the interior spaces outside and into the landscape. The idea of spatial continuity was later continued in the more formal period revival estates on Long Island in which extended vistas continued the interior axes for great distances out into the landscape, as in the John S. Phipps Estate, Westbury House (1906–24), at Old Westbury (see page 123), and in the William R. Coe Estate, Planting Fields (1919), at Upper Brookville (see page 155).

The original design for Sagamore Hill closely followed the typical shingle-cottage format. La Farge's addition of the trophy room emphasized the linear organization of the plan by continuing an axis beginning at the entry and vestibule area and by creating a spatial progression that moved straight through to the new major space of the house. By 1905, when this addition was designed, Beaux-Arts architects were already working in more formal modes, and the trophy room reflects this change. Although its exterior appears as a modest extension of the older portion of the house, the interior is decidedly grander, reflecting both the attitudes of the times and the new status of the owner. The floor level of the new room is lower than that of the main first floor, and the design of the connecting stairs creates an open balcony overlooking the new space

21–1 (opposite above) View from the southwest

21–2 (opposite below) Main-floor plan. Drawing by Historic American Buildings Survey, National Park Service

with its trophies. The lower floor level in the addition also achieves a greater ceiling height in the room without disturbing the exterior profile of the house. Ionic columns are used to frame the main axis of the space, as well as a cross-axis that is defined by a fireplace and by a large bay-window alcove.

The architectural firm of Lamb & Rich was well known in New York both for its designs of country homes and for its urban, residential, and educational projects. Hugh Lamb (1849–1903), a native of Scotland, lived in East Orange, New Jersey, and designed many homes in the New Jersey area. Lamb began his New York partnership with architect Charles A. Rich in 1882. Rich (1855–1943), born in Beverly, Massachusetts, was a graduate of Dartmouth College. He studied architecture both in the United States and in Europe (1879–82) and later practiced in New York. He remained a partner in the firm until Lamb's death in 1903.

In addition to Sagamore Hill, Lamb & Rich designed several large residences on Long Island, including the Shingle Style S. P. Hinckley House, Sunset Hall (1883), in Lawrence; the Tudor-influenced Talbot J. Taylor Residence, Talbot House (c. 1903), in Cedarhurst; and the Charles Gates Residence (c. 1902) at Peacock Point. Rich planned his own Shingle Style home, Old Rider Farm (c. 1889), in Bellport, and he later designed the rusticated-stone Ward Clock Tower (1895), in Roslyn.

In New York City, the firm designed the Richardsonian-Romanesque main building of Pratt Institute (c. 1887) in Brooklyn and the Astral Apartments (1886), commissioned by Charles Pratt to provide low-cost workers' housing, in Brooklyn. In Manhattan, Lamb & Rich planned several row-houses or brownstone developments, including Henderson Place (c. 1882), now a New York City historic district; it was designed as a single urban composition in variations of the Queen Anne Style. The firm also planned the French-inspired Beaux-Arts Studio Building (c. 1901) on West Fortieth Street, later known as the Beaux-Arts Hotel and in which many well-known artists and architects had their New York studios, and the Berkeley School (c. 1890) on West Forty-fourth Street, now known as the Mechanics Institute.

Rich later worked on large-scale educational facilities, including the Dartmouth College campus (c. 1915) in Hanover, New Hampshire, and individual buildings for Barnard, Smith, Amherst, and Colgate colleges. He con-

21–3 (opposite) Entrance or south elevation, showing the use of ornamental shingles

tinued to practice until 1933 as the senior partner in the firm of Rich, Mathesius & Koyl.

Christopher Grant La Farge (1862–1938) was the son of the noted American painter John La Farge. He studied painting with his father and received his architectural education at Massachusetts Institute of Technology. La Farge served his apprenticeship in the office-atelier of H. H. Richardson in Brookline, Massachusetts. In 1884 he opened an office in New York City with his classmate George L. Heins, and in 1892 these two architects won a national competition for the design of the Cathedral of St. John the Divine in New York City. The firm designed several other large churches, including St. Matthew's Roman Catholic Church (1893) in Washington, D.C., and St. Patrick's Church (1915) in Philadelphia, the latter in association with Benjamin Wistar Morris. Heins & La Farge also designed many subway stations (1884–1938) in New York City. This firm also laid out the master plan and designed the main buildings of the New York Zoological Park (1899–1910), commonly called the Bronx Zoo, in New York City.

21–4 (opposite above) West elevation

21–5 (opposite below) North room or trophy room. Designed by C. Grant La Farge, 1905

21–6 (above) Entrance or south elevation. Drawing by Historic American Buildings Survey, National Park Service

22

Marshall Field III Estate, Caumsett, Lloyd Neck

John Russell Pope, architect, c. 1925; Alfred Hopkins and Warren & Wetmore, associate architects; Marian C. Coffin, landscape architect; estate now Caumsett State Park, owned by the Long Island State Park Commission; grounds open by appointment for nature walks; located off Lloyd Harbor Road

22–1 (opposite above) Main house, entrance or south elevation

22–2 (opposite below) Main house, main-floor and second-floor plans

Marshall Field III (1893–1956), publisher and corporate director, was born in Chicago, Illinois. He was the grandson of Marshall Field, Sr., who had founded the famous Chicago department store that still bears his name. The younger Field was educated in England at Eton School and at Cambridge University. He returned to the United States in 1914 and became president of Field Enterprises, an organization that owns the *Chicago Sun Times* and *World Book Encyclopedia.* Marshall Field III also owned and operated Simon & Schuster, the New York publishers, and their subsidiary organization, Pocket Books, Inc.

In 1921 Field moved to New York, and he purchased more than 1,750 acres in Lloyd Neck that were soon to become Caumsett, his country estate. The house, designed by architect John Russell Pope, was modeled on the large English country homes that Field had known in Great Britain. He christened the estate Caumsett after the original American Indian name for his property. Field's estate was developed as a self-sufficient rural community and included twenty-five miles of roads, independent sources of electricity and water, and a dairy farm where prize-winning cattle were raised. The large stable complex, garages, and servants' quarters created the impression of a remote country village situated in the vast wilderness of the estate. Athletic facilities were also an important part of this microcosm, and they included riding stables, polo fields, indoor and outdoor tennis courts, and a large dock for Field's yacht, *The Coursande.*

During World War II the estate was used by the Office of War Information, and after Field's death in 1956, his widow, Ruth, sold Caumsett to the Long Island State Park Commission. Eventually the property will become Caumsett State Park, and while this transition takes place the grounds are open for nature walks by appointment only. Nearby, on the same property, is the Henry Lloyd Manor, a Colonial manor house built in 1711 by an early English settler of Lloyd Neck. This house is administered by the Society for the Preservation of Long Island Antiquities and is open to the public.

The scope of the Caumsett Estate was so great that three architectural firms were involved in its design. John Russell Pope made the overall master plan and designed the main house and the polo-stable complex. Alfred Hopkins also worked on the stables as well as on the garages and the dairy-farm group, and Warren & Wetmore were responsible for the large indoor tennis stadium. Marian C.

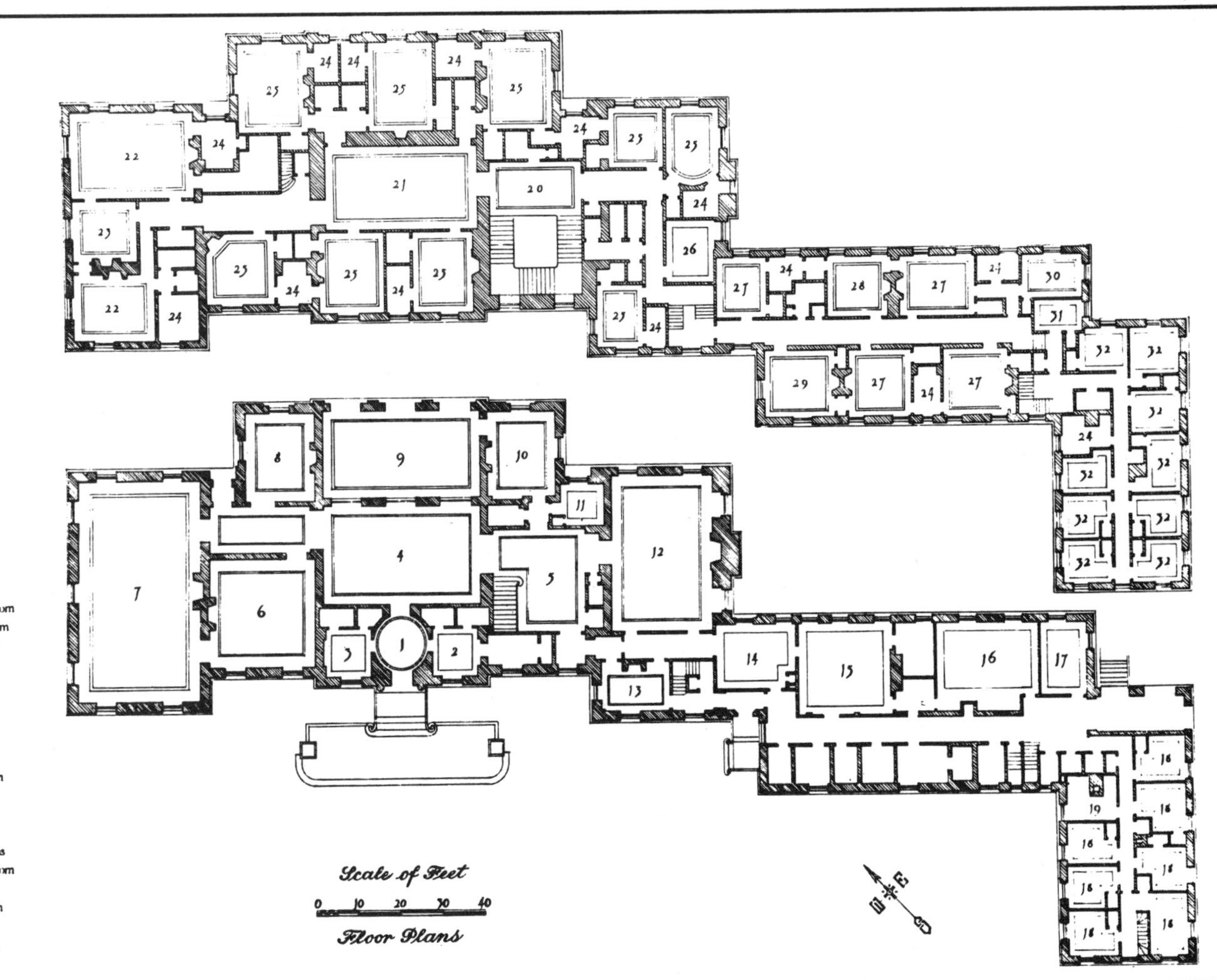

First Floor
1. Vestibule
2. Men's room
3. Ladies' room
4. Entrance hall
5. Stair hall
6. Library
7. Living room
8. Card room
9. Loggia
10. Gun room
11. Flower room
12. Dining room
13. Breakfast room
14. Butler's pantry
15. Kitchen
16. Servants' dining room
17. Servants' sitting room
18. Servants' bed rooms
19. Servants' bath
Second Floor
20. Stair hall
21. Main hall
22. Owner's bed rooms
23. Owner's sitting room
24. Bath rooms
25. Guest bed rooms
26. Linen room
27. Children's bed rooms
28. Children's sitting room
29. Day nursery
30. Governess' bed room
31. Sewing room
32. Servants' bed rooms
Scale of Feet
0 10 20 30 40
Floor Plans

Coffin designed the landscaping, and the Whitney Construction Company was the chief contractor for the entire development.

The main house is organized around a central great hall. The primary living areas radiate from this major space. The living room and library are located to the west of the hall, and the dining room, stair hall, and service areas lie to the east. To the north the hall expands into a large open-air loggia, which is set within the main form of the house and enclosed or defined on three sides by the interior rooms. It appears as an outdoor space, a large outdoor living room, although it is located within the house. The vista from here is a romantic one, leading to a lagoon and to Long Island Sound in the distance.

The exterior of the house recalls the Dutch influence on the early Palladian period of English architecture, also known as the Stuart period (1603–1714), which preceded the English Georgian period. The broad, hipped roof with

22–3 Main house, loggia, as it was originally designed, c. 1925

overhanging eaves is typically Dutch. The façade combines brick with limestone detailing, and horizontal bands of limestone divide each story. Stone quoins adorn each corner of the house, and limestone columns, or pilasters, are attached to the exterior. Dutch influence is also apparent in the design of the polo-stable complex, which exhibits double-curved gables and a skylighted cupola over the central space.

The Palladian aspect of the design may be seen in the central portion of the waterfront elevation of the house, which is characterized by four great double-story attached columns bearing Ionic capitals topped by a triangular classical pediment with an elliptical window. The first story of this central portion contains the open arcaded loggia that leads to the interior central hall. This design recalls the form and composition of such English country houses as Eltham Lodge at Bromley, Kent, designed in 1663 by the English architect Hugh May.

22–4 Main house, detail of north elevation, showing loggia as it appears today

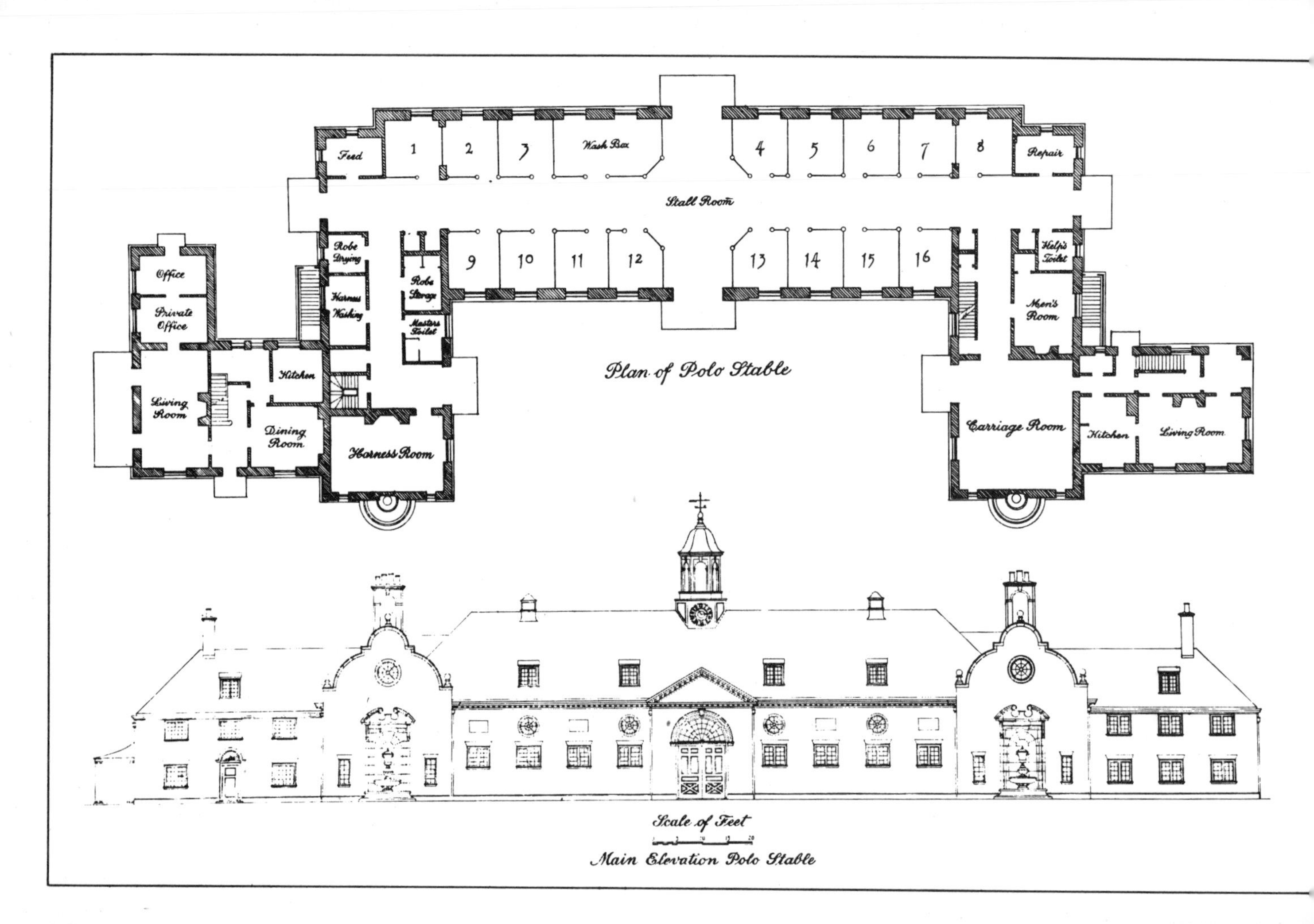
Feed
1
2
3
Wash Box
4
5
6
7
8
Repair
Stall Room
Robe Drying
Harness Washing
Robe Storage
Masters Toilet
9
10
11
12
13
14
15
16
Help's Toilet
Men's Room
Office
Private Office
Living Room
Kitchen
Dining Room
Harness Room
Plan of Polo Stable
Carriage Room
Kitchen
Living Room
Scale of Feet
Main Elevation Polo Stable

The scale of the house is enormous, and it has a public, rather than a residential, character. The formal entrance leads into a circular vestibule set within a rectangular frame, and large toilet rooms are located on either side. The oversized scale of the main rooms surrounding the open-air core of the loggia, and the convenient arrangement of the service facilities, make the house ideally suited for eventual public use as a museum and/or pastoral restaurant-inn within the state park. The William Bayard Cutting Estate, Westbrook, at Great River (see page 191), now the Bayard Cutting Arboretum, is also administered by the Long Island State Park Commission, and the main house furnishes a good example of a successful conversion from mansion to modest park restaurant.

Caumsett was altered for Field's wife, Ruth, in the 1950s by the architectural firm of O'Conner & Delaney, who removed two far-end wings and made some interior changes. The demolished west wing had contained the original living room on the first floor and the master-bedroom suite above. A new living room was created by O'Conner & Delaney from the former library. The demolished wing to the far east had contained servants' bedrooms on both floors. The exterior appearance of the house was carefully restored at both ends in order to reflect Pope's original design.

John Russell Pope (1874–1937) was one of America's most famous Beaux-Arts architects (see the article on the Robinson/Gossler/Hutton Residence at Brookville for a discussion of Pope's career, page 144). Warren & Wetmore were equally well known for their work on Grand Central Station in New York City (1903–13). This firm also planned the William K. Vanderbilt, Jr., Estate, Eagle's Nest, in nearby Centerport (see page 185). The office records of Warren & Wetmore now form part of the collections of Avery Library, Columbia University, New York City.

Alfred Hopkins (1870–1941) studied architecture at the Ecole des Beaux-Arts and opened his own office in 1913. He became known for his large-scale designs of farm groups and garage complexes for estates and institutions. He also published several articles and books on the technical details and concepts underlying these special building types. On Long Island, Hopkins's work includes a dairy farm for the Arthur Bourne Estate (c. 1919) in Oakdale and buildings (1914–16) for the C. V. Brokaw Estate in Glen Cove, for the Mortimer Schiff Estate (c. 1914) in

22–5 (opposite above) Polo stable complex, plan and main elevation

22–6 (opposite below) Polo stable complex, view George McKesson Brown Estate, Huntington

Oyster Bay, and for the George S. Brewster Estate (c. 1916) in Brookville.

The landscape architect Marian C. Coffin also designed the gardens at the Lloyd Bryce/Childs Frick Estate, Clayton, at Roslyn Harbor (see page 83), and at the Marjorie Merriweather Post/Edward F. Hutton Estate, Hillwood, in Brookville (see page 138).

23
George McKesson Brown Estate, Huntington

Clarence Luce, architect, 1910–11; estate now houses the Harbor Arts Center and the Suffolk County Archeological Museum; endangered; administered by the Suffolk County Department of Parks; museum exhibit open on Sundays and for scheduled events; located on Brown's Road, off Southdown Road

George McKesson Brown was a member of the McKesson family, the owners of the McKesson Chemical Company of Connecticut. He was a civic leader in the town of Huntington and served as head of the Taxpayers' Association there. On the same membership roster could be found the names of Henry L. Stimson, Brown's neighbor and a former Secretary of War, Walter Jennings of Standard Oil, and Gerald M. Livingston, another neighbor whose estate is now owned by Friends World College.

In 1910 Brown commissioned architect Clarence Luce to design a large French Château Style house on a dramatic waterfront site facing Huntington Harbor. J. V. Schafer was listed as the contractor. In addition to the main house, the design for the original estate included a large stable and a garage and service complex, the latter now owned by the Universalist Unitarian Fellowship. A boathouse and servants' quarters, located at the waterfront edge of the estate, still forms a part of the property, and this building is now used by the Suffolk County Police. Until recently the main house was part of a Roman Catholic boys' school and was known as Coindre Hall. In 1973 the estate was taken over by the Suffolk County Department of Parks, and it has since found new life as the Harbor Arts Center, a community center for cultural events. The main house also contains the exhibits of the newly organized Suffolk County Archeological Museum. Although the county currently owns this facility, there are insufficient funds to continue its maintenance, and the future of the entire property is uncertain.

The design of the main house was influenced by the French Château Style that first became popular in the United States during the late nineteenth century. The distinctive composition of towers and roofscape combines those Late French Gothic and Renaissance design elements that were characteristic of the Château Style, also called the Francis I Style after King Francis I (reigned 1515–47). This style is best exemplified by the sixteenth-century châteaux of the Loire Valley, including Azay-le-Rideau (1518–27), Chenonceaux (1515–76), and Blois (1498–1524).

In the Brown Estate tall circular towers with conical roofs, a dominant hipped roof, elongated brick chimneys, and steeply pointed masonry gables reflect the Château Style. A second-story porch that projects over the entrance serves as a bridge to connect the two tower forms. This porch is topped by a prominent central gable that has elaborate side brackets at the roof level.

The central gable is composed of a steep triangular pedi-

23–1 (above) Detail of ornamental roof gable above main entrance

23–2 (right) Entrance or south elevation, view from the southeast

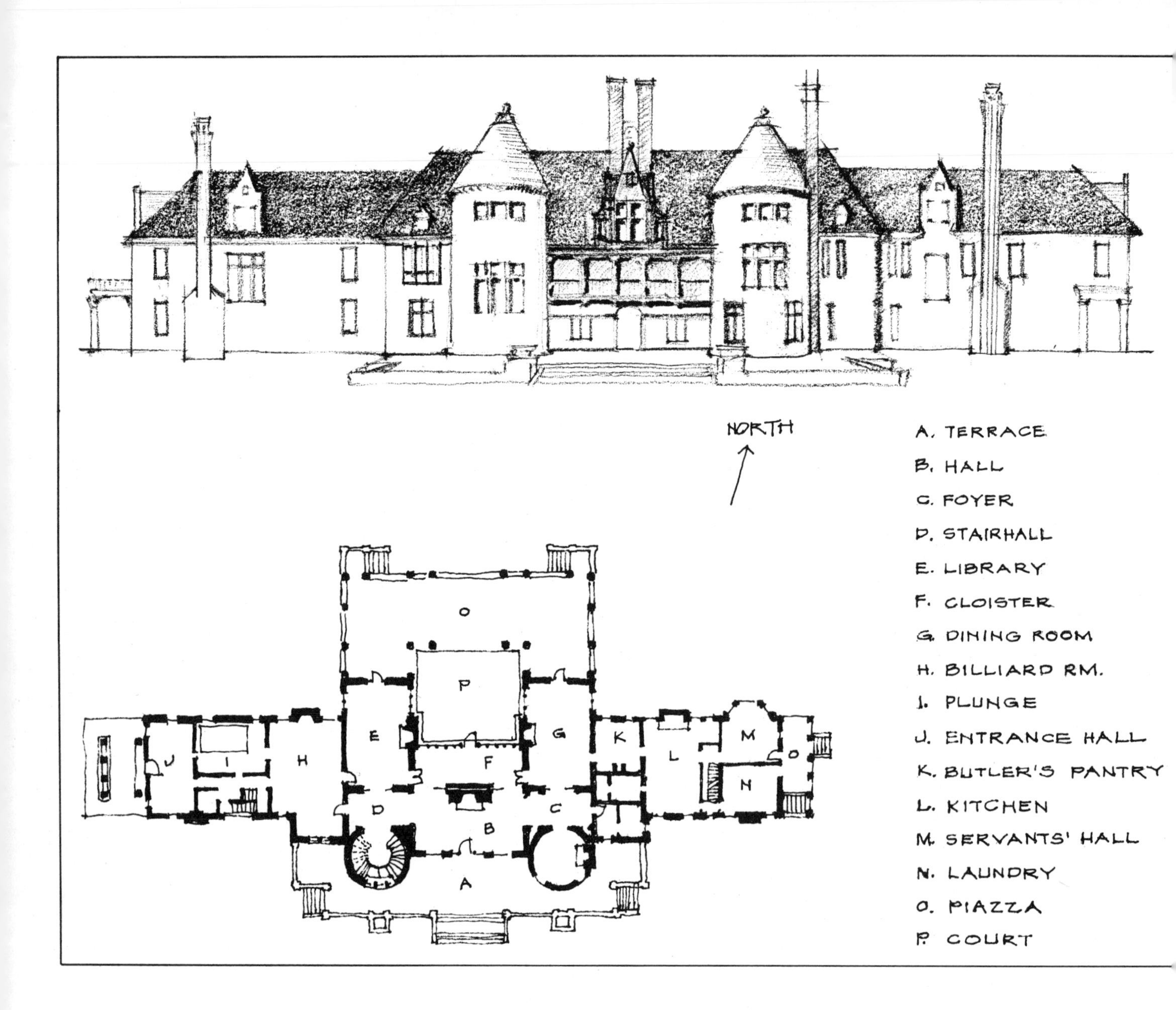

23–3 (top) Drawing of entrance or south elevation

23–4 (above) Main-floor plan

ment with an ogee-arched ornamental window. The brackets are sculpted with medieval crockets, or foliated hooks, and finials, or end points. Heraldic fish gargoyles are positioned as Renaissance scrollwork on either side of the pediment, and open balustrades at the ends of the gable also show a classical influence.

The service buildings on the estate were designed to complement the main house. The stable group is dominated by a large square tower, the top of which is supported by corbels, or stone projections, and from which a smaller round turret rises. The boathouse complex has a central octagonal tower with a steep gabled roof.

The French Château Style was first popularized in the United States by architect Richard Morris Hunt, who designed the William K. Vanderbilt, Sr., Château (1881) on Fifth Avenue in New York City. Although early examples of the Château influence in America were often a part of asymmetrical or picturesque designs, later examples, such as the George McKesson Brown Estate, have the strong symmetrical and axial organization that then reflected Beaux-Arts training. This spatial formality could also be seen in the Late French Château Style designs for the Clarence H. Mackay Estate, Harbor Hill (1902–1905), at Roslyn (see fig. I–26), by McKim, Mead & White (now demolished), and in the Otto Kahn Estate (c. 1923) in Woodbury, by Delano & Aldrich (now Eastern Military Academy).

The plan of the Brown house is a long narrow configuration that stretches out along the crest of a hill that overlooks the harbor. The major living spaces project on either side of an axis that is perpendicular to the linear plan. This axis follows a progression that begins in the large entry hall, passes through a cloister or living hall, and then moves out into a small sheltered court that opens onto a covered outdoor piazza (now glass-enclosed) that overlooks the waterfront. From here, one has access to the projecting library and dining rooms.

The waterfront side of the house was altered and expanded during the years of school ownership, but the entrance elevation is still well preserved. The stair hall and study occupy the ground floor of the symmetrical towers. The two end wings of the linear plan extend out from either side of the central block of the house. One wing originally held the kitchen and service areas, and the other contained an indoor pool and a billiard room.

Both Luce and Brown were genuinely interested in the mechanical aspects of the building. At the entry terrace two large brick planters doubled as coal chutes that led into the basement. There ceiling-mounted tramway tracks held cars that picked up the coal from the chutes, delivered it to the boilers, and transported the ashes to the far end of the house, dumping them at a garbage pickup point. Other elements included sophisticated electric panel boards and specially designed details of brick, terra-cotta, and hollow-tile-block construction.

The architect Clarence Luce (1851–1924) originally practiced in the Boston area, and he designed several country residences in the Shingle Style during the 1880s. These homes include the Lyman C. Joseph Residence (1882–83) and the Conover Residence (1888), both in Middletown, Rhode Island, and the W. H. Wesson Residence (1882–

84) in Springfield, Massachusetts, designed completely in shingles but which has some of the same tower forms and angles that were used later in the George McKesson Brown Estate. Luce's entry for the Toronto Court House competition of 1885 shows the French medieval influence of H. H. Richardson's civic projects, and it also contains the details and ornamentation that he later used on the Brown house. An early apprentice in Luce's Boston office was Joseph M. Wells, a young architect who later became one of the chief designers for McKim, Mead & White. He worked on the Henry Villard Houses (1882–85) and the Century Club, all in New York City.

Luce eventually moved his office to New York City, and in 1891 he was one of the architects who worked on the King Model Houses (also called Strivers' Row and now known as the St. Nicholas Historic District). Other architects who took part in this project were McKim, Mead & White, Bruce Price, and James Brown Lord. This development also included several blocks of row houses on the Upper West Side, between Seventh and Eighth avenues, which were planned by David H. King. Clarence Luce collaborated with Bruce Price on the block between 138th and 139th streets.

During his career Luce planned several large exposition buildings. The Massachusetts State Building at the Philadelphia Centennial Exposition (1876) and the New York State Building at the St. Louis Louisiana Purchase Exposition (1904) were both designed by him. In New York City he planned commercial and office structures, including the "Night and Day" Bank Building (c. 1906) at Forty-fourth Street and Fifth Avenue.

23–5 Boathouse

24
William K. Vanderbilt, Jr., Estate, Eagle's Nest, Centerport

Warren & Wetmore, architects, 1928; museum-wing addition, 1934–36; estate now the Vanderbilt Museum; open to the public; located off Little Neck Road

William K. Vanderbilt, Jr. (1878–1944), was the son of William K. Vanderbilt, Sr., and Alva Vanderbilt (see page 209) and the great-grandson of Commodore Cornelius Vanderbilt (1794–1877), the founder of a transportation empire that eventually controlled more than a few of the major shipping lines and railroads in the United States. Commodore Vanderbilt had taken over the New York Central Railroad in 1867 and had built the first Grand Central Terminal in New York City in 1873. His great-grandson was educated at Harvard University and took up a position with the New York Central in 1903. He became president of that railroad in 1918.

William, Jr., was also a well-known sportsman who participated in both yachting and auto racing. He inaugurated the Vanderbilt Cup Automobile races in 1904 and constructed the Long Island Motor Parkway in 1908 as the first high-speed motorway on the island. As a young boy, William had developed a love of the sea and of boating. He served in the U.S. Navy during World War I and later studied navigation, receiving a license in 1927. He was well educated in all aspects of sea life, including marine biology, natural history, astronomy, and marine engineering. Vanderbilt navigated his own boats and ships on several scientific expeditions that collected marine specimens from around the world.

Eagle's Nest, his waterfront estate at Centerport, was planned as a personal retreat and as a special place to house his marine collections. His earlier home at Great Neck (now demolished) had been designed by Carrère & Hastings (c. 1900) shortly after his first marriage to Virginia Graham Fair in 1899. Vanderbilt's residence in Centerport was completed in 1928 from plans by Warren & Wetmore, the architectural firm that later designed the museum-wing addition to the house (1934–36). William lived at his Centerport estate with his second wife, Rosamund Lancaster Warburton, following their marriage in 1927.

After Vanderbilt's death in 1944, the estate property was donated to Suffolk County to serve as a museum of natural history. A portion of the main house has been maintained in its original condition, and the wings now contain the museum's natural history exhibits and administrative offices. Two separate buildings, the Hall of Fishes and a planetarium, also form part of Vanderbilt Museum.

The entry to Eagle's Nest is marked by a prominent bell tower. Visitors approach the main house along a cobble-

24–1 (opposite) View from entrance tower into courtyard

stoned entry road that passes over a small arched bridge, through a great arched opening in the bell tower, and into the central courtyard of the house. From here the house appears to be quite small in scale and modest in appearance, with plain stuccoed walls, low, gently sloping, tiled roofs, and a single-story, glass-enclosed arcade or cloister.

The plan of the house was developed in phases into the existing courtyard parti, with the major residential wing facing Long Island Sound, the side wings containing the kitchen and service areas, and a final wing, built in 1934–36, enclosing the courtyard and containing Vanderbilt's personal collections. Although the design details give the house a Spanish Colonial character, its overall site plan is quite modern in the sense that only continued movement around and through the complex of elements gives one an understanding of the relationship of the house to the site.

24–2 (above) Waterfront or north elevation

24–3 (opposite below) Aerial perspective view from the southeast. Drawing by Santo Vitale, Vanderbilt Museum

The design is multileveled with the house and surrounding hillside tied together by a series of terraces and bridges.

The ground level around the house, particularly on the waterfront side, is much lower in elevation than that of the interior courtyard. When viewed from the waterside, the house can be seen at the crest of a steep, terraced hillside. This dramatic image is in sharp contrast to the intimate enclosure of the interior court. This waterfront view, which greeted Vanderbilt as he climbed up the hill from the dock where he moored his large yacht, *The Alva*, may have inspired the estate's name, Eagle's Nest.

The architectural ornamentation on the exterior elevations of the house recalls the Spanish Baroque Style of architecture as it was adapted in the American colonies. Sculpted cartouches, medallions, and heraldic emblems are concentrated around the door and window openings. Broad expanses of white-stuccoed wall surfaces and characteristic wrought-iron window grilles and ornamental balcony railings complete the overall impression. The bell tower and courtyard cloister also recall traditional designs of early Spanish missions and convents in America.

Other buildings on the estate grounds include the similarly Baroque-styled Hall of Fishes, which is located at the edge of the property off Little Neck Road. Here Vanderbilt housed many of his marine specimens. A shingled, Tudor-styled waterside cottage, resembling a boathouse, lies at the end of an estate service road. It is presently boarded up, but it could easily be adapted for public use as a coffeehouse or visitors' center. A small farm group on the estate is designed in the same style as the waterfront cottage.

The architect Whitney Warren (1864–1943), a cousin of the Vanderbilts, was educated at Columbia University and later graduated from the Ecole des Beaux-Arts in Paris, where he worked for ten years before joining Charles D. Wetmore (1867–1941), a graduate of Harvard University, in an architectural practice.

Many of Warren & Wetmore's most famous projects were commissioned by the Vanderbilt family. The firm designed New York City's Grand Central Station (1903–13), in association with Reed & Stem. It also planned all of the major buildings in the vicinity of the station—the Biltmore Hotel (c. 1914), the Hotel Commodore (c. 1919), the Vanderbilt Hotel (1912), the New York Central (General) Building (1928), and the Grand Central Post Office (c. 1906). In addition to Eagle's Nest, Warren & Wetmore also designed a New York City residence for William K.

Vanderbilt, Jr., at 49 East Fifty-second Street (1908–1909), Vanderbilt's original residence by McKim, Mead & White having been first demolished. The firm also planned the Deepdale Club (c. 1926) for Vanderbilt at Lake Success, Long Island (now Lake Success Village Office and Golf Course). Other New York City commissions of the firm include the New York Yacht Club (1899); the James A. Burden Residence (1902), which now forms part of the Convent of the Sacred Heart; R. Livingston Beekman's Mansion (1905), now the Yugoslav Mission; and the Mrs. Marshall Orme Wilson Residence (1903), now India House.

Warren & Wetmore became famous for their designs of grand hotels and resorts, including The Broadmoor Hotel (c. 1918) in Colorado Springs, Colorado; The Homestead Hotel in Hot Springs, Virginia, in association with Elzner & Anderson; the Newport Country Club (1894) in Newport, Rhode Island; and the Biltmore Country Club (c. 1922) in Rye, New York.

Other country residences were also planned by Warren & Wetmore, including the William Starr Miller Estate (1900) at Newport and the Joseph Stevens Estate in Westbury. In addition, the firm designed several large stable, athletic, and service complexes for the Isaac Guggenheim Estate in Sands Point; for the Marshall Field III Estate, Caumsett, in Lloyd Neck (see page 170); for the Clarence H. Mackay Estate, Harbor Hill, in Roslyn; and for the William K. Vanderbilt, Sr., Estate, Idle Hour, in Oakdale (see page 209).

24–4 West elevation

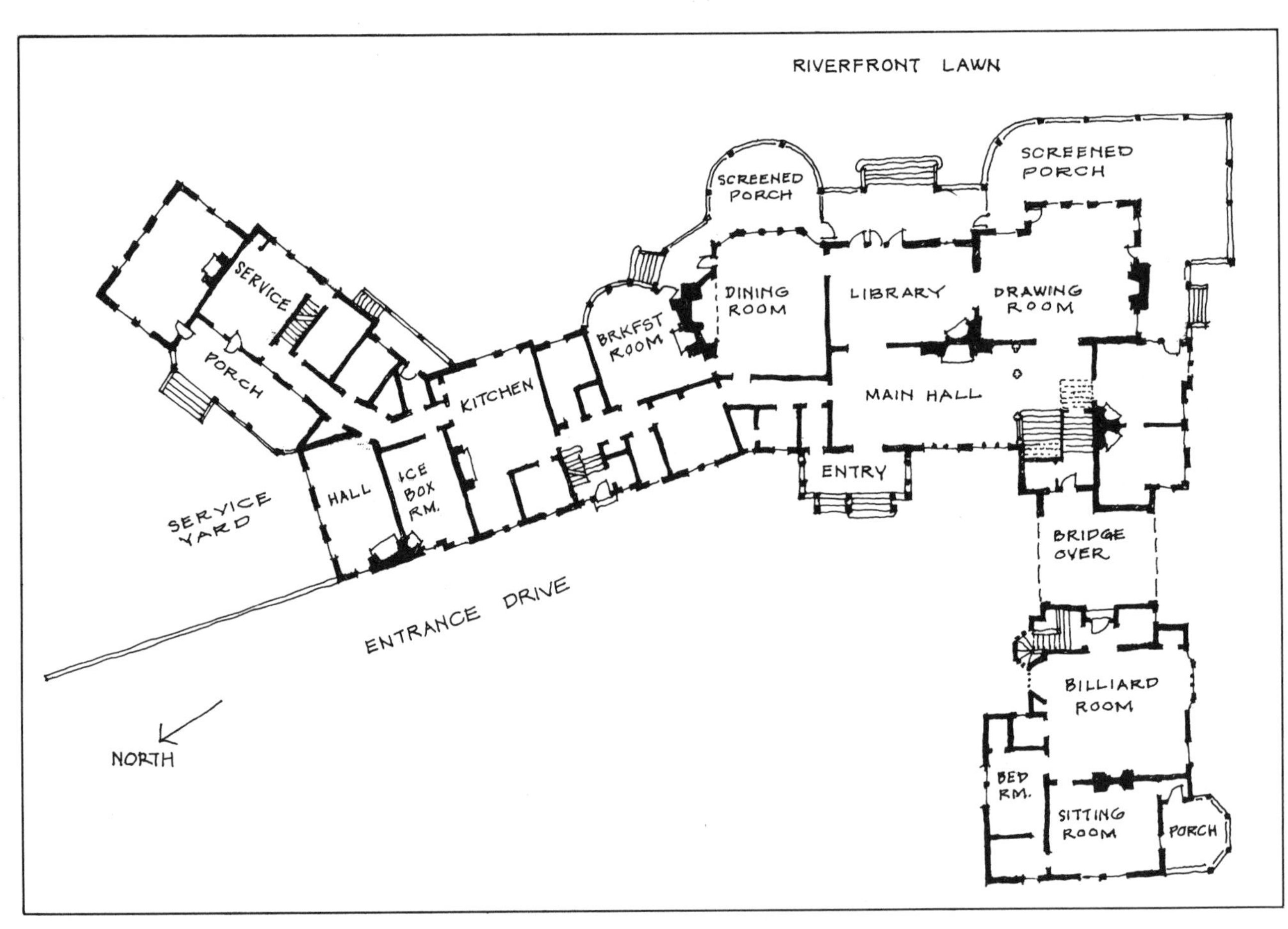
RIVERFRONT LAWN
SCREENED PORCH
SCREENED PORCH
SERVICE
PORCH
DINING ROOM
LIBRARY
DRAWING ROOM
BRKFST ROOM
KITCHEN
MAIN HALL
ENTRY
HALL
ICE BOX RM.
SERVICE YARD
BRIDGE OVER
ENTRANCE DRIVE
BILLIARD ROOM
NORTH
BED RM.
SITTING ROOM
PORCH

25 William Bayard Cutting Estate, Westbrook, Great River

Charles C. Haight, architect, 1886; Frederick Law Olmsted, landscape architect; estate now the Bayard Cutting Arboretum, administered by the Long Island State Park Commission; arboretum grounds open to the public; a portion of the main house open in the summer as a park restaurant; located off South Country Road (Route 27A)

William Bayard Cutting (1850–1912), who was trained as a lawyer, was born in New York and educated at Columbia University (1869–72). The Bayard side of his family traced its history in America back to the days of the Dutch East India Trading Company. The Bayards later acquired controlling interests in railroads at the time when lines were rapidly moving westward across the country. By the time that William was twenty-eight years old, he had become president of three rail lines and director of two others, the St. Louis and Southern Pacific railways. He also served as a director of several corporations, including the American Exchange National Bank and the Commercial Union Insurance Company.

Work on Westbrook, Cutting's estate at Great River, began in 1886. He commissioned New York architect Charles Coolidge Haight to design the elongated, wood-shingled house with broad porches overlooking the Connetquot River. The land had originally been owned by the Lorillard family (see the article on Westbrook Farm, page 198), and Cutting converted the former racing stables on the property into a model dairy farm. In addition to scientific farming, he was also interested in horticulture and in natural history, and he was a founder of the New York Botanical Garden and Zoological Society. Cutting commissioned Frederick Law Olmsted, America's most noted landscape architect, to design a naturalistic environment for his new estate. Olmsted's design incorporated both distinctive local trees and plants and unusual and rare horticultural specimens from around the world.

Cutting lived at Westbrook until his death in 1912. His widow continued to spend her summers there until 1949, when she died at the age of ninety-four. Mrs. Cutting bequeathed the estate to the Long Island State Park Commission, and Westbrook is now open to the public as a park and arboretum.

The design of the house shows several influences, including those of the English Queen Anne and Tudor styles as well as the later American Shingle Style. The floor plan is a rambling and asymmetrical configuration, with the main living spaces of the house contained in two wings perpendicular to each other. The service area takes up two additional wings, which are set at oblique angles to the L-shaped living spaces. The main ridgeline of the gabled roof follows this plan as it changes direction, rising or falling in height as the plan turns, as the grade changes, and as the activities within the wings vary.

A series of screened porches, each one serving a different

25–1 (opposite above) Main entrance

25–2 (opposite below) Main-floor plan

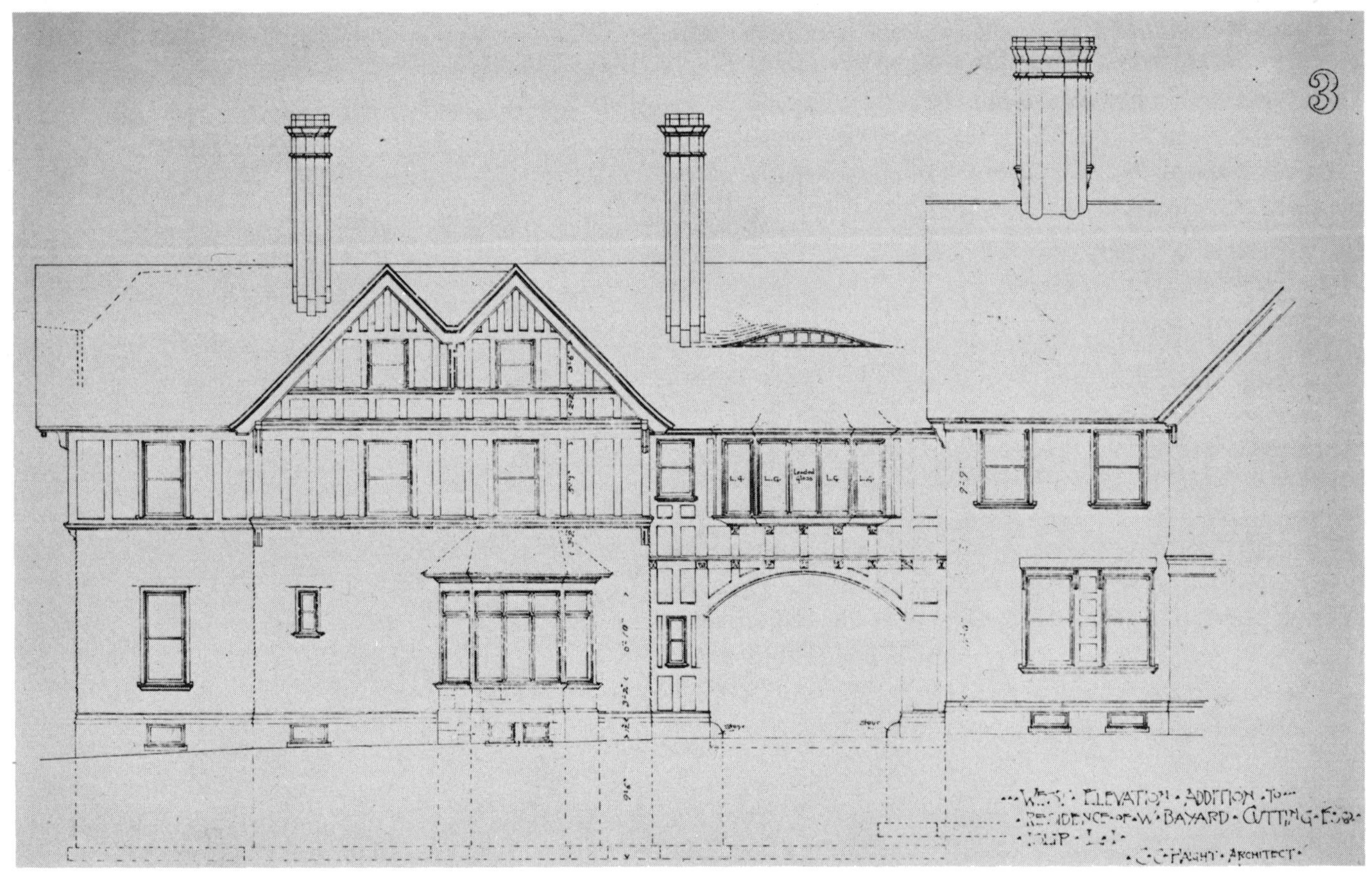
3
WEST · ELEVATION · ADDITION · TO
RESIDENCE · OF · W · BAYARD · CUTTING · ESQ ·
ISLIP · L · I ·
C · C · HAIGHT · ARCHITECT ·

room, opens up the house and makes it seem a part of the landscape. The porches and projecting bays clearly articulate each of the major living spaces, extending them into the great landscaped meadow that slopes gently down toward the river. An indented porch, off the library, serves as a waterfront entrance to the house and leads to a covered drawing room porch on one side and to a circular screened dining-room porch on the other. This circular porch is an extension of the interior dining room space, and it complements the solid, projecting circular form of the adjacent breakfast room and creates a contrast of solids and voids on the waterfront elevation. The wide openings between all of the main living areas in the interior, together with the spacious porch circulation outside, reinforce the open feeling of the design and aid the circulation of welcome summer breezes.

The waterfront, or southeast, elevation of the house, is dominated by two large half-timbered roof gables that rise from behind the porches, and the inland, or northwest, elevation is shaped inwardly to imply a sheltered or protected entrance court. A carriage driveway passes beneath the arching, bridged connection to a guest wing, creating a framed access to this entry area.

Fireplaces and chimneys were given special attention by Haight. Shaped bricks on the chimney stacks accentuate their height and importance in the building's silhouette. A terra-cotta panel set into a major chimney near the entryway charmingly proclaims: "William Bayard Cutting—he built me—1886." On the interior another chimney with a large double fireplace is used as a connecting link between the dining and breakfast rooms, at which point there is a change in direction of the building's wings. Another massive double fireplace also defines and separates the main hall of the house from the library and drawing rooms.

The estate grounds are organized into a variety of naturalistic woodland and waterfront landscapes. They are now maintained as nature walks by the Long Island State Park Commission. The pinetum, wild flower walk, rhododendron park, bird watchers' walk, and swamp cypress grove all form part of an extensive master-plan layout and, together with the waterfront great lawn, cover most of the 690 acres of the estate.

One of the delightful aspects of Westbrook's conversion into a public park is the summer restaurant that has been set up in the former drawing room and library of the main house. The large glass-enclosed porch off the drawing room has tables and chairs where one can sit with refreshments

25–3 (opposite above) Guest-wing or southwest elevation, showing entry drive

25–4 (opposite below) Architect's drawing of guest-wing or southwest elevation

25–5 (overleaf) Waterfront or southeast elevation

and gaze at the river, becoming totally immersed in the Romantic park setting as it was created by Olmsted.

The architect Charles Coolidge Haight (1841–1917), like Cutting, had also studied law at Columbia University. Haight left school during the Civil War, however, to serve as a captain in the same company as Emelyn T. Littell, a New York architect. After the war Haight entered Littell's office and received his architectural training there. When H. H. Richardson arrived in New York, after attending the Ecole des Beaux-Arts, he shared his first architectural office space with Emelyn T. Littell, before joining Charles Gambrill as a partner in 1867. Haight also left Littell's office in order to start his own practice in 1867; he designed many country residences early in his career, including the Shingle Style Cutting Residence (1886) and the Georgian Revival Walter Breese Smith Residence (1889) in Tuxedo, New York. Haight eventually developed a large practice that concentrated on educational and commercial facilities.

Haight's early large-scale projects are represented by several Collegiate Gothic-styled buildings at Columbia University (1874–84), including the School of Mines and Hamilton Hall (now demolished). At Yale University he designed Vanderbilt and Phelps halls (1898), and he collaborated with Alfred W. Githens on the College Library and the Sheffield Scientific School (c. 1914).

Haight designed many large projects in New York City, including the General Theological Seminary (1883–1900) on West 20th Street and the New York Cancer Hospital (1887) on West 106th Street. This large French Château Style structure later became the Towers Nursing Home and is now threatened with demolition. He also designed the Richardsonian-influenced H. O. Havemeyer Residence (1890) at 66th Street and Fifth Avenue and the Downtown Club (1887) on Pine Street.

Frederick Law Olmsted (1822–1903), was born in Hartford, Connecticut, and educated at Yale University. Olmsted shared Cutting's interest in agriculture and in scientific farming methods, and he had traveled in Europe and throughout the United States, studying agricultural and horticultural developments. Olmsted became America's foremost landscape architect and park planner. In recent years much has been written about his life and work. In 1857 he entered and won the competition for the design of New York's Central Park with architect Calvert Vaux, an associate of Andrew Jackson Downing. He also collaborated with Vaux on other famous projects, including Pros-

pect Park (1865) in Brooklyn and Riverside Park (1869) in Chicago. In addition, he planned the United States Capitol grounds (1875–78) in Washington, D.C.

Olmsted later moved to Brookline, Massachusetts, and continued his practice there. His large-scale, master-plan projects include the Boston and Chicago municipal parks systems (1886–87) and the World's Columbian Exposition in Chicago (1891–93). Olmsted designed many private residential parks and gardens in addition to the Cutting Estate. In Massachusetts, he collaborated with H. H. Richardson on the Dr. John Bryant Residence (1880) in Cohasset and on the C. J. Hubbard Residence (1883) in Weston. On the G. N. Black Residence (1883) in Manchester, Massachusetts, he worked with Peabody & Stearns, and in association with Richard Morris Hunt, he designed the Cornelius Vanderbilt Estate, The Breakers (1892–95), in Newport, Rhode Island (see fig. I–9), and the George W. Vanderbilt Estate, Biltmore (1888–95), in Asheville, North Carolina.

Olmsted trained his stepson, John, and his younger son, Frederick, Jr., as landscape architects. At first they worked with him and later they carried on Olmsted's practice as Olmsted Brothers of Brookline, Massachusetts (see page 162).

25–6 Architect's drawing of waterfront or southeast elevation

26
Westbrook Farm, Farm Group of the William Bayard Cutting Estate, Westbrook, Great River

Attributed to Stanford White, architect, 1895; farm now owned by the Long Island State Park Commission; damaged by vandalism; not open to the public; endangered status; may be seen from South Country Road (Route 27A)

The acreage of the William Bayard Cutting Estate, Westbrook, at Great River (see page 191), was originally owned by George L. Lorillard, who had a summer home there (now demolished) and a large racing stable complex (c. 1875), which was shared with members of the nearby Southside Sportsmen's Club in Oakdale. Lorillard and his brothers Pierre and Louis were active members of this club, and they trained many famous race horses at these stables, including Iroquois, the first American horse to win England's Epsom Derby (1881).

After Lorillard's retirement in 1884, William Bayard Cutting purchased the property. Pursuing his interests in agriculture and in scientific farming, he converted the stables into a model dairy farm, adding a cow barn (1889) and a brick horse stable (1892). The complex was severely damaged by fire in 1895, and the buildings were redesigned in that year. Cutting's granddaughter, Iris Origo, later remembered the Sunday ritual of distinguished visitors, as well as relatives, taking a grand tour of the model farm, newly rebuilt. Under Cutting's leadership, the guests inspected and duly admired the prize-winning dairy cows that were raised there.

The Long Island State Park Commission owns both Westbrook Farm and the separate, main portion of the Cutting Estate, now the Bayard Cutting Arboretum, which is located on the other side of South Country Road. Unfortunately, the state's budget is not large enough to provide funds to maintain a full-time caretaker or security guards or even to take care of the complex at a minimal level. The buildings are relatively unsecured and have been badly damaged by vandalism.

A proposal has been made to restore the stables as a productive horse-breeding farm to be run by a private group. A Board of Cooperative Educational Services (B.O.C.E.S.) training center has also been proposed as a new use for the farm complex. This project would involve an agricultural and occupational school similar to the one at the former F. Ambrose Clark Racing Stables at Old Westbury (see page 131), which now form part of the State University of New York, College at Old Westbury.

The Westbrook Farm complex was recently given National Landmark status, largely through the efforts of the Vanderbilt Historical Society in Oakdale. As of this writing, however, the property remains on the endangered list, a victim of ongoing deterioration.

The design of Westbrook Farm is characterized by a combination of Queen Anne and Shingle Style elements, with its individual structures arranged in a village-like cluster. The farm is comparable to the earlier stable and barn groups, probably by Richard Morris Hunt, of the William K. Vanderbilt, Sr., Estate, Idle Hour, in nearby Oakdale (see page 209). However, the Vanderbilt barns were designed with prominent exterior wall buttresses, and they also show a regular or consistent series of roof dormers as opposed to the irregular roof configuration of the Cutting barns. Westbrook also has the same large scale as the great dairy-farm complexes that were later designed on Long Island by Alfred Hopkins, including the "Chinese"-influenced dairy for the Arthur Bourne Estate (c. 1919), also in Oakdale, and the Georgian Revival farm group for the Marshall Field III Estate, Caumsett, in Lloyd Neck (see page 170). The open street system at Westbrook is also similar to the arrangement of the Marshall Field III dairy, although the buildings are quite different in style.

The huge barns at Westbrook Farm are rectangular in plan with massive red brick walls and broad arched openings. The entries to the stall areas are identified by projecting brick bays, topped by steep hipped or mansard-tower roofs. Although the ground-level walls are of brick, the second story, with its haylofts and storage areas, is entirely contained within a dominant, sloping roof. This serves as a backdrop for an elaborate and fanciful shingled roofscape composition characterized by groupings of curvilinear and polygonal projections that are tied together by the continuous use of wood shingles. Varied roof gables and wall dormers form part of the design along with cylindrical turrets and cupolas and conical overhanging tower caps. These fanciful structures provide access to the haylofts and are sources of natural light and ventilation. The cylindrical forms of the turrets and some of the dormers playfully echo the forms of the giant double-cylinder silos adjacent to the barns.

Although these buildings are basically utilitarian structures without "applied" decorative ornamentation on their façades, they have a sense of "picturesque" activity in their intricate manipulation of roof forms as well as in such structural details as the brick patterns of the arches and the thick-dimensioned, rough-wood shingles.

Queen Anne and Shingle Style elements in the design include the detailing of the red brick walls and arches, which is continued in the shingles above. The use of

cylindrical-tower forms with projecting turrets and the steep hipped roof also show the French Château Style's influence on the Queen Anne Style in the United States. These influences may also be seen in the George McKesson Brown Estate (1910–11) at Huntington (see page 177), designed by Clarence Luce.

Although the design of Westbrook Farm was attributed to Stanford White by Mrs. Cutting, no positive confirmation has been found in the existing office records of McKim, Mead & White, nor do the buildings strongly resemble other projects designed by White. In addition, by 1895, when the new Westbrook barns were built, McKim, Mead & White had largely abandoned the picturesque Queen Anne manner. However, in Newport, Rhode Island, the Samuel Coleman House (1882–83), an earlier design by McKim, Mead & White, shows a variety of dormers that are similar to some of those at Westbrook Farm, where White might possibly have worked over the foundations and brick walls that perhaps survived the fire of 1895. In that case the elaborate roofscape could be more closely associated with White's work, and he may also have wished to keep the new design sympathetic to the Queen Anne and Shingle Style aspects of the main house on the estate.

Additional discussions of McKim, Mead & White and their Long Island projects are contained in the articles on the James L. Breese Estate, The Orchard (1898–1906), at Southampton (see page 229), and the Association Houses (1882–84) at Montauk Point (see page 237).

26–1 (opposite above) Main building, south elevation, seen from the east

26–2 (opposite below) Main building, south elevation, detail

27 Southside Sportsmen's Club, Oakdale

Isaac H. Green, architect, c. 1885–90; club now Connetquot River State Park; club administered by the Long Island State Park Commission; grounds open for fishing by permit only and for nature walks by appointment; located off Sunrise Highway

Mrs. John King Van Rensselaer referred to the members of the Southside Sportsmen's Club in her book *The Social Ladder* as several of the wealthiest and most influential men in the country. The club roster included Vanderbilts, Lorillards, Cuttings, Whitneys, James Gordon Bennett, Frederick G. Bourne, O. H. P. Belmont, Robert and Ogden Goelet, and Charles L. Tiffany.

The club was originally organized in the 1860s as a game preserve "dedicated to hunting and fishing." Earlier, in the 1820s, a tavern and inn had thrived on the site. This older building still exists as one wing of the main clubhouse. Nearby, between the Main Pond and the Connetquot River, is an even older structure, a Revolutionary period gristmill, now being restored by the Long Island State Park Commission.

The facilities of the club have undergone alterations and expansion over the years. In the 1960s an annex was built to the south, opposite the original tavern section of the clubhouse, in order to provide additional lodgings. It now houses park administration offices. In the 1880s the main clubhouse building was enlarged to incorporate the old tavern at its southern end and to provide game and billiard rooms, lockers, dining rooms, and kitchen facilities on the ground floor. The upper floors contained additional guests' and members' lodgings and bathrooms. In addition, another annex was constructed to the north on nearby Main Pond, the so-called North Annex. This building was designed to contain lodgings for married members.

The design for most of the Southside Sportsmen's Club (c. 1885–90), including the present main clubhouse and the later annex, is attributed to architect Isaac H. Green. The existing buildings and 3500 acres of the club grounds now form part of Connetquot River State Park, which is maintained as a nature preserve and as a wildlife refuge by the Long Island State Park Commission. The grounds are open for fishing, by permit only, and for guided nature walks by appointment.

The Southside Sportsmen's Club complex is an unusual example of Shingle Style and Colonial Revival design elements as they developed during the late nineteenth century in the United States. The original tavern and the gristmill provide glimpses of early shingled buildings. This style was indigenous to Long Island, beginning with the first Colonial settlements. The additions made to the club in the 1860s and 1880s show an historic progression from the rural, utilitarian, shingled design of the 1860s annex, to the matured Shingle Style main clubhouse, and finally to

27–1 (opposite) Entrance or east elevation, detail

27–2 *(opposite above) Entrance or east elevation, view from the southeast*

27–3 *(opposite below) Drawing of entrance or east elevation*

the Shingle style as it was combined with the later Colonial Revival period elements in the 1880s annex. This progression roughly parallels the development of estate architecture on Long Island (see pages 21–34).

The plan of the main clubhouse buildings is based on a linear parti, with the major ground-floor spaces aligned in sequence, parallel to the water, and interconnected by broad access doors. This interior circulation is directly paralleled outside by an open-air porch running the length of the building, with an entrance into each club room, and serving, in effect, as an open-air main corridor.

The exterior of the clubhouse building is characterized by a multigabled roof with two high-pitched gables over the central portion of the building that are perpendicular to the main roof line. The old two-story tavern is clearly visible at the southern end of the building. At the northern end, a covered porch projects off the dining and kitchen wing. The open wood porch deck runs the length of the building and connects the tavern to the covered porch.

The overall composition of the clubhouse is asymmetrical, with the various elements of the building tied together by a continuous sheathing of wood shingles. There is a deliberate sense of movement in the wall surface, which undulates or projects out over the window openings to create overhanging eaves. This feeling of movement is reinforced by wall projections that appear as bays, with prominent curvilinear supporting brackets and interconnected window openings below. The windows, instead of appearing as isolated holes in an unbroken plane, are located at the juncture or intersection of a break or undulating projection in the wall.

The clubhouse contrasts with the 1880s North Annex building, which was probably designed somewhat later than the main clubhouse. The influence of Colonial Revival elements on the earlier Shingle Style is reflected in the more formal, symmetrical plan of the building. A centrally located roof gable is developed as a triangular pediment, with a denticulated cornice and fanlight. Although most of the house is shingled, the central bay beneath the pediment is sheathed in raised wood paneling on the upper floor, and on the first floor a covered open-air entry porch with classically detailed columns is attached. The rear façade of the building also has a triangular pediment with a Palladian window arrangement and a smaller porch that locates the rear of the central-hall parti within the building. The interior is symmetrical to either side of the central hall, unlike the linear, asymmetrical parti of the main clubhouse.

The architect Isaac H. Green (1858–1937) was born in Riverhead and was a descendant of early Colonial settlers on Long Island. His daughter, Henriette, married a member of the Snedecor family, who had owned and run the original tavern. Later, this family managed the Southside Sportsmen's Club. Green practiced in Sayville and designed many country houses on Long Island, especially along the South Shore. His work includes a Tudor-styled lodge (c. 1885), originally with a thatched roof, on the William Bayard Cutting Estate, Westbrook, at Great River (see page 191), as well as buildings on the Frederick G. Bourne and Wagstaff estates.

In Islip, Green planned the half-timbered Parish House (1890) adjacent to St. Mark's Episcopal Church, a shingled building designed by Richard Morris Hunt in 1878. About 1895 Green designed a major Colonial Revival addition to Sagtikos Manor in Bay Shore, which had been the Van Cortlandt family home and dated from 1693. One of his largest projects was a Palladian design for the Brandish Johnson Estate, Woodland (c. 1906), in Islip.

Isaac H. Green's Southside Sportsmen's Club stands out as one of the most impressive building complexes remaining on Long Island. The Long Island State Park Commission deserves credit for preserving the club buildings as publicly owned resources.

27–4 (opposite above) Entrance or east elevation, view looking south

27–5 (opposite below) North Annex, east elevation

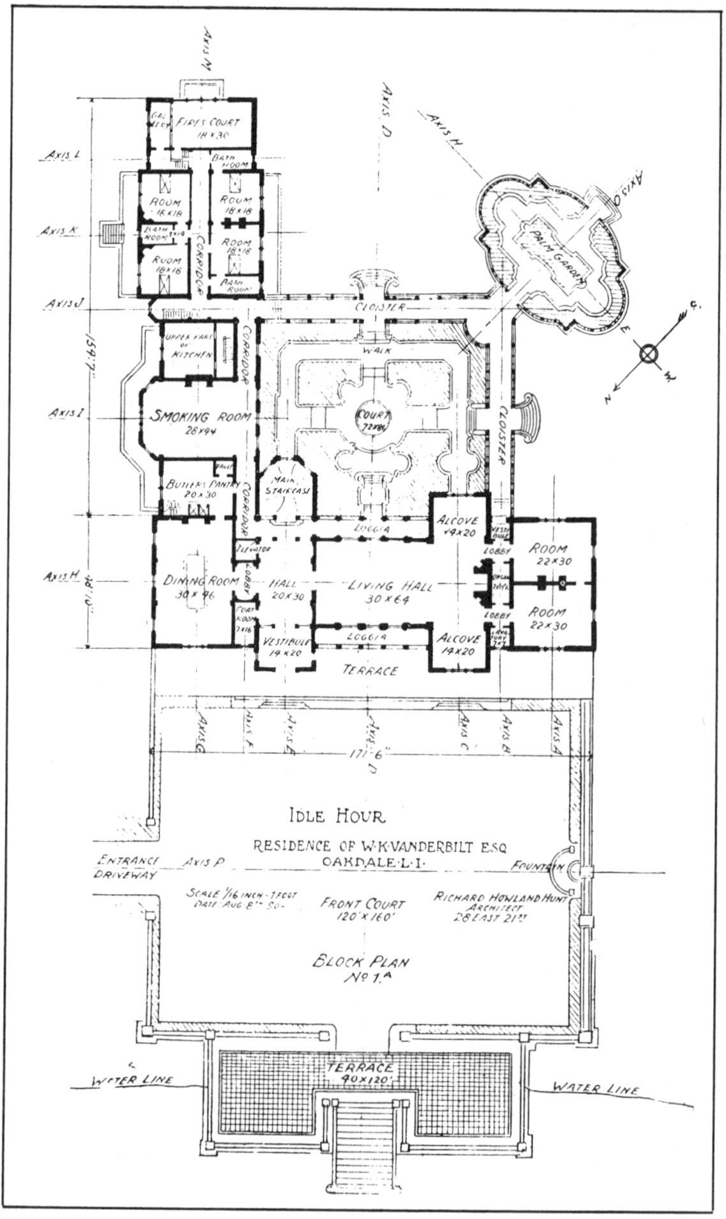

28–1 (above) View from the north, showing northeast (left) and northwest or waterfront (right) elevations

28–2 (right) Main-floor plan

IDLE HOUR

RESIDENCE OF W·K·VANDERBILT ESQ

OAKDALE·L·I·

RICHARD HOWLAND HUNT ARCHITECT 28 EAST 21ST

BLOCK PLAN No 1.A

28
William K. Vanderbilt, Sr., Estate, Idle Hour, Oakdale

Richard Howland Hunt, architect, 1899; estate now owned by Dowling College; building undergoing renovation after being damaged by fire; located off Idle Hour Boulevard

William K. Vanderbilt, Sr. (1849–1920), was the son of William H. Vanderbilt and the grandson of Commodore Cornelius Vanderbilt (1794–1877). Born in New York and educated in Switzerland, the younger William began working on the family-owned Hudson River Railroad line at the age of nineteen. By 1877 he had become the vice-president of the New York Central and Hudson River lines, and by 1882 William K. Vanderbilt, Sr., was president of the New York, Chicago & St. Louis Railways. After the death of his father in 1885, he and his brother Cornelius took over the direction of the Vanderbilt railroad and financial empire.

William K. was also a competitive sportsman. He owned several yachts and participated in the America's Cup sailing races. He also maintained racing stables both on Long Island and in France. In 1875 Vanderbilt married Alva Smith, and in the following year he commissioned architect Richard Morris Hunt to plan their new country estate, Idle Hour, at Oakdale. Shortly after this, in 1881, Hunt designed Vanderbilt's French Château Style mansion in New York City, a project that established his reputation as a major Beaux-Arts architect in the United States and Mrs. Vanderbilt's as a fashionable patron of the arts.

When the original Idle Hour was destroyed by fire in 1899, Vanderbilt commissioned Hunt's office, then run by Hunt's elder son, Richard Howland Hunt, to redesign the house on the same site. Later additions (c. 1902–1904), which were constructed to provide a guest wing, or "bachelors' quarters," and a large indoor tennis court, were planned by architects Warren & Wetmore. The estate grounds included the main house, a large coach house, a powerhouse, gate lodges, greenhouses, and boathouses, as well as a farm group of stables, barns, and service buildings, probably designed by Richard Morris Hunt. The latter structures eventually became known as "The Artists' Colony" when several of the buildings were converted into artists' summer studios and residences. The cow barns were recently occupied by a boat building company. They now form part of an historic district in Oakdale.

Vanderbilt's property was near several other large estates, including the William Bayard Cutting Estate, Westbrook (1886), at Great River (see page 191), directly across the Connetquot River, and the Frederick G. Bourne Estate (c. 1902) in Oakdale, designed by Ernest Flagg. The Bourne Residence at that time was considered to be the largest mansion on Long Island. It is now occupied by LaSalle Military Academy.

Vanderbilt's daughter, Consuelo, who later married the

28–3 *Northwest or waterfront elevation*

Duke of Marlborough, recalled her early childhood days at Idle Hour in her autobiography *The Glitter and the Gold* as among her happiest memories. His son, William K., Jr., had his own country retreat on the North Shore of Long Island, Eagle's Nest, at Centerport (see page 185).

Idle Hour is now owned by Dowling College and was an administrative center until 1974 when fire damaged the interior of the building. The structure is undergoing renovations and repairs and will eventually reopen as a campus facility. Other estate buildings also used by the college include the coach house, now a gymnasium, and the former powerhouse, which has been converted into a performing arts center.

Richard Howland Hunt's design for Idle Hour, completed in 1899, is a good example of the strong influence that academic Beaux-Arts planning principles had on American architecture at that time. The house is sited parallel to the waterfront edge of the property, with the entrance elevation facing the Connetquot River. The site plan is developed

as a formal progression of axially aligned rectangular spaces. These spaces begin with the water terrace, or boat dock, which projects out into the river, and continue up terrace steps to a large rectangular entry court, where carriages or coaches arrived at the house. The axial progression continues through the court and up shallow steps to an entry terrace and arcaded loggia that open directly into the major interior space of the house, the living hall. This space spanned the entire width of the building and extended outside through an arcaded cloister into a sheltered, rectangular garden court. The interior and exterior spaces were aligned to create a continuous progression from the water's edge through the house, moving along the major organizing axis of the master plan. In reverse, a reciprocal axial vista extended back toward the water when one stood within the house looking out. The water terrace, located at the river, was often a main point of entry to the house since many guests arrived by boat after sailing or fishing expeditions.

The floor plan of the house is based on an L-shaped

parti, with the main living spaces laid out symmetrically about the living hall and located in the primary wing facing the water. The service areas were set at a right angle in a secondary wing. The entrance hall, located between the living and dining spaces, also led to the projecting wing, which contained a lounge, or smoking room, as well as the kitchen and service facilities. The great living hall of the house, which opened onto the waterfront terrace on one side and onto the sheltered cloister on the other, was designed to receive a breezy cross-ventilation during summer months.

A glass-enclosed rectangular cloister, or covered colonnaded walkway, creates the central garden court to the rear of the house. At the far corner of this courtyard is the entrance to the palm garden, a glass pavilion set on an axis at a diagonal to the rest of the house. The plan of the pavilion is composed of elliptical and circular forms projecting from a rectangular space. The main roof outline is that of a rectangle, and the curving projections are treated as lower bays. Both the glass-enclosed palm garden and the open garden court were planned with a southern exposure in order to obtain the maximum amount of sunlight. This plan created a protected garden environment in contrast to the open carriage court and the exposed waterfront terrace at the entrance to the house. The palm garden was originally the terminating point of the walkway around the cloister, but the guest wing and indoor tennis court structure were added later beyond the palm garden along the same diagonal axis.

The importance of academic principles of composition in the design of Idle Hour can be seen in the symmetrical layout of the main spaces about the central living hall and in the use of at least twelve organizing cross and parallel axes in the plan. In several areas the interior spaces flow out into adjacent loggias or passageways. This is seen in the living hall connections to the waterfront loggia and garden cloister and in the smoking room, where an ornamental carved wood screen defines the space while leaving it open to the adjacent circulation. The articulation of spaces in the design was also an important planning principle. To achieve this, each major room or functional area was brought forward or set in back of the space beside it so that the building could be clearly "read" on the exterior. In this aspect Idle Hour resembles the later F. W. Woolworth Estate, Winfield Hall (1916), at Glen Cove (see page 91), designed by C. P. H. Gilbert.

The stylistic detailing of Idle Hour shows a Beaux-Arts assimilation of both medieval and Renaissance design in-

28–4 (opposite) Central courtyard, showing exterior of stair hall

fluences from several different countries. The house has a prominent sloping roof with splayed, overhanging roof eaves and exposed rafter ends. Two symmetrical projecting bays, which are topped by ornate, stepped, and double-curving gable ends, show a Flemish influence and may have playfully recalled the Dutch origin of the Vanderbilt family. The rectangular form of the entrance elevation, which ends in symmetrical hipped-roofed bays, is seen in many English country houses as well. An English influence can also be seen in the interior of the house, where there are elaborate molded-plaster ceilings, exposed wood ceiling beams, and carved wood dividing screens.

The exterior walls of the house are constructed of brick with horizontal bands of limestone at the floor lines and dressed stone quoins and lintels at the door and window openings. At the second-floor level the limestone band projects out to form balcony parapets off the master bedroom suites. The central arcaded loggia off the living hall space is detailed with marble columns and circular medallions, in addition to limestone trim that recalls Italian Renaissance designs. This loggia, as well as the curvilinear gable form, is repeated on the courtyard elevation. The main staircase of the house forms a polygonal bay that also projects out into the garden courtyard. Unfortunately, the interior of this staircase was destroyed by the fire of 1974, but a pictorial record remains. The elaborate staircase was inspired by French prototypes and recalled the sixteenth-century double-staircase in the Church of St. Etienne-du-Mont in Paris. It had an ornate carved wood balustrade combining heraldic patterns and Renaissance details.

Richard Morris Hunt (1827–1895), who designed the original Idle Hour and several of the estate's outbuildings, was the first American architect to attend the Ecole des Beaux-Arts in Paris. He later designed many of the most famous projects of the Vanderbilt family, including Marble House (1892) in Newport, Rhode Island, also for William K. Vanderbilt, Sr.; The Breakers (1892–95) in Newport for Cornelius Vanderbilt; and Biltmore (1888–95) in Asheville, North Carolina, for George W. Vanderbilt. Hunt's elder son Richard Howland Hunt (1862–1931) was educated at Massachusetts Institute of Technology and at the Ecole des Beaux-Arts. He worked with his father, at first as his associate, later carrying on the firm after his father's death in 1895. He completed much of the work Richard Morris Hunt had begun on the main portion of the Metropolitan Museum of Art (1895–1902) in New

York. In 1901 his younger brother Joseph Hunt (1870–1924), who also attended the Ecole, joined him to form the firm of Hunt & Hunt, Architects. Together, they became well known for their designs of large urban and country houses, including the George W. Vanderbilt Residence (c. 1906) in New York City and the Howard Gould/Daniel Guggenheim Estate, Castlegould (1909), in Sands Point (see page 58). They also planned campus facilities for several colleges, including the Alumni Building and Williams Hall at Vassar College, Poughkeepsie, New York.

28–5 Main stairway, c. 1903

29

The Robin/Wagg/ Meyer Residence, Driftwood Manor, Baiting Hollow, near Wading River

Henry Hornbostel of Palmer & Hornbostel, architect, 1906–1908; estate now part of Wildwood State Park, administered by the Long Island State Park Commission; damaged by vandalism; building not open to the public; endangered status; park grounds open to the public; park entrance off North Wading River Road

Driftwood Manor was designed in 1906–1908 for J. G. Robin, a Wall Street investor. Robin was the model for Mr. X, a character in the story "Vanity, Vanity" by his friend Theodore Dreiser. Apparently, Dreiser had visited Robin at the time Driftwood Manor was under construction, and in his story he gives a beautiful and fitting description of the house—"It was so unpretentiously pretentious, so really grand in a limited and yet poetic way."

The estate was later owned by Alfred Wagg, another financial investor, but Wagg lost the property during the Depression. Driftwood Manor was held by several banks and mortgage companies until it was acquired by Arthur G. Meyer, whose family operated lace mills in Patchogue, Long Island, as well as both wool and lace manufacturing plants in Massachusetts. The Meyers entertained many well-known friends, including the actor Edward G. Robinson, during the summers they spent at the house. After Meyer's death in 1934, his widow maintained the house until she died in 1968, after which the Long Island State Park Commission took over the property.

The original presentation drawings for the house by architect Henry Hornbostel show a preliminary design that is very close in plan and concept to the house as it was constructed. A major change, however, was made in the roof. A high-pitched, hipped roof is shown in the early drawings. This high-pitched roof, plus the stuccoed concrete wall texture, the small door and window openings, and a projecting hexagonal tower bay, gave the early design a French Provincial character, somewhat similar to that of the Mr. and Mrs. Roderick Tower Residence at Old Westbury (see page 114). As built, however, the house has a shallow or truncated hipped roof with a simplified number of roof and wall breaks, or setbacks. The lower roof line and the streamlined elevations give the house, as built, a horizontal emphasis that is quite different from the original sketches. Hornbostel must have been pleased by the "modern" effect he achieved because he used the same design elements in several later projects, including buildings for the Carnegie Institute of Technology (1904–12), Pittsburgh, Pennsylvania.

The house is constructed of reinforced concrete walls into which ornamental shells and small stones were hand-set. The overall appearance is reminiscent of the white-stuccoed villas of the Mediterranean area. At the time of its construction new uses for concrete were being explored, both as a residential building material and as a new fire-proofing method.

The house has a linear parti. The main living spaces are axially aligned, with a service wing shifted off the main axis but paralleling it and emphasizing the length of the house. At the center of the composition an elliptically shaped living room was set within the rectangular frame of the building. It opened out onto a garden terrace that was framed on either side by open-air, covered piazzas, or porches. These porches were defined by rectangular concrete piers that, because of their unadorned geometric character, added to the modern aspect of the house. One of the porches connected to the dining room and served as a breakfast area, and the other extended off the waterfront side of the house and overlooked Long Island Sound to the north.

A hexagonal smoking room between the living room and the polygonal configuration of the dining room was designed as an interconnecting formal link. It also related to the stair hall space on the opposite side of the house, off the entrance. This designed interconnection between different forms was an important element of academic planning principles and illustrated an intentional use of "positive and negative" spaces.

29–1 Entrance or southwest elevation

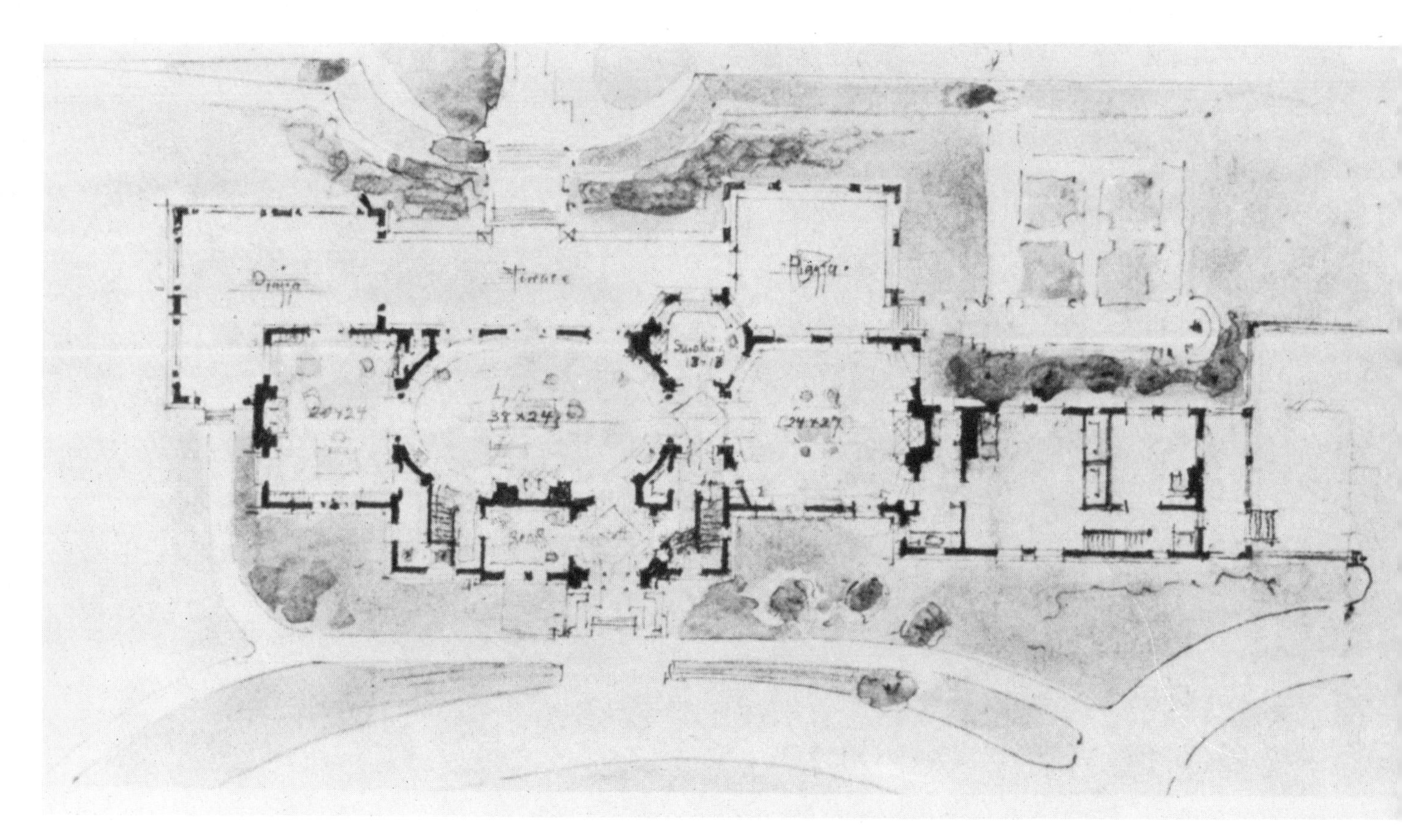
20×24
38×24
24×27

The principal designer of the firm of Palmer & Hornbostel was Henry Hornbostel (1867–1961), an architect who received his training at Columbia University (1891) and at the Ecole des Beaux-Arts in Paris (1893–97). Hornbostel made his reputation as a spectacular, large-scale designer and as an exuberant renderer. This combination of talents enabled him to win many national architectural competitions, including those for the master plan for the new campus of the Carnegie Institute of Technology (1904) in Pittsburgh, Pennsylvania; the New York State Education Building (1908) in Albany, New York; and the Queensborough Bridge (1903–1909) in New York City. He also won commissions for Hell's Gate Bridge (c. 1907) and for city halls and municipal buildings (c. 1910–12) in Pittsburgh, Pennsylvania; Wilmington, Delaware; Oakland, California; and Hartford, Connecticut. Hornbostel also made the master plans (1908–15) for the University of Pittsburgh, Northwestern University at Evanston, Illinois, and Emory University at Atlanta, Georgia.

Before World War I, Hornbostel maintained his office and teaching atelier in New York City and was affiliated with Columbia University. He was considered one of the great professors, or design critics, of the American Beaux-Arts educational system, and he also served as president of the Beaux-Arts Institute of Design in New York (see page 10). Harry Sternfeld, F.A.I.A., the eleventh Paris Prize winner (1914), and a former professor of architecture at the University of Pennsylvania, later recalled: "The office of Palmer & Hornbostel was well known to the sophisticated draftsmen of cities all over the United States. First of all, because of the tremendous volume of important projects which it handled, it seemed like the promised land for those seeking top-grade experience; secondly, it was famed for the atelier which it housed—Atelier Hornbostel—where the architectural Bohemian could study under its dynamic and successful Patron. Finally it ranked with the Bowery and Chinatown as a sight-seeing Mecca. To have visited it was a 'must' for all draftsmen of standing and sophistication."

After 1904, when Hornbostel won the competition for the Carnegie Institute of Technology campus plan, he spent much of his time in Pittsburgh, supervising the site-work, designing many of the campus structures, and eventually becoming head of the school of architecture there. Many of his students and apprentices later became well-known architects. For example, Hornbostel trained Raymond Hood, who after working for his teacher on buildings at Carnegie Tech and on the New York State Education Build-

29–2 (opposite above) Garden or northeast elevation

29–3 (opposite below) Main-floor plan. Drawing by Henry Hornbostel, architect, 1906–1908

29–4 *Garden or northeast (left) and entrance or southwest (right) elevations. Design renderings by Henry Hornbostel, architect, 1906–1908*

ing, later won the competition for the Chicago Tribune Building (1922) with a rendering very much in the spirit of Hornbostel. Hood became internationally known as one of the chief architects of Rockefeller Center (1931–40) in New York City.

Between 1901 and 1914 Hornbostel designed several country houses and urban residences in the New York area, including the William H. Moffit Estate in Islip, the Arthur S. Dwight Estate in Great Neck, the W. W. Caswell Estate in Mamaroneck, and the Countess Leary Residence on Fifth Avenue in New York City. The design for the Moffit house showed several similarities to that of Driftwood Manor, including a shallow, longitudinal, sloping roof; the use of reinforced concrete walls with flattened arched openings; and concrete piers that project above the porch roofs to form parapet walls.

Driftwood Manor is now administered by the Long Island State Park Commission. However, the state has provided no budget for caretakers, security, or maintenance of the property, and the building has been badly damaged by vandalism. The property now forms part of Wildwood State Park, and the adjacent area was originally the site of the Roland G. Mitchell Estate, Wildwood (c. 1906). Designed by McKim, Mead & White, Wildwood was acquired by the Long Island State Park Commission in 1925. No attempt to convert the main house for public purposes was made, and the building was torn down in 1934. The grounds, which had been laid out by the Olmsted Brothers (see page 162), were developed as a public park with

summer campgrounds. A barn from the estate still remains and is now used as a park administration center. Driftwood Manor, located on a wooded site overlooking the water, could easily be converted into a beautiful summer restaurant similar to the one operated at the Bayard Cutting Arboretum (see page 191). The house could easily accommodate park police or summer employees' lockers or lodgings on its upper floor.

[*Authors' note: Driftwood Manor has recently been demolished.*]

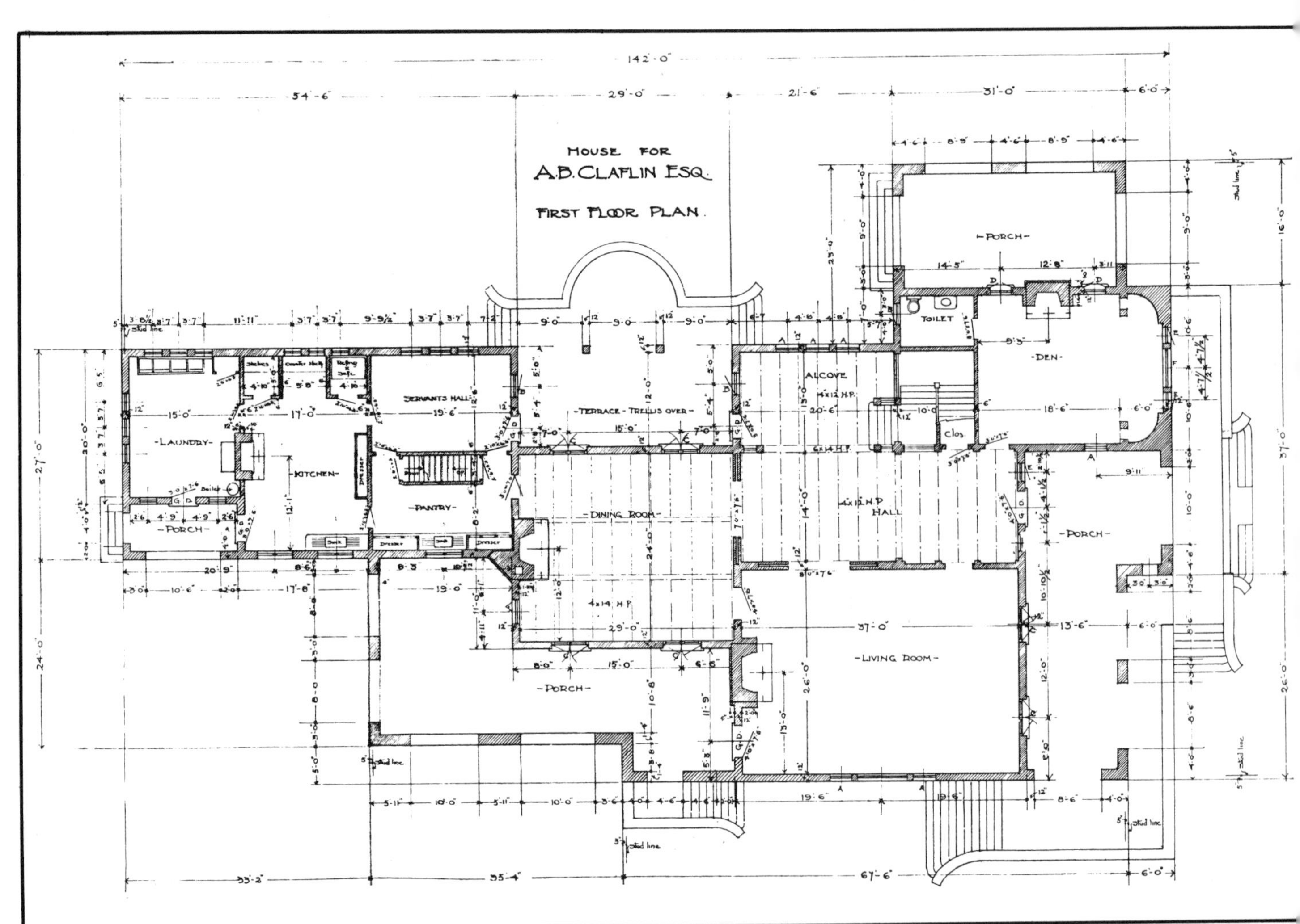
HOUSE FOR
A.B. CLAFLIN ESQ.
FIRST FLOOR PLAN.
142'-0"
-PORCH-
TOILET
-DEN-
ALCOVE
-TERRACE-TRELLIS OVER-
SERVANTS HALL
-LAUNDRY-
KITCHEN
-PANTRY-
-DINING ROOM-
HALL
-PORCH-
-PORCH-
-LIVING ROOM-
-PORCH-
Clos

30
Arthur B. Claflin Residence, Shinnecock Hills

Grosvenor Atterbury, architect, 1896–98; property now part of Southampton College Center, Long Island University; located off Montauk Highway (Route 27A)

Arthur B. Claflin was a textile manufacturer from Lakewood, New Jersey. Work began on his summer home at Shinnecock Hills, just west of Southampton, in 1896. The property had previously been owned by Mrs. William Hoyt and was distinguished by an early-eighteenth-century windmill that she had had transported to the site in 1890. Claflin commissioned a young architect, Grosvenor Atterbury, to design his new house adjacent to the old windmill and on top of a large rolling hill that looked out over the dunes toward Shinnecock Bay and the Atlantic Ocean.

The house, which was completed in 1898, can be seen for miles around because of the exposed, elevated nature of its site, and its silhouette soon became a distinctive local landmark. Nearby, also in Shinnecock Hills, was the shingled residence of William Merritt Chase, the American Impressionist painter. Chase's home, built c. 1892, has been attributed to McKim, Mead & White. His studio and art school there, originally called the Shinnecock Art School and now known as Art Village, became famous as the training center of many young and later well-known artists, including Rockwell Kent and Joseph Stella.

The Claflins maintained their summer residence in Shinnecock Hills until the Depression. The house was later converted into Tucker Mill Inn (1949), and the windmill served as a guest cottage in which playwright Tennessee Williams reportedly summered. In 1963 the property was acquired by Southampton College, and the house is now the administration center of the college campus.

The original floor plan of the main house is related to the designs of earlier Shingle Style residences. An entry terrace on the north side, opposite the waterfront elevation, opens into an alcove off a central hall. The large hall (14′ x 37′) connects all the main living spaces on the first floor, and a wide, open stair leads from the alcove to the second floor. Large double doors open directly into the living room and dining room spaces, which face the waterfront vista.

To catch the summer breezes coming off the water, the main rooms jut in and out in plan, giving each space a corner exposure or floor-through ventilation. Shaded porches, or verandas, surrounded the house, penetrating the interior rather than projecting from the exterior walls. They were treated as open-air interior rooms with views in all directions. Each major room in the house had its complementary exterior porch, and each corner was defined

30–1 (opposite above) Waterfront or south elevation, as it was originally designed

30–2 (opposite below) Main-floor plan, as originally designed by Grosvenor Atterbury, 1896–98

30–3 Waterfront or south elevation, as it looks today

by one. The porches opened onto the grounds, providing a very open and informal plan with a great sense of freedom of movement. They also provided shaded and sheltered outdoor areas, which were important on such an exposed site where only low scrubs or brushwood grew. The large and airy bedrooms on the upper floor projected in and out in plan, extending over the porches below to achieve a similar cross-ventilation.

The exterior of the house is an asymmetrical composition that is dominated by a tall hipped roof with multiple gable projections and dormers. A prominent, hipped-roofed, projecting bay defines the major living room space on the waterfront elevation. The porches were an integral part of the overall form of the house, and they were created by elongated wall piers with flat, or shallow, arches.

The entire building was raised above the sloping grade of the hill on the waterfront side to ensure uninterrupted vistas and to catch the sea breezes. The dramatic nature of the site was complemented by the high, sloping roof forms and by the balloon-like outline of the sandy-colored, stuccoed walls. The house seemed to rise up from the surrounding hills and dunes like a great ship with billowing sails looking out toward the Atlantic Ocean.

With new owners and new uses, alterations were made

to the house. The location of the entrance was shifted from the entry hall to the dining room, and the lawn in front of the dining-room porch was cut away to make room for a parking lot. The gentle, flat-arched openings in the verandas seen in early photographs were changed to semicircular arches, and the elevations were altered by additions and fire escapes. The concept of the original design is still clearly visible, however, and the true character of the building has not been lost.

Grosvenor Atterbury (1869–1956) was born in Detroit, Michigan, and educated at Yale and Columbia universities. He worked as a young draftsman in the office of McKim, Mead & White and went on to attend the Ecole des Beaux-Arts in Paris in 1894. Atterbury opened his own office after returning to the United States. His earliest commissions were several large Shingle Style and Tudor-influenced country houses (c. 1898), including the W. Swayne Residence in Shinnecock Hills and the Dr. C. C. Rice Residence in East Hampton. The Claflin Residence is very similar in plan and concept to both of these houses, although its exterior was designed with the plain, stuccoed wall surfaces that became very common in the next decade. Atterbury also designed the well-known Parrish Art Museum (c. 1897), in nearby Southampton, for Samuel Parrish, the patron of William Merritt Chase's Shinnecock Art School.

Atterbury was a contemporary of Henry Hornbostel, and like him he won several competitions as a young architect. His design for the Claflin Residence resembles Hornbostel's early designs for the Robin/Wagg/Meyer Residence, Driftwood Manor (1906–1908), in Baiting Hollow (see page 216), in the use of a prominent hipped roof, flat-arched openings, and stuccoed walls. However, Hornbostel used later design characteristics in his emphasis on the horizontal and in his employment of a simple rectangular composition. Following Hornbostel's example, Atterbury's plans for the H. O. Havemeyer Estate (c. 1909) in Islip used concrete, unadorned planar walls and piers and an uncompromising abstract geometry of form. As an Early Modern house, the Havemeyer Estate was one of his most published and widely admired projects.

Atterbury designed the John S. Phipps Residence (c. 1904) in New York City and also planned the Phipps Model Houses, Tenement #1 (c. 1906), a prototype low-cost housing project in New York City. He developed a long-standing interest in the planning and cost problems of housing and designed early forms of prefabricated building systems. Atterbury was the chief architect, along

with landscape planner Frederick Law Olmsted, Jr., of Forest Hills Gardens (c. 1913) in Queens, New York City, still considered a landmark American residential and commercial development.

Later in his career Atterbury planned several large-scale medical and institutional facilities, including the Johns Hopkins Psychiatric Clinic and Medical Library at Baltimore, Maryland, and the School of Medicine at Yale University, New Haven, Connecticut. He also served as a professor of architecture at Yale University School of Architecture. One of Atterbury's apprentices was a young architect, Elizabeth Coit, who shared his interest in planning and analyzing the problems of New York City housing projects. Elizabeth Coit became famous for this work and was one of the pioneers in the development of current American social theories concerning housing design.

30–4 (opposite) Early-eighteenth-century windmill, moved to its present site in 1890

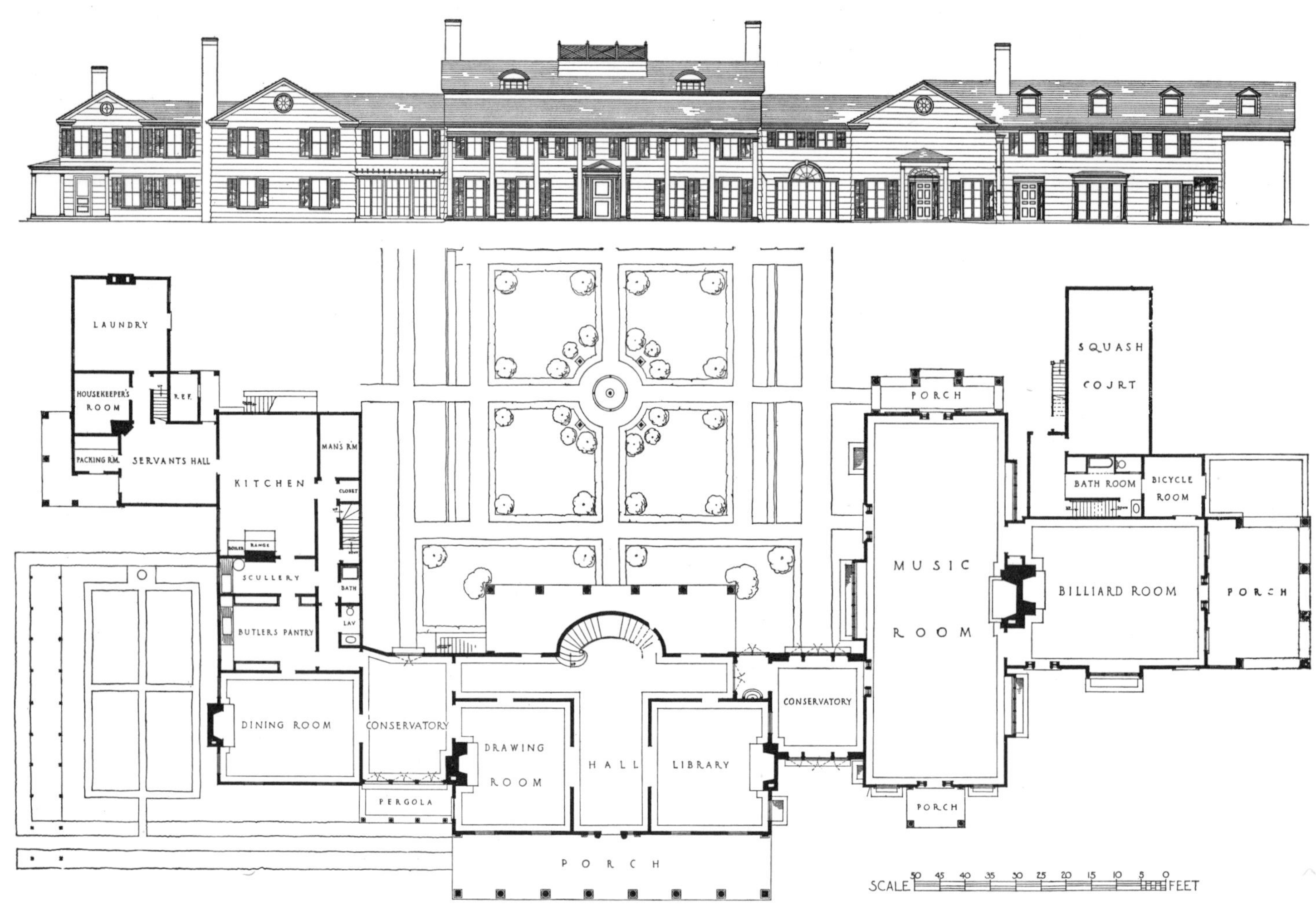
LAUNDRY
HOUSEKEEPER'S ROOM
REF.
PACKING RM.
SERVANTS HALL
KITCHEN
MAN'S RM.
CLOSET
BOILER
RANGE
SCULLERY
BATH
LAV.
BUTLERS PANTRY
DINING ROOM
CONSERVATORY
PERGOLA
DRAWING ROOM
HALL
LIBRARY
CONSERVATORY
PORCH
PORCH
MUSIC ROOM
PORCH
SQUASH COURT
BATH ROOM
BICYCLE ROOM
BILLIARD ROOM
PORCH
SCALE 50 45 40 35 30 25 20 15 10 5 0 FEET

31
James L. Breese Estate, The Orchard, Southampton

McKim, Mead & White, architects, 1898, 1906; estate formerly occupied by the Nyack Boys' School; property for sale; not open to the public; status endangered; may be seen from Hill Street

James Lawrence Breese (1854–1934), although educated to be an engineer, became a partner in the Wall Street brokerage firm of Breese and Smith. He was an enthusiastic sportsman who participated in auto races, and at one time he constructed and drove his own racing cars. He also experimented with photography and became one of the first photographers in the United States to work with color-film processing, experiments he conducted at his studio in New York City.

Breese's far-ranging interests must have been a common bond with architect Stanford White, who became a close friend and who designed the Breese Estate, The Orchard (1898–1906), in Southampton. Breese was also interested in architecture and reportedly had considered at one time becoming an architect himself.

The Orchard has had several owners other than the Breese family. It was first purchased by C. E. Merrill, a stockbroker, financier, and senior partner in the brokerage firm of Merrill, Lynch, Pierce, Fenner and Smith. The house was subsequently owned by Amherst College, and until recently it was occupied by the Nyack Boys' School, a private school in Southampton. The estate property is now for sale.

James L. Breese acquired the property in the 1890s from the Drake family. In 1898 he commissioned Stanford White to design a summer home for his family that would incorporate the existing farmhouse, built c. 1858. (Both dates—1858 and 1898—are inscribed over the entrance to the house.) This older building appears to be the present west wing of the main residence, and it now contains the dining and kitchen areas.

The central block of the house, with its broad Doric-columned portico, contains the entry and the central hall, flanked by the drawing room and study. An open elliptical stair leads from the north end of the hall to the bedrooms on the upper floor. In 1906 a large addition was constructed. This east wing includes the music room, or ballroom, a billiard room, and an open, double-level porch. Both the original west wing, or dining and service area, and the east wing are separated from the central block of the house by glass-enclosed and trellised garden rooms, or conservatories. One serves as a breakfast area off the dining room, the other as a palm court off the ballroom.

The design was influenced by Georgian Colonial and Federal period prototypes. These influences may be seen in the generally symmetrical massing of the plan and composition and in the use of a central-hall parti with sym-

31–1 (opposite above) Entrance or south elevation, detail showing main entrance

31–2 (opposite below) Main-floor plan and entrance or south elevation

metrical double chimneys, features that were common to Southern Colonial country houses. Classical details and elements include the Doric-columned porticoes topped by a triangular pediment on the eastern elevation, the balustraded roof access above the entry, dormers topped by segmental pediments, and the circular or bull's-eye windows at the roof gable ends. Palladian windows are used in the east-wing conservatory and in the elliptical stair-hall bay facing the gardens. The north or garden elevation is characterized by a series of projecting wings, also with gable roofs. The kitchen and service projections are to one side of the garden, and the music room and squash court projections are to the other side.

The exterior of the music room, or ballroom, appears as a modest, two-story-high wing with a small entry porch and a fanlight over the entrance door. Although the music room is actually the largest space within the house, it appears subservient in elevation to the central block of the house, which has an imposing main portico. The subdued exterior of the music room also helps to achieve the balanced appearance of the elevation. The enormous interior space of the music room is almost seventy-five feet in length, and it is designed with Elizabethan and Renaissance elements. Linen-fold wood paneling covers the wall surfaces, which formerly were hung with tapestries on either side of the great stone fireplace. The two-story-high ceiling is designed with exposed and articulated wood beams and with elaborately carved coffered panels.

The grand scale of the music room contrasts dramatically with the modest character of a typical Colonial country house. The other rooms are defined by changes in ceiling height, in scale, and in stylistic detail. They show a freedom from the strict historic use of style and an emphasis on the interrelationship of spaces in the plan. The progression or sequence through these spaces is another important characteristic of Beaux-Arts planning.

The master plan for the site is designed along a north-south axis. Almost 700 feet in length, it is the organizing spine of the house as well as of the entire property. This axis begins at the entrance drive off Hill Street, extends north along the drive to the front entry portico and through the central hall of the house, and exits through the the projecting bay of the elliptical stair, which identifies it on the garden elevation of the house. The second floor overlooks the formal garden that was designed to continue this axial progression, and the garden is framed by an elaborate system of pergolas. A fountain and pool are located at the intersection of the major axis and a minor, or east-west,

axis. Beyond the end of the garden the linear vista was originally continued by a farm quadrangle that ran to the far boundary of the property, appropriately called White's Lane.

McKim, Mead & White introduced and popularized the Georgian Colonial, or Colonial Revival, Style during the late nineteenth century. The partners' joint trip through New England in 1877 was spent sketching and documenting examples of Colonial architecture. Later, in Newport, Rhode Island, they designed the H. A. C. Taylor House

31–3 Music room, c. 1915

31–4 *View from the northeast*

(1885–86), now demolished, which was one of their earliest fully developed Colonial Revival houses. Its formal, symmetrical plan, designed with classical open porticoes, expressed the desire for a system of order that contrasted with the sometimes picturesque tendencies of the Shingle Style and with the ornate, overscaled tendencies of the French Château Style.

The Colonial Revival James L. Breese Estate in Southampton is the last existing example of the Long Island estates designed and published by McKim, Mead & White in their monograph of 1915 *(A Monograph of the Works of McKim, Mead & White, 1879–1915)* as their most important projects. The others published in the monograph have been demolished. These included the French Renaissance château for Clarence H. Mackay, Harbor Hill (1902–1905) in Roslyn (see fig. I–26), whose remaining gatehouse now belongs to a swimming club, and the Edwin D. Morgan Estate (1891–1900) in Wheatley Hills (see fig. I–24), whose three remaining corner fragments have been turned into development houses. The Morgan Estate was also designed in the Colonial Revival Style and was one of McKim, Mead & White's largest commissions on Long Island. The main house was constructed of naturally weathered shingles and classically detailed white trim, and it was composed of a formal, rectangular central-hall block with two lower, symmetrical side wings. The gable roofs of the wings were perpendicular to the main roof line, and their splayed, overhanging eaves recalled early Dutch Colonial farmhouses in the New York area. In 1898–1900 this complex was extended into a quadrangle with additional buildings—a chapel, poolhouse, gymnasium, and service structures. Although the inspiration of a Colonial farm group was maintained, the scale was that of the largest Newport mansions.

Other houses by McKim, Mead & White not published in the 1915 monograph still exist; however, the James L. Breese Estate was and remains a unique project. At present it is on the endangered list. Potential future uses might easily accommodate several functions, including those of an educational facility, historical museum, community arts center, and/or historic restoration project similar to those maintained by the Newport Preservation Society in Newport, Rhode Island.

The firm of McKim, Mead & White is discussed and mentioned throughout this volume. It ranks as one of the most prominent Beaux-Arts architectural firms in American cultural history. Many young architects considered it essential to serve their apprenticeship at McKim, Mead & White. Several of these later went on to establish well-known offices of their own. The apprentices, designers, and associates that began their career with this firm include John M. Carrère, Thomas Hastings, Cass Gilbert, George F. Babb (later of Babb, Cook & Willard), Terence Koen (later of Hoppin & Koen), Henry Bacon, John Galen Howard, and Arthur L. Harmon, later of Shreve, Lamb & Harmon, the architects of the Empire State Building (1931) in New York City.

Charles Follen McKim (1847–1909), born in Pennsylvania, was educated at Harvard University and graduated from the Ecole des Beaux-Arts in 1870. McKim apprenticed under H. H. Richardson in the New York office of Gambrill & Richardson, and he began his own practice in 1872. William Rutherford Mead (1846–1928), born in Vermont and educated at Amherst College, served his apprenticeship under architect, critic, and historian Russell Sturgis, in whose atelier McKim had also worked at one time. Mead traveled and studied in Italy from 1871 to 1873 and became McKim's partner in 1877. Stanford

White (1853–1906), born in New York and educated at New York University, also received his architectural training under H. H. Richardson. White traveled extensively in France and through Europe, joining McKim and Mead as a partner in 1879 at the age of twenty-six.

In addition to the Breese, Morgan, and Mackay estates, some of the other country homes and estates that the firm designed on Long Island include a Queen Anne and Shingle styles residence for Mrs. Anna C. Alden (1879–80) at Lloyd Neck (see page 240), now privately owned; the Association Houses (1882–84) at Montauk Point (see page 237), now privately owned; the Roland G. Mitchell Estate, Wildwood (c. 1906), at Wading River (see page 220), now demolished; the William C. Whitney Estate (c. 1902) in Old Westbury (see page 109), the main house now demolished; and the Mrs. K. A. Wetherill Residence (1894–96) in St. James (see page 28), now privately owned. Stanford White's own home, Box Hill (1892–1902), in St. James (see fig. I–25), continues to be owned by the White family.

Some of the nonresidential projects designed by McKim, Mead & White on Long Island include the Garden City Hotel (1898–1901) in Garden City (see fig. A–2), now demolished; the Trinity Episcopal Church (1906) in Roslyn (see fig. A–3); the Shinnecock Hills Golf Club (1895) in Shinnecock Hills; and Westbrook Farm (1895), for William Bayard Cutting, in Great River (see page 191).

The firm designed many other important country estates in the northeastern United States: the Charles J. Osborn Estate (1884–85) in Mamaroneck, New York (a portion still exists as a private club); the Whitelaw Reid Estate, Ophir Court (1893), in Purchase, New York (now Manhattanville College); the Frelinghuysen Residence (1912) in Morristown, New Jersey (now a museum); the Frederick W. Vanderbilt Mansion (1899) at Hyde Park, New York (now owned by the National Park Service); the Herman Oelrichs Residence, Rosecliff (1900–1902), in Newport, Rhode Island (see fig. I–11), now owned by the Newport Preservation Society; the A. A. Pope Residence (1898) in Farmington, Connecticut (now the Hill-Stead Museum); and the Joseph H. Choate Estate, Naumkeg Gardens, in Stockbridge, Massachusetts.

A large number of the firm's buildings were erected in New York City, where some of their most famous projects still exist—the Pierpont Morgan Library (1906) on East Thirty-sixth Street (open to the public); the Henry Villard Houses (1882–85) on Madison Avenue (endangered); the master plan for Columbia University and the design for Columbia's Low Library (1895–97); and the New York City Municipal Building (1912), near City Hall. The firm also designed several club buildings in addition to private residences—the University Club (1899) at Fifty-fourth Street and Fifth Avenue; the Harvard Club (1902, 1915) on West Forty-fourth Street; the Metropolitan Club (1894) on East Sixtieth Street; and the Racquet and Tennis Club (1915) on Park Avenue. In many respects McKim, Mead & White created the physical appearance of New York City at the turn of the century. Even today many people think of their buildings when they are asked to describe the most distinctive physical landmarks of the city.

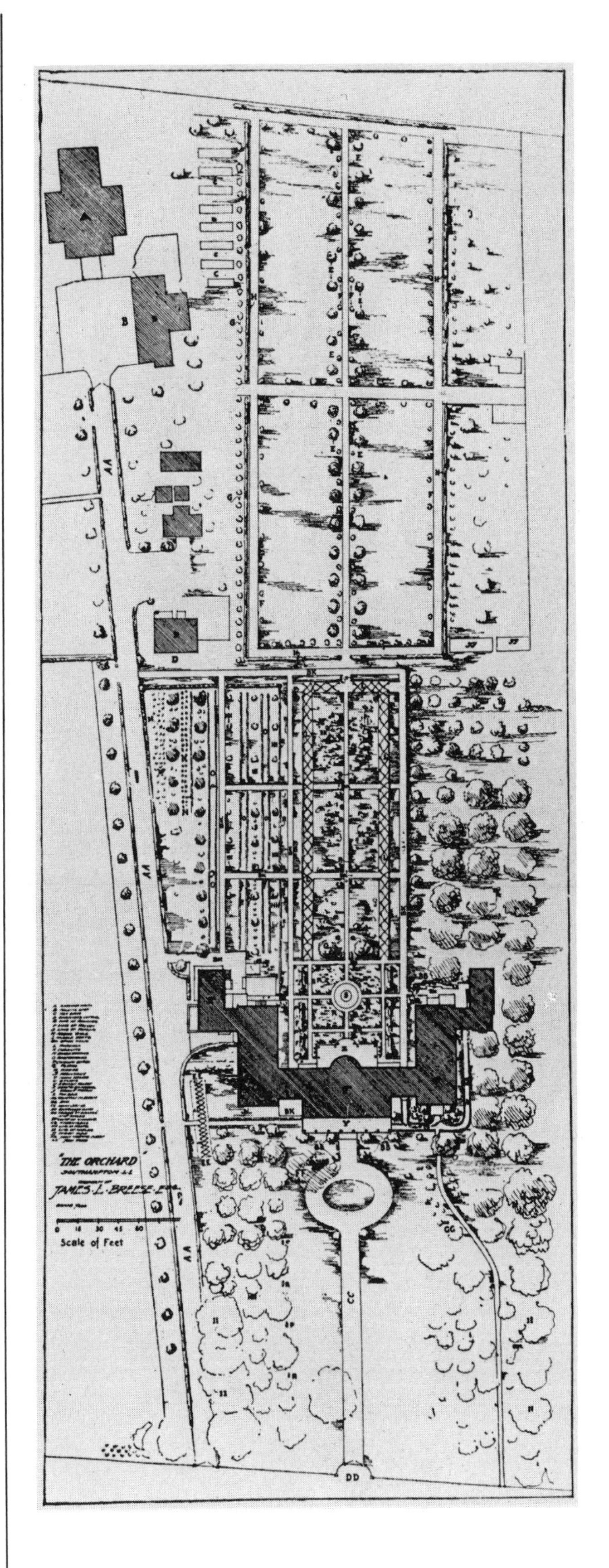

31–5 Site plan

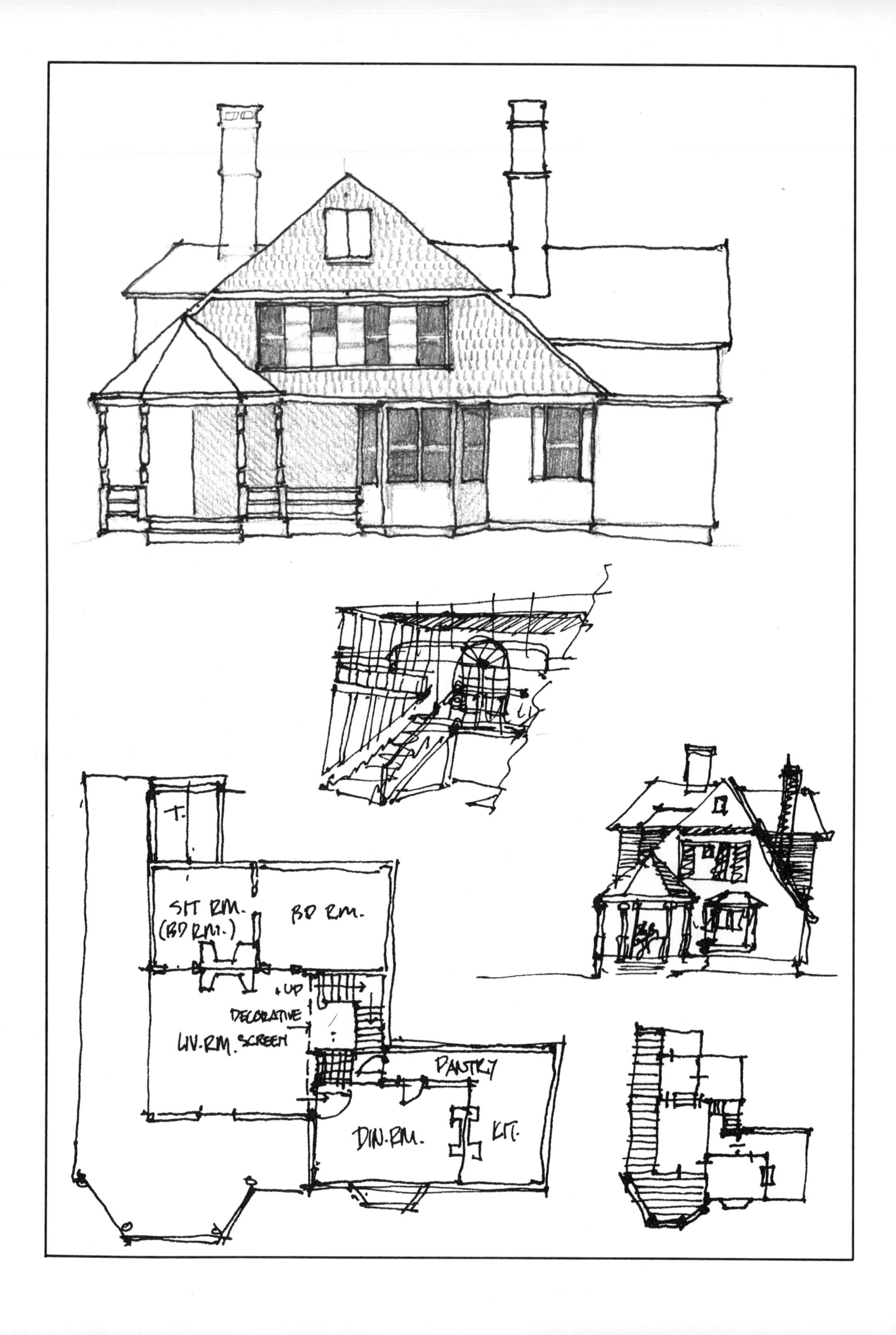

T.
SIT RM.
(BD RM.)
BD RM.
UP
DECORATIVE
SCREEN
LIV. RM.
PANTRY
DIN. RM.
KIT.

32
The Association Houses, Montauk Point

McKim, Mead & White, architects, 1882–84; landscaping attributed to Frederick Law Olmsted; a development of privately owned houses, except for Sharon's Inn (operated by Mr. and Mrs. Frank Hourtal), open during the summer as a tourist inn; located off Ditch Plains Road

Arthur W. Benson was a wealthy New York financier who developed much of the Bensonhurst section of Brooklyn. He acquired two hundred acres of property in the Ditch Plains area of Montauk Point in 1879. There he and a group of friends from Brooklyn and Manhattan built fishing and hunting cottages that overlooked the ocean, along with a central clubhouse known as the Montauk Association. Between 1882 and 1884 McKim, Mead & White designed individual cottages for Henry G. deForest, Alexander E. Orr, Henry Sanger, Alfred M. Hoyt, William L. Andrews, and Dr. Cornelius R. Agnew. In 1882 the firm also designed a central-hall clubhouse, which was destroyed by fire in 1933. The naturalistic landscape design surrounding the houses has been attributed to Frederick Law Olmsted.

In the 1920s the cottages were bought by developer Carl Fisher and several of his friends. Fisher envisioned a large tourist resort at Montauk Point and built a high office-building headquarters, called Fisher's Tower, in the center of Montauk. He also constructed a large Tudor-styled resort hotel, the Montauk Manor Hotel (c. 1926), on Montauk Point (see fig. A–4), which was designed by Schultze & Weaver, the architects of the Waldorf-Astoria Hotel in New York City. The Manor has recently been converted into apartments.

The Association Houses at Montauk Point are under consideration for designation as a national historic district. Weathered by constant, heavy exposure to winds and ocean spray, they are protected only by dunes and by rocky cliffs that rise high above the water. The cottages of the Association are still privately owned, with one exception, Sharon's Inn. Operated by Frank and Helen Hourtal, the inn is open during the summer months. At Montauk Point, at the very end of Long Island, one thus has the surprising and unanticipated opportunity of spending a summer night in a cottage planned by McKim, Mead & White.

Large areas of natural vegetation, including low-lying bushes and trees, separate the cottages. The original character of the rolling dunes with their protective scrub growth has been maintained. Although the designs of the individual cottages vary in plan, they are related by several common features—their exterior surfaces of shingled and clapboard sidings, and their overall physical massing, which is based on a square central section two stories tall with a prominent, sloping gable roof. On the first floor the central square includes the main living areas and an elaborate open stair hall. These areas are defined by

32–1 (opposite) Sharon's Inn, one of the Association Houses. Drawing of east elevation (above) and sketches of main-floor plan, stair hall, and east elevation (below)

32–2 *Association Houses, view from the south*

screened openings and by fireplace masses. Lower projecting spaces include the kitchen and service areas, with a large porch opening off the main block. The wide gable roofs, which appear on all of the cottages, as well as the deeply recessed porches and the prominent chimneys seem to anchor the buildings to the ground, while leaving the shifting character of the sand dunes undisturbed.

The shingled roof and wall surfaces of the cottages were weathered naturally with painted trim. Sharon's Inn has been painted white, but several of the other cottages have maintained their natural finishes. A broad, continuous porch runs along the front of the inn, with a polygonal projection locating the main entrance. This projection is echoed by the bay window of the dining room. Both the porch roof and the entrance projection extend the line or slope of the main roof. This plane dominates the form of the house and is punctuated by several hipped-roofed dormers of varying sizes that are sheathed in shingles.

These shingles were originally the same color and texture as those of the roof and thus created a continuous horizontal roofscape underlined by the recessed main porch. The window opening in one of these dormers has been altered and enlarged.

The floor plan of the inn is based on a combined entry hall, living hall, and stair hall that creates a major interior space that contrasts with the small and sealed appearance of the exterior. The living hall, with its large fireplace, is at once spacious and informal, and this room ties together all of the main living functions of the house, at the same time extending outward in several different directions. To one side of the living hall are the dining and kitchen areas and to the other are the sitting room and bedroom, or study, areas. The living hall extends out to the surrounding veranda on two sides and into the stair hall space, the latter framed by turned-wood screens. Both the open stair hall and the exterior porch are treated as extensions of the liv-

32–3 Sharon's Inn, east elevation

ing hall. This shared flow of spaces and this openness in plan were characteristic of the Shingle Style and were appropriate to an informal life-style featuring outdoor activities.

The cottages combine Queen Anne and Shingle Style design elements. The Queen Anne characteristics include the use of clapboard and shingled surfaces, with clapboards below and shingles above, and articulated wall breaks that employ changes in the exterior surfacing at each story level. Windows are usually located at these wall projections or indentations. The small-paned sash patterns of the dining-room bay windows and of the windows facing the veranda are typical Queen Anne details. The interior wood paneling at the front door and entryway and the use of turned woodwork for columns and balusters are also characteristic of this style. The Shingle Style elements include the continuous surfaces of shingles on the upper walls and roof, with the main roof gable encompassing the porch roof, and the use of grouped or interconnected windows.

Other design details have become identified with the work of Stanford White and the firm of McKim, Mead & White. Distinctive wood spindled screens, used to define interior spaces without separating them by walls, form part of the stair hall. The treatment of the stair hall includes a high arched window at the landing, with an eyebrow-dormer light above and vertically grooved wide-board wainscoting on the walls. A sitting nook is also part of the stair hall composition at the ground-floor level. Distinctive exterior detailing includes windows interconnected by coffered wood panels and by ornamental changes in the cut-shingle patterns. This detailing may be seen on the largest of the roof dormers on the main elevation, in which the window openings are interconnected by triangular- and diamond-cut shingle patterns and by curved cuts in the line of shingles above the windows connecting them to the fascia strip at the roof line.

Some of the design details can be associated with the work of Stanford White, but the overall designs of the Association Houses resemble the drawings of Queen Anne cottages made by Charles F. McKim in the 1870s when he was still associated with Gambrill & Richardson. These drawings are on file at the New-York Historical Society.

McKim, Mead & White also designed several other projects on Long Island about the same time that the Association Houses were being planned. These included the Mrs. Anna C. Alden Residence, Fort Hill (1879–80), in Lloyd Neck, planned by McKim, Mead & Bigelow (the firm's name before White became an official partner), and the Walter C. Tuckerman Residence (1881–82) in Oyster Bay. In the Alden house the central, gable-roofed bay of the entrance elevation is similar in proportion to that of several of the Montauk cottages, as are the clapboard and shingled wall surfaces and the employment of turned-wood screens.

In Newport, Rhode Island, the Samuel Tilton Residence (1881–82) and the Isaac Bell Residence, Edna Villa (1881–82), also show some similarities in detail. The Tilton house has a wide gable-roof pitch with similar window treatments on the exterior and an open interior stair hall with spindled wood screens and vertical board paneling. The Bell house is designed with elongated and articulated porches on the exterior and with a spacious central living hall combined with an adjacent open stair hall on the interior. At about the same time the firm designed the Robert Goelet Residence (1882–83) in Newport and the Newport Casino (1879–81). These projects, though much larger in scale than the Association Houses, also show related design elements, including the use of ornamental cut-shingle patterns and carved wood panels and, in the Goelet house, the characteristic central living hall. Additional information on McKim, Mead & White's work is given in the article on the James L. Breese Estate, The Orchard, at Southampton (see page 229).

32–4 Sharon's Inn, stair hall

Chronological Listing of the Estates

(arranged by date of construction, 1882–1932)

1882–84	The Association Houses, Montauk Point; McKim, Mead & White, architects; Frederick Law Olmsted, landscape architect (attributed)
1884–86 1905	Theodore Roosevelt Residence, Sagamore Hill, Oyster Bay; Lamb & Rich, architects; 1905 addition, C. Grant La Farge, architect
c. 1885–90	Southside Sportsmen's Club, Oakdale; Isaac H. Green, architect
1886	William Bayard Cutting Estate, Westbrook, Great River; Charles C. Haight, architect; Frederick Law Olmsted, landscape architect
1895	Westbrook Farm, farm group of the William Bayard Cutting Estate, Westbrook, Great River; Stanford White, architect (attributed)
1895 1919	Lloyd Bryce/Childs Frick Estate, Clayton, Roslyn Harbor; Ogden Codman, Jr., architect; 1919 additions, Sir Charles Carrick Allom, architect; Marian C. Coffin, 1930, landscape architect
1896–98	Arthur B. Claflin Residence, Shinnecock Hills; Grosvenor Atterbury, architect
1898 1906	James L. Breese Estate, The Orchard, Southampton; McKim, Mead & White, architects
1898–99	William C. Whitney Racing Stables and Gymnasium, Old Westbury; George A. Freeman, architect
1899	William K. Vanderbilt, Sr., Estate, Idle Hour, Oakdale; Richard Howland Hunt, architect
1902 1909	Howard Gould/Daniel Guggenheim Estate, Castlegould, Sands Point; 1902, stables and outbuildings, Augustus N. Allen, architect; 1909, Hunt & Hunt, architects
1903–1904	Egerton L. Winthrop, Jr., Estate, Syosset; Delano & Aldrich, architects
c. 1904	Foxhall Keene/William Grace Holloway Estate, Old Westbury; George A. Freeman and Francis G. Hasselman, architects; Charles W. Leavitt, landscape architect
1906–24	John S. Phipps Estate, Westbury House, Old Westbury; George Crawley, architect; Alfred C. Bossom and Edward Hinkle,

	associate architects; 1911 addition, Horace Trumbauer, architect; Jacques Gréber, landscape consultant
1906–1908	The Robin/Wagg/Meyer Residence, Driftwood Manor, Baiting Hollow, near Wading River; Henry Hornbostel of Palmer & Hornbostel, architect
1910–11	George McKesson Brown Estate, Huntington; Clarence Luce, architect
1912	F. Ambrose Clark Racing Stables, Old Westbury; Rogers & Zogbaum, architects
1912	Herbert L. Pratt Estate, The Braes, Glen Cove; James Brite, architect; James Leal Greenleaf, landscape architect
1916	F. W. Woolworth Estate, Winfield Hall, Glen Cove; C. P. H. Gilbert, architect
1916	Henri Bendel/Walter P. Chrysler Estate, Kings Point; Henry Otis Chapman, architect; Charles W. Leavitt, c. 1929, landscape architect
1916–17	Alfred I. Du Pont/Mrs. Frederick Guest Estate, Templeton, Brookville; Carrère & Hastings, architects
c. 1917 1929	William S. Barstow Residence, Kings Point; original architect unknown; 1929 addition, Greville Rickard, architect
c. 1917 1926	The Robinson/Gossler/Hutton Residence, Brookville; John Russell Pope, architect; Ellen B. Shipman, c. 1926, landscape architect
1919	William R. Coe Estate, Planting Fields, Upper Brookville; Walker & Gillette, architects; Olmsted Brothers, landscape architects
1921	Marjorie Merriweather Post/Edward F. Hutton Estate, Hillwood, Brookville; Hart & Shape, architects; Marian C. Coffin, landscape architect
1923	Harry F. Guggenheim Estate, Falaise, Sands Point; Frederick J. Sterner, architect; Polhemus & Coffin, associate architects
1924	Mr. and Mrs. Roderick Tower Residence, Old Westbury; Delano & Aldrich, architects
c. 1925	Marshall Field III Estate, Caumsett, Lloyd Neck; John Russell Pope, architect; Alfred Hopkins and Warren & Wetmore,

	associate architects; Marian C. Coffin, landscape architect
1927–28	J. Randolph Robinson Residence, Brookville; William L. Bottomley, architect
1928 1934–36	William K. Vanderbilt, Jr., Estate, Eagle's Nest, Centerport; Warren & Wetmore, architects
1929	Mrs. Christian R. Holmes Estate, The Chimneys, Sands Point; Edgar I. Williams, architect
1932	Mrs. Daniel Guggenheim Residence, Mille Fleurs, Sands Point; Polhemus & Coffin, architects

Appendix/Other Beaux-Arts Buildings on Long Island

A study of the thirty-two estates on Long Island discussed and illustrated in this guide will have given some measure of the richness and diversity of Beaux-Arts architecture in this field. A brief look at some representative examples of nonresidential Beaux-Arts architecture that developed concurrently with the estates on Long Island will serve to give a more complete picture of Beaux-Arts architecture during the period of estate building.

These examples reflect and extend the historic development of styles illustrated in the estates, as well as incorporate characteristic variations that express the public, ecclesiastic, or commercial nature of the individual facilities. Many of the architects of these buildings, beginning with Richard Morris Hunt, had either a direct Beaux-Arts education or were trained under graduates of the Ecole des Beaux-Arts. This academic background is described in detail in the Introduction (see pages 9–12).

The Shingle Style and Tudor design influences on Long Island, beginning in the 1870s and 1880s, have been illustrated in this guide in the articles on the Theodore Roosevelt Residence, Sagamore Hill, at Oyster Bay (see page 163) and on the William Bayard Cutting Estate, Westbrook, at Great River (see page 191). The influences of these styles may also be seen in Richard Morris Hunt's design for St. Mark's Church (1878–80) in Islip (see fig. A–1); in the Soldiers' and the Sailors' Memorial Building (1891) in Huntington, designed by Henry Bacon, later the architect of the Lincoln Memorial, Washington, D.C.; and in the later projects of Aymar Embury, including his design for the East Hampton Public Library (c. 1912).

The widespread influence of H. H. Richardson's work on Long Island may be seen in the Brooklyn Waterworks (c. 1888–1910), located near Freeport, which may have been the work of architect Frank Freeman. Freeman also designed the Brooklyn Fire Department Headquarters (1892) on Jay Street, as well as the Eagle Warehouse (1910), also in Brooklyn. Other buildings on Long Island in which the Richardsonian-Romanesque style was employed include the Pratt Institute Free Library (1896) in Brooklyn, designed by William B. Tubby, as well as the main building of Pratt Institute (c. 1887) and the Ward Clock Tower (1895), in Roslyn, both of which were planned by Lamb & Rich, the architects of the Theodore Roosevelt Residence, Sagamore Hill, in Oyster Bay (see page 163).

The Shingle Style was later combined with Colonial Revival design elements as in Isaac H. Green's Southside Sportsmen's Club (c. 1885–90), at Oakdale (see page

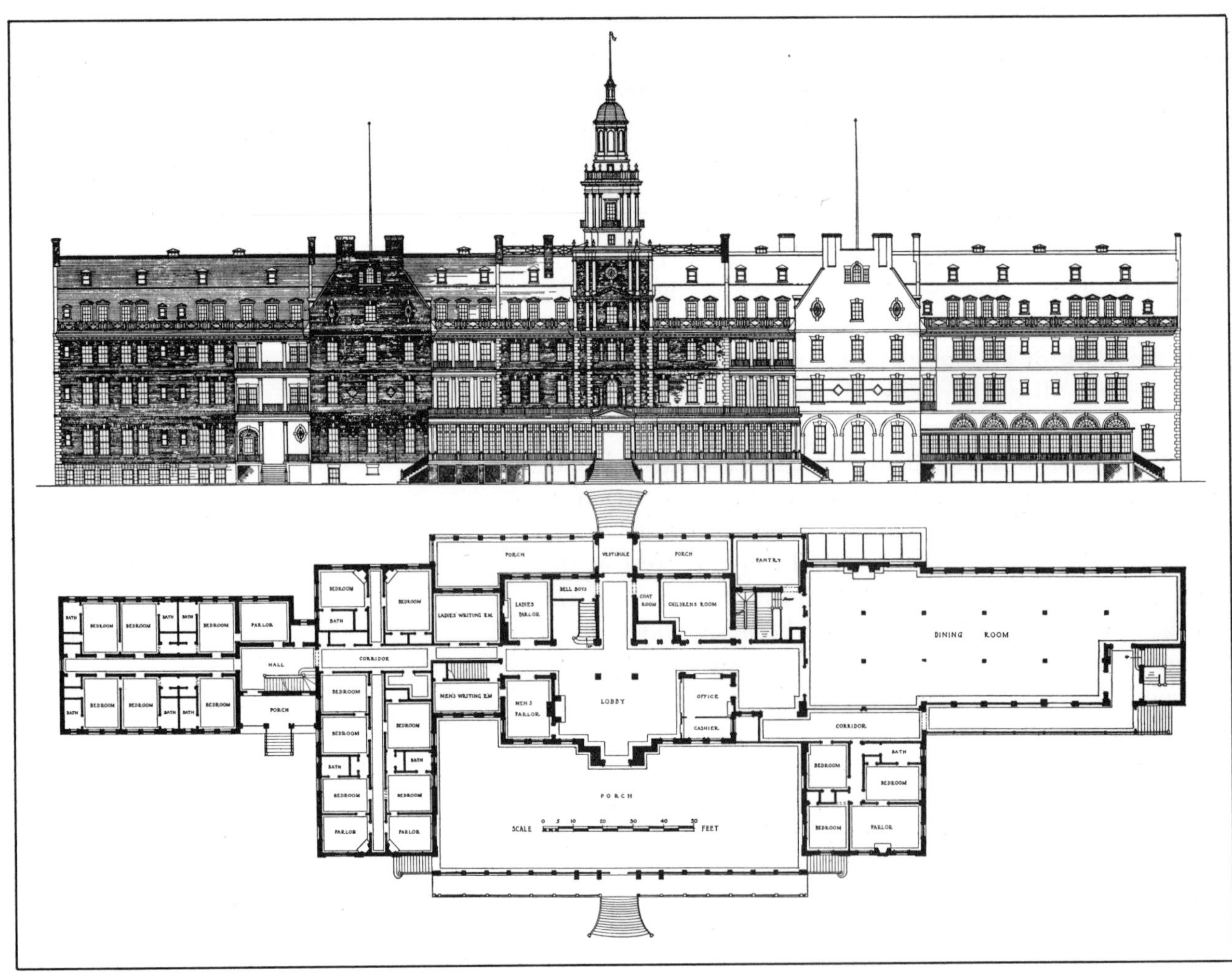
PORCH
VESTIBULE
PORCH
PANTRY
BEDROOM
BATH
LADIES WRITING RM.
LADIES PARLOR
BELL BOYS
COAT ROOM
CHILDRENS ROOM
DINING ROOM
PARLOR
HALL
CORRIDOR
MEN'S WRITING RM.
MEN'S PARLOR
LOBBY
OFFICE
CASHIER
CORRIDOR
PORCH
SCALE 0 5 10 20 30 40 50 FEET

203), and in the Shinnecock Hills Golf Club (1895), near Southampton, which was designed by McKim, Mead & White. The fully developed Colonial Revival Style was represented by McKim, Mead & White's now-demolished Garden City Hotel (1898–1901) at Garden City (see fig. A–2) and by some of this firm's later buildings for Adelphi College. Colonial and Palladian elements were also used in William B. Tubby's design for the Nassau County Court House (1901) in Mineola and in the work of Peabody, Wilson & Brown, including their design for the Huntington Town Hall (1912).

Although the Colonial Revival and Palladian styles became popular for the design of public buildings and estates on Long Island at the turn of the century, the Tudor and medieval styles remained influential in the planning of ecclesiastic projects, as seen in Trinity Episcopal Church (1907) in Roslyn (see fig. A–3), designed by McKim, Mead & White with great exposed wooden roof trusses. Medieval detailing could also be seen in such commercial buildings as the Doubleday, Page and Company headquarters (1910) in Garden City, planned by architects Kirby and Petit.

French and Italian Renaissance design influences on Long Island architecture were represented by the now-demolished Château des Beaux-Arts Casino (1905) in Huntington, designed by Delano & Aldrich, and by the design for the Heckscher Museum (1920), also in Huntington, by architects Maynicke and Franke. Other buildings that employed classical design elements included the Parrish Art Museum (c. 1897) at Southampton, planned by architect Grosvenor Atterbury, and the Cold Spring Harbor Laboratories (c. 1914), originally the Carnegie Institute, which was designed by Peabody, Wilson & Brown.

Subsequent Eclectic or period revival styles, such as the Eclectic Tudor Style, influenced the design of large, suburban housing developments on Long Island. A good example is Forest Hills Gardens (c. 1913) in Queens, New York City, which was planned by Grosvenor Atterbury in collaboration with the Olmsted Brothers, and another is the Kensington development (1912–16) in Great Neck, with houses designed by Aymar Embury. At the farther tip of Long Island this influence was seen in the Montauk Manor Hotel (c. 1926), designed by Schultze & Weaver, the architects of the Waldorf-Astoria Hotel in New York (see fig. A–4), and in the Maidstone Club (c. 1925) at East Hampton, designed by Roger H. Bullard.

Representative examples of the later Colonial and Georgian Eclectic styles on Long Island include the design for

A–1 (opposite above) St. Mark's Church, Islip, Long Island. Richard Morris Hunt, architect, 1878–80

A–2 (opposite below) Garden City Hotel, Garden City, Long Island. Entrance elevation and main-floor plan. McKim, Mead & White, architects, 1898–1901. The building has been demolished

A–3 (above) Sketch of Trinity Episcopal Church, Roslyn, Long Island. McKim, Mead & White, architects, 1906

the Timber Point Yacht Club (c. 1924) at Great River by Hart & Shape, which completely altered an earlier Shingle Style clubhouse. Charles M. Hart was also the architect of the Marjorie Merriweather Post/Edward F. Hutton Estate, Hillwood (1921), at Brookville (see page 138). Colonial influence may be seen in William L. Bottomley's design for the Canoe Place Inn (c. 1921), near Southampton, and in Southampton High School (c. 1914), planned by Hewitt and Bottomley.

The impact that the Art Deco and Art Moderne styles had on Long Island architecture may be seen in the design of William Van Alen for the Lido Beach Hotel (c. 1920), at Long Beach. Van Alen, a Beaux-Arts graduate and the designer of the Chrysler Building (1929–31) in New York (see fig. I–13), was in partnership with H. Craig Severance at the time. Severance & Van Alen also designed the O'Donahue Residence (c. 1918) in Huntington. Harvey Corbett, another important Beaux-Arts architect, with a well-known atelier in New York, was the planning consultant on the Jones Beach Recreational Complex (1926–32), executed by Robert Moses and the Long Island State Park Commission. Corbett, in collaboration with the State Park Commission design team headed by Herbert Magoon and Clarence Combs, employed Beaux-Arts master-planning principles in laying out this major public park.

Although the building styles employed in public architecture during the Beaux-Arts period generally paralleled those of the estates, public facilities added an additional dimension by introducing some of the more urban forms of design to Long Island. These included the Richardsonian-Romanesque style of the 1880s and 1890s and the Art Deco and Art Moderne phases of the 1920s and 1930s. These public buildings, in addition to the great estates and the country houses, have become important visual landmarks created by those Beaux-Arts–trained architects who practiced on Long Island.

Although this guide concentrates on those estates that are publicly owned and are open or visible to the public, a few examples of other estates can be mentioned here as these projects also represent the work of nationally prominent Beaux-Arts architectural firms and are historically related to the houses discussed in separate articles.

Charles A. Platt, the noted architect and landscape designer whose Beaux-Arts training included painting and sculpture, designed several large projects on Long Island. The most important include the Georgian-styled John T. Pratt Estate (1909) in Glen Cove, now a private conference center (see fig. A–5); the Francis Weld Estate (1912) in

A–4 (opposite above) Rendering of Montauk Manor Hotel, Montauk Point, Long Island, by Floyd Yewell. Schultze & Weaver, architects, c. 1926

A–5 (opposite below) John T. Pratt Estate, Glen Cove, Long Island. Charles A. Platt, architect, 1909

A–6 Drawing of Harold I. Pratt Estate, Welwyn, Glen Cove, Long Island. Babb, Cook & Willard, architects, c. 1906; alterations, Delano & Aldrich, architects, c. 1914

Huntington; the C. V. Brokaw Estate (1912) in Glen Cove; and the Ralph Pulitzer Residence (1913) in Manhasset. Three of Platt's sons, Charles C., William, and Geoffrey, trained as architects and joined their father's firm. The French Provincial-styled Frederick B. Pratt Estate, Poplar Hill (1917), in Glen Cove, now owned by a nursing home, was largely the work of William and Geoffrey Platt.

George F. Babb had worked in the 1880s with McKim, Mead & White, and his partner, Walter Cook, had graduated from the Ecole des Beaux-Arts in 1869. The Long Island projects of Babb, Cook & Willard include the original design for the Paul D. Cravath Estate (c. 1908) in Locust Valley, a building later altered into the Creek Club by Walker & Gillette, and the original Shingle Style Harold I. Pratt Estate, Welwyn (c. 1906), in Glen Cove, later (c. 1914) adapted into a Georgian design by Delano & Aldrich (see fig. A–6). Babb, Cook & Willard were also the architects of the Andrew Carnegie Mansion, now the Cooper-Hewitt Museum, in New York City.

Arthur Little received a Beaux-Arts education at Massachusetts Institute of Technology in 1875 and later studied in France. He and his partner, Herbert W. C. Browne, designed many Shingle Style and Colonial Revival houses near Boston, in addition to planning the C. E. Proctor Residence (c. 1912) in Great Neck. Wilson Eyre, a Philadelphia architect who was educated along with Arthur Little at M.I.T., designed the Roland Conklin Estate (c. 1905) in Huntington. It is now a seminary.

Francis V. L. Hoppin and Terrence A. Koen, partners

in Hoppin & Koen, had both trained at the Ecole des Beaux-Arts and had worked for McKim, Mead & White. They were the architects of Edith Wharton's Residence, The Mount, in Lenox, Massachusetts, and their work on Long Island included the Palladian design for the Ormond Smith Estate, Shoremonde (c. 1914), in Oyster Bay; the Iselin Estate (1912–13) in Upper Brookville; and the Roslyn Memorial Building (c. 1920). Howard Van Buren Magonigle, another former apprentice in McKim, Mead & White's office, designed the Isaac Guggenheim Estate, Villa Carola (c. 1920) in Sands Point; it is now the IBM Country Club.

A founder of the Beaux-Arts Institute of Design, S. B. Parkman Trowbridge graduated from Columbia University in 1886 and studied at the Ecole des Beaux-Arts. The firm of Trowbridge & Livingston, architects of the St. Regis Hotel in New York City, on Long Island designed the country manor house of George S. Brewster (c. 1919) in Brookville (now the Charter Oaks Country Club). Ernest Flagg, one of the most important Beaux-Arts architects in New York and the designer there of the Singer Office Tower (now demolished) and Scribner's Bookstore on Fifth Avenue, also planned the Frederick G. Bourne Estate (1902) at Oakdale for the president of the Singer Sewing Machine Company (see fig. A–7).

The Philadelphia architect Horace Trumbauer, whose chief designer was the black architect and Ecole graduate Julian Abele, also executed several projects on Long Is-

A–7 Frederick G. Bourne Estate, Oakdale, Long Island. Ernest Flagg, architect, 1902

A–8 Samuel A. Salvage Estate, Rynwood, Glen Head, Long Island. Roger H. Bullard, architect, c. 1928. This residence is now endangered

land. These include the Howard Brokaw Estate (c. 1920) in Brookville and the Henry C. Phipps Residence, Bonnie Blink, in Great Neck (now owned by the Great Neck Board of Education). Several other nationally prominent Beaux-Arts firms designed large estates on Long Island. John Mead Howells was the architect of the Albert G. Milbank Estate, Panfield (c. 1915), in Lloyd Neck; Howard Van Doren Shaw of Chicago designed the Davison Residence (c. 1917) in Locust Valley; F. Burrall Hoffman, Jr., architect of the James Deering Estate, Vizcaya (c. 1912), in Dade County, Florida (see fig. I–17), designed the Mrs. C. C. Rumsey Residence (c. 1916) in Wheatley Hills and planned several houses between 1914 and 1923 at Southampton and at East Hampton; Addison Mizner, the architect and planner of Palm Beach, Florida, designed his own house in Whitestone Landing (c. 1915); and Theodate Pope, a prominent woman architect who practiced in Connecticut and New York, designed the Charles C. Gates Residence (c. 1918) in Locust Valley.

Several other New York firms were noted for their projects on Long Island. Harrie T. Lindebergh, of the firm of Albro and Lindebergh, designed the Doubleday Estate (c. 1923) in Oyster Bay and the H. L. Batterman Residence (c. 1914) in Mill Neck, and James W. O'Connor designed the W. R. Grace Estate (c. 1918) in Westbury and the Sidney Mitchell Residence (c. 1926) in Locust Valley. Clinton & Russell were the architects of the Mrs. Robert L. Dodge Estate (c. 1923) in Mill Neck, and Cross & Cross planned a residence (c. 1916) for W. Seward Webb, Jr., in Manhasset and a residence for F. S. von Stade (c. 1914) in Westbury. Finally, Roger H. Bullard designed the presently endangered Samuel A. Salvage Estate, Rynwood (c. 1928), in Glen Head (see fig. A–8).

Although most of these residences remain privately owned and are not generally accessible to the public, they form an important part of the history of Beaux-Arts architecture during the Gilded Age. Together with the estates discussed and illustrated in this guide, they show the wide scope of Beaux-Arts architecture on Long Island.

Selected Bibliography

BOOKS

Wayne Andrews. *Architecture, Ambition and Americans.* New York: Macmillan, 1947

Wayne Andrews. *Architecture in New England.* Brattleboro, Vermont: Stephen Greene Press, 1973

Wayne Andrews. *Architecture in New York.* New York: Harper & Row, 1973

John C. Baker. *American Country Homes and Their Gardens.* Philadelphia: John Winston Company, 1906

Charles C. Baldwin. *Stanford White.* New York: Dodd, Mead Company, 1931

Reyner Banham. *Theory and Design in the First Machine Age.* New York: Praeger, 1960

Albert Bush-Brown. *Louis Sullivan.* New York: George Braziller, 1960

Ettore Camesasca. *History of the House.* New York: G. P. Putnam's Sons, 1971

Eugene Clute. *Drafting Room Practice.* New York: Pencil Points Press, 1928

Carl W. Condit. *American Building, Materials and Techniques from the First Colonial Settlements to the Present.* Chicago: University of Chicago Press, 1968

Marc Connelly. *The Most of John Held, Jr.* Brattleboro, Vermont: Stephen Greene Press, 1972

Marshall B. Davidson and Margot P. Brill. *The American Heritage History of Notable American Houses.* New York: American Heritage Publishing Company, Inc., 1971

Barr Ferree. *American Estates and Gardens.* New York: Munn and Company, 1904

Sir Banister Fletcher. *A History of Architecture on the Comparative Method.* New York: Charles Scribner's Sons, 1961 edition

Donald A. Fletcher. *Introduction to Architectural Design.* New York: Privately published, 1947

David Gebhard and Harriette Von Breton. *Architecture in California, 1868–1968.* Santa Barbara: University of California Press, 1968

Harmon Goldstone and Martha Dalrymple. *History Preserved, A Guide to New York City Landmarks and Historic Districts.* New York: Simon & Schuster, 1974

John F. Harbeson. *The Study of Architectural Design with Special Reference to the Program of the Beaux-Arts Institute of Design.* New York: Pencil Points Press, 1926

Thomas S. Hines. *Burnham of Chicago, Architect and Planner.* New York: Oxford University Press, 1974

Walter H. Kilham, Jr. *Raymond Hood, Architect, Form through Function in the American Skyscraper.* New York: Architectural Book Publishing Company, 1973

Esther McCoy and Randall L. Makinson. *Five California Architects.* New York: Reinhold, 1960

Massachusetts Avenue Architecture: Northwest Washington, D.C., Vol. 1. Washington, D.C.: U. S. Government Printing Office, 1973

Denys Peter Meyers and Eva Ingersoll Gatling. *The Architecture of Suffolk County.* Huntington, New York: Heckscher Museum, 1971

Monograph of the Work of Charles A. Platt. New York: Architectural Book Publishing Company, 1913

Monograph of the Works of McKim, Mead & White, 1879–1915. New York: Architectural Book Publishing Company, 1915

Charles Moore. *The Life and Times of Charles Follen McKim.* Boston and New York: Houghton Mifflin Company, 1929

Noted Long Island Homes. Babylon, New York: E. W. Howell and Company, 1933

Martin Pawley and Yukio Futagawa. *Frank Lloyd Wright, Public Buildings.* New York: Simon & Schuster, 1970

Mark L. Peisch. *The Chicago School of Architecture, Early Followers of Sullivan and Wright.* New York: Random House, 1964

Joseph Pennell. *Pen Drawing and Pen Draughtsmen.* New York: Macmillan, 1920

The Architecture of John Russell Pope. Vol. 3. New York: W. Helbrun, Inc., 1930

Portraits of Ten Country Houses by Delano & Aldrich. New York: Doubleday, 1924

Anne Randall. *Newport, A Tour Guide.* Newport, Rhode Island: Catboat Press, 1970

Frederick Ruther. *Long Island Today.* Hicksville, New York: Privately published, 1909

Vincent J. Scully, Jr. *The Shingle Style, Architectural Theory and Design from Downing to the Origins of Wright.* New Haven, Connecticut: Yale University Press, 1955

Edward J. Smits. *Long Island Landmarks.* Albany, New York: New York State Office of Planning Coordination, 1969

Edward J. Smits. *Nassau, Suburbia U.S.A.* New York: Friends of the Nassau County Museum and Doubleday, 1974

Louis H. Sullivan. *The Autobiography of an Idea.* New York: American Institute of Architects, 1924. Reprinted, Dover Press, New York, 1956

Mrs. John King Van Rensselaer and Frederick Van deWater. *The Social Ladder.* New York: Henry Holt and Company, 1924

Mariana Griswold Van Rensselaer. *Henry Hobson Richardson and His Works.* Boston: Houghton Mifflin Company, 1888. Reprinted, Dover Press, New York, 1969

Edith Wharton. *A Backward Glance.* New York: Charles Scribner's Sons, 1933

Marcus Whiffen. *American Architecture Since 1780, A Guide to the Styles.* Cambridge, Massachusetts: MIT Press, 1969

Norval White and Elliot Willensky. *A.I.A. Guide to New York City.* New York: Macmillan, 1967

Winning Designs, 1904–1963, Paris Prize in Architecture. New York: National Institute for Architectural Education, 1964

Frank Lloyd Wright. *Genius and the Mobocracy.* New York: Horizon Press, 1949. Reissued, 1971

Richard Saul Wurman and John Andrew Gallery. *Man-made Philadelphia, A Guide to Its Physical & Cultural Environment.* Cambridge, Massachusetts: MIT Press, 1972

GENERAL REFERENCES

American Institute of Architects' Members' Directory. Washington, D.C.: American Institute of Architects, 1956 edition

Britannica Encyclopaedia of American Art. New York: Simon & Schuster, 1974

Dictionary of American Biography. New York: Charles Scribner's Sons, 1928

Who Was Who in America. Chicago, Illinois: Marquis, 1973 edition

Henry Withey and Elsie Withey. *Biographical Dictionary of American Architects (Deceased).* Los Angeles, California: New Age Publishing Company, Los Angeles, California: 1956

ARTICLES

Walter Cook, "The Story of Design in the Ecole des Beaux-Arts," *Architectural Record* (January 1901), pp. 57–63

Paul Cret, "The Ecole des Beaux-Arts; What Its Architectural Teaching Means," *Architectural Record* (May 1908), pp. 367–371

Ernest Flagg, "The Ecole des Beaux-Arts," *Architectural Record* (July–September 1894), pp. 38–43

Ernest Flagg, "The Influence of the French School on Architecture in the United States," *Architectural Record* (October–December 1894), pp. 213–228

Ernest Flagg, "American Architecture as Opposed to Architecture in America," *Architectural Record* (October 1900), pp. 178–181

A. D. F. Hamlin, "The Influence of the Ecole des Beaux-Arts on Our Architectural Education," *Architectural Record* (April 1908), pp. 241–247

Thomas Hastings, "The Influence of the Ecole des Beaux-Arts Upon American Architecture," *Architectural Record* (January 1901), pp. 66–89

Thomas Hastings, "How the Beaux-Arts Institute Has Helped Our Architectural Schools," *Architecture* (May 1918), pp. 115–116

John Mead Howells, "From Nouveau to Ancien at the Ecole des Beaux-Arts," *Architectural Record* (January 1901), pp. 35–55

Eugène Muntz, "The Ecole des Beaux-Arts," *Architectural Record* (January 1901), pp. 1–34

Percy Stuart, "The Columbia University School of Architecture," *Architectural Record* (July 1900), pp. 5–21

Francis S. Swales, "Master Draftsmen XVII, Henry Hornbostel," *Pencil Points* (February 1926), pp. 72–92

"The Works of Ernest Flagg," *Architectural Record* (April–July 1902), pp. 65–75

PERIODICALS

Architectural Forum (1917–1974)

Architectural Record (1891–1979)

Architectural Review, Boston edition (1891–1921)
(absorbed by *The American Architect and Building News*)

Architecture (1900–1935)

Brickbuilder (1892–1917)
(absorbed by *Architectural Forum*)

The American Architect and Building News (1876–1938)

The Architect, New York edition (1923–1931)

The New York Architect (1908–1912)

Pencil Points (1920–1945)
(absorbed by *Progressive Architecture*)

American Country Houses of Today (1911–1935) (annuals published by Architectural Book Publishing Company, New York)

COLLECTIONS

New York Public Library, New York. Artists' File; Architecture Collection

Avery Library, Columbia University School of Architecture, New York

New York Historical Society, New York. McKim, Mead & White Archives

Dowling College Historical Collection, Dowling College, Oakdale, New York

Barbara Van Liew, The Van Liew Register of Long Island Landmarks, Society for the Preservation of Long Island Antiquities

C. W. Post Center Rare Books Collection, Long Island University, Greenvale, New York

Nassau County Historical Museum, Eisenhower Park, New York

Suffolk County Historical Museum, Riverhead, New York

Illustration Sources

The map of Long Island, as well as all of the other uncredited drawings and photographs in this volume, was made by the authors. The sources of the other illustrations are as follows:

INTRODUCTION

I–1 *Architectural Record* (January 1901), p. 3
I–2 Marshall B. Davidson and Margot P. Brill, *The American Heritage History of Notable American Houses* (New York: American Heritage Publishing Co., Inc., 1971), p. 280
I–3 Mariana Griswold Van Rensselaer, *Henry Hobson Richardson and His Works* (Boston, Mass.: Houghton Mifflin Co., 1888). Reprinted by Dover Press, New York, 1969, frontispiece
I–4 Charles C. Baldwin, *Stanford White* (New York: Dodd, Mead Co., 1931), p. 115
I–5 Martin Pawley and Yukio Futagawa, *Frank Lloyd Wright, Public Buildings* (New York: Simon & Schuster, 1970), p. 6
I–6 John F. Harbeson, *The Study of Architectural Design with Special Reference to the Program of the B.A.I.D.* (New York: Pencil Points Press, 1926), p. viii
I–7 John F. Harbeson, *The Study of Architectural Design with Special Reference to the Program of the B.A.I.D.* (New York: Pencil Points Press, 1926), p. 7
I–8 *The Bulletin of the Beaux-Arts Institute of Design*, vol. 8, no. 10 (August 1932), p. 14
I–16 *Architectural Record* (January 1901), p. 95
I–18 *Architectural Record* (October 1900), p. 143
I–24 *A Monograph of the Works of McKim, Mead & White, 1879–1915* (New York: Architectural Book Publishing Co., 1915), plate 147. Reprinted by Benjamin Blom, Inc., New York, 1973
I–25 John C. Baker, *American Country Homes and Their Gardens* (Philadelphia, Pa.: John Winston Co., 1906)
I–26 *A Monograph of the Works of McKim, Mead & White, 1879–1915* (New York: Architectural Book Publishing Co., 1915), plates 166, 168
I–27 Marc Connelly, *The Most of John Held, Jr.* (Brattleboro, Vt.: Stephen Greene Press, 1972), p. 37. Originally published in *The New Yorker* (July 16, 1927)
I–28 *Architecture* (September 1912), p. 168
I–29 *Architectural Record* (May 1903), p. 459
I–30 *Architectural Record* (May 1903), p. 478
I–32 *The New York Architect*, vol. 2, no. 4 (April 1908)
I–40 *Architecture* (November 1914), p. 258
I–42 *Architectural Annual, 1929* (New York: Architectural League of New York, 1929)

THE ESTATES

1–2 Plan based on data from U.S. Merchant Marine Academy, Kings Point, courtesy of Martin P. Skrocki, director of external affairs
1–5 Working drawing section on file at the U.S. Merchant Marine Academy, Kings Point, courtesy of Martin P. Skrocki, director of external affairs
2–2 Plan based on data from U.S. Merchant Marine Academy, Kings Point, courtesy of Martin P. Skrocki, director of external affairs
3–3 *Architecture* (September 1912), p. 168

3–4 *Architecture* (September 1912)
3–5 Drawing by Sidney L. Katz, F.A.I.A., of Katz Waisman Weber, New York
3–6 Original drawing by Augustus N. Allen on file at Sands Point Park and Preserve, courtesy of Leonard Johnson, supervisor
4–2, 4–5, 4–6 *The Architect* (October 1925)
4–3 Elevation drawing based on original working drawings on file at E. W. Howell and Company, Babylon, New York, courtesy of Ralph Howell, Sr.
5–1, 5–2 Elevation and plan are based on original working drawings on file at E. W. Howell and Company, Babylon, New York, courtesy of Ralph Howell, Sr.
6–2 *Pencil Points* (April 1933)
6–3 Plan based on blueprints of original working drawings by Edgar Williams
7–2 Plan based on original drawing by Ogden Codman, Jr., courtesy of Nassau County Office of Cultural Development, John Maerhofer, director
8–2 *Architectural Record* (March 1920)
9–1 *Architecture* (November 1914), p. 258
9–4 Drawing of west elevation on file at Webb Institute of Naval Architecture, courtesy of Rear Admiral C. N. Payne, U.S.N. (ret.), president
9–5 *Architecture* (November 1914)
10–2 Plan based on drawings on file at the New York Institute of Technology, courtesy of William Donaldson, superintendent of buildings and grounds
10–3 Carrère & Hastings Archives, Avery Library, Columbia University, New York
10–4 *The American Architect and Building News* (September 15, 1917)
11–3 Elevation drawing on file at the New York Institute of Technology, courtesy of William Donaldson, superintendent of buildings and grounds
12–2 Plan based on working drawings on file at the New York Institute of Technology, courtesy of William Donaldson, superintendent of buildings and grounds
13–1 *The New York Architect*, vol. 2, no. 4 (April 1908)
15–1 *Architecture* (April 1918), p. 106
16–1 Plan based on drawings on file at C. W. Post College, Long Island University, courtesy of Joseph Halligan, department of buildings and grounds
17–2 Plan based on drawings on file at C. W. Post College, Long Island University, courtesy of Joseph Halligan, department of buildings and grounds
17–5 *Noted Long Island Homes*, privately published by E. W. Howell and Company, Babylon, New York, 1933
18–3 *Architecture* (December 1926)
19–1 *The American Architect* (July 28, 1915)
19–6 *Architecture* (April 1920)
20–2, 20–6 *Architectural Record* (March 1921)
20–3 Plan based on drawings on file at the Long Island State Park Commission, courtesy of James E. Arles, assistant commissioner
21–2, 21–6 Drawings courtesy of Historic American Buildings Survey, National Park Service
21–5 Photograph by Jack E. Boucher, Historic American Buildings Survey, National Park Service

22–2, 22–3, 22–5 Royal Cortissoz (intro.), *The Architecture of John Russell Pope*, vol. 3 (New York: W. Helburn, Inc., 1930)
23–4 Plan based on working drawings on file at Harbor Arts Center, courtesy of Richard Jorgensen, superintendent
24–3 Aerial perspective drawing by Santo Vitale, curator, Vanderbilt Museum
25–2 Plan based on data furnished by the Long Island State Park Commission, courtesy of James E. Arles, assistant commissioner
25–4, 25–6 Original drawings on file with the Long Island State Park Commission, courtesy of James E. Arles, assistant commissioner
28–2, 28–5 *Architectural Record* (May 1903)
29–3, 29–4 *Architectural Annual, 1906* (New York: Architectural League of New York, 1906)
30–1, 30–2 *The American Architect and Building News* (August 26, 1908)
31–2, 31–3 *A Monograph of the Works of McKim, Mead & White, 1879–1915* (New York: Architectural Book Publishing Co., 1915)
31–5 John C. Baker, *American Country Homes and Their Gardens* (Philadelphia, Pa.: John Winston Co., 1906)
32–2 Photograph by Estelle F. Strizhak

APPENDIX/OTHER BEAUX-ARTS BUILDINGS ON LONG ISLAND

A–2 *A Monograph of the Works of McKim, Mead & White, 1879–1915* (New York: Architectural Book Publishing Co., 1915), plate 72
A–4 *The Architect* (July 1926), p. 422
A–5 *A Monograph of the Work of Charles A. Platt* (New York: Architectural Book Publishing Co., 1913), p. 77
A–7 *Architectural Record* (April 1902), p. 68
A–8 *Architectural Annual, 1929* (New York: Architectural League of New York, 1929)

Index